T5-CRR-266

COPING WITH CRISES

How Governments Deal with Emergencies

Edited by Shao–chuan Leng

Volume II
The Miller Center Series
on Asian Political Leadership

UNIVERSITY
PRESS OF
AMERICA

Lanham • New York • London

The Miller Center

University of Virginia

Copyright © 1990 by

University Press of America®, Inc.

4720 Boston Way
Lanham, MD 20706

3 Henrietta Street
London WC2E 8LU England

All rights reserved

Printed in the United States of America

British Cataloging in Publication Information Available

"Emergency Powers in Northern Ireland"
copyright 1989 by J.C. Garnett

Library of Congress Cataloging-in-Publication Data

Coping with crises : how governments deal with emergencies /
edited by Shao–chuan Leng.
p.   cm. — (The Miller Center series on Asian political leadership ; v. 2)
Sponsored by the White Burkett Miller Center of Public Affairs.
1. War and emergency powers.   I. Leng, Shao Chuan, 1921–
II. White Burkett Miller Center.   III. Series.
K3344.C67   1989   342'.062—dc20   89–16734 CIP
[342.262]

ISBN 0–8191–7584–6 (alk. paper)
ISBN 0–8191–7585–4 (pbk. : alk. paper)

The views expressed by the author(s) of this publication do not necessarily
represent the opinions of the Miller Center. We hold to Jefferson's dictum that:
"Truth is the proper and sufficient antagonist to error, and has nothing
to fear from the conflict, unless by human interposition, disarmed
of her natural weapons, free argument and debate."

Co-published by arrangement with
The White Burkett Miller Center of Public Affairs,
University of Virginia

The paper used in this publication meets the minimum requirements of American
National Standard for Information Sciences—Permanence of Paper for Printed Library
Materials, ANSI Z39.48–1984.   ∞

DEDICATED TO

NORA AND DAVID

Table of Contents

Preface

KENNETH W. THOMPSON

Crises are the rule rather than the exception in international relations. Within organized and more stable national systems, insurrections and civil conflict signal the breakdown of the political and legal order. They involve the substitution of force and violence for the political process. They constitute, to use the core concept or the informing thesis of this little book, an emergency requiring emergency powers.

Coping with emergencies, even when they are the exception rather than the rule, is a perennial problem for sovereign nation states. In some parts of the world, the threat of emergencies is more pressing than in others. Israel and Northern Ireland are caught in a vortex of unending conflict that make emergencies more commonplace. The problems of emergencies in Italy take on a different character, as Professor Robert Evans demonstrates, with different legal responses.

The great merit of this collection of scholarly inquiries is its value in comparing emergencies in various nation states in far-flung corners of the world. Whereas the Miller Center has concentrated on the study of the American presidency and executive power within the United States, this treatise contains papers that help us understand alternative approaches to coping with crises and emergencies.

Professor S. C. Leng is uniquely qualified to conceive, organize, and edit such a volume. From 1983-85, he was president of the American Association of Chinese Studies. He has been chairman of the Committee on Asian Studies at the University of Virginia. Trained in law and political science, he has been a consultant to U.S. government agencies as well as the International Commission of Jurists. Above all, he is the Compton Professor of Government and Foreign Affairs at the Miller Center and the Woodrow Wilson Department of Government and Foreign Affairs. He is an important member of the Miller Center staff. In this capacity, he has helped broaden and strengthen the Center's studies of presidential and executive power contributing, for example, an important paper to a volume on *The U.S. Constitution and the Constitutions of Asia* as well as being a principal intellectual architect.

More than 40 years ago, Arnold G. Toynbee justified what he called the comparative method in historical studies. As I wrote in the book *Toynbee's Philosophy of World History and Politics*:

> In some ways, this method is more a rule of thumb than a science. In its most elementary form, it is simply an attempt to look at a historical question from as many sides as possible—as Toynbee did in dealing with contemporary diplomatic problems: "By taking the bearings of his contemporary object of study from various local observation-posts and then combining these several readings into a single formula, the student [of foreign policy] is able to bring the object into focus and to calculate its position and to measure its dimensions with some approach to objectivity even though the time-vista is denied to him." With civilizations, he takes his bearings in both time and space. Having made certain readings, he examines these for elements of recurrence and novelty between the genus civilization and the particular one he is observing. The fruits of these comparisons are of little value until they are pondered by the imaginative mind. Even then, their purpose is to illuminate the understanding rather than to provide ready-made previews of events. For the sanguine scientist of society, this may suggest craven incompetence. For someone who will settle for the rewards of

greater insight and deeper understanding, the use of this method is not without value.

In this spirit, the Miller Center looks on the forums and publications being developed by Professor Leng as a contribution intended to deepen comprehension of governance and the presidency. In turning to the study of emergency powers in the United States, his inquiries can provide pointers to neglected issues and problems. Other areas for comparative research suggest themselves including executive-legislative relationships, the executive and the media, and the electoral process. Such inquiries can continue into the future as comparative studies under the guidance and leadership of S. C. Leng.

Introduction

SHAO-CHUAN LENG

International law recognizes the right of a government to use emergency powers that limit the enjoyment of recognized political and civil rights by the population under exceptional circumstances threatening the security and survival of the state. Yet, the administration of such powers is at times controversial. The dilemma posed by emergency powers is that they invariably interfere with approved rights and freedoms in a democracy and may strengthen authoritarian tendencies in a society with a fragile democratic base.

This volume is a comparative study to examine both in theory and in practice the employment of constitutional emergency powers in five polities to combat internal and/or external threats. Our focus is only on limited governments and not on absolutist governments free of legal constraints. In a constitutional state, a political emergency calls for a *temporary* suspension of normal rules and concentration of power in the executive in response to particular conditions. The extraordinary measures are taken for special purposes with a certain time-limit and are not intended to be institutionalized on a permanent footing. With these criteria in mind, we have selected for study three Western democracies: Israel, Italy, and Northern Ireland. For diversity's sake, we have also included two new economic powers in Asia: South Korea and Taiwan, each of which is moving from a "guided democracy" to a more open, democratic society. All five have used exceptional measures in one form or another to cope with threats to their order and security. Compared with Italy and Northern Ireland, however, Israel, South Korea and Taiwan are confronted with more formidable opponents threatening their survival.

In this volume, we shall analyze the nature of emergencies and emergency powers in historical and political context. Among the issues to be addressed wherever appropriate are the propriety and effectiveness of such powers, the rationale for their invocation, the scope and frequency of their use, the mechanisms of decision-making and control, and the move to reform or remove emergency measures.

Professor Alan Dowty, in his chapter on Israel, first examines the circumstances under which a state of emergency was proclaimed in 1948 by the new state of Israel and the unusual pressures with which Israel has contended throughout its four decades of existence. Then he proceeds to survey Israeli law and practice on emergency powers in great detail. According to him, emergency powers have not challenged the normal functioning of government in Israel and there has been a trend to a greater regularity in the use of emergency powers and greater reliance on legal and judicial procedures governing them. Still, on the balance between demands of security and those of law and liberty, Dowty argues, one can criticize Israel for the weight assigned to emergency powers. On the other hand, he says that an act of balance is taking place in Israel which has managed to maintain the rule of law despite extraordinary pressures.

In Chapter 2, Professor J. C. Garnett explores emergency powers in Northern Ireland. At the outset he makes it clear that while undoubtedly interested in reconciling the embittered Protestant and Catholic communities in Northern Ireland, the British government faces the immediate imperative of maintaining law and order against violence. In pursuit of the short term objective, it has been necessary to enact, over the years, a body of emergency powers legislation to enable the British to combat terrorism and civil disorder.

Much of Garnett's discussion focuses on the military and political effectiveness of the emergency legislation and the implications of this legislation for democratic values. In his view, the main concern should be with the extent of the legislation and the manner in which it is enforced rather than with the fact of the legislation itself. Despite the curtailment of individual rights and clear evidence of a degree of police and army brutality, contends the author, Northern Ireland remains an essentially "open" society. He cites the presence of a number of safeguards against abuses, namely, a free press, public enquiries, the right of every individual citizen with a grievance to complain, and the watchful eye of the British government.

The unique way in which Italy has dealt with terrorism and subversion is treated in Chapter 3 by Professor Robert Evans. Starting with a brief examination of the development of terrorism in Italy, the author turns his main attention to Italian *legal* responses to terrorist attacks, focusing on legislative provisions and changes in the Italian penal code. Despite over 14,000 episodes of violence between 1969 and 1987, he describes Italy's initial reaction to terrorism as a slow and fragmented one, for which a heavy price was paid in deaths and injuries. Once the emergency was declared, however, the state responded, the government legislated, the police enforced, and together they thwarted terrorism. The vigor of the state response increased as terrorism advanced, heightening police power and punishment, while offering incentives as the emergency diminished. At the same time, he emphasizes, fundamental civil liberties were maintained. In conclusion, Evans suggests that the Italian case provides interesting perspectives on how even a weak democratic system such as Italy's, given its anti-authoritarian political culture, can defeat a serious terrorist threat without curtailing the basic constitutional rights of the citizens.

In his chapter on Korea, Professor Young C. Kim analyzes what he labels as the politics of emergency powers. Part I of the chapter begins with an examination of the existing legal provisions on emergency powers under the Fifth Republic (1981 to the present), followed by a discussion of comparable provisions under the Fourth Republic (1961-1981). Brief references are also made to the legal provisions under previous regimes. Part II reviews briefly eight actual cases in which emergency powers were employed. He notes the circumstances and the purposes for which emergency powers were invoked as well as the consequences of their use. Although the author presents no overall conclusion, his summary and conclusions of the eight individual cases indicate mixed results. In some instances, the exercise of emergency powers appeared necessary in defense of national security and the existing constitutional order, but in others, it tended to result in the increasing involvement of the military in politics and the adoption of more authoritarian and restrictive political practices.

Laws on emergency powers in Taiwan are examined in Chapter 5 by Drs. Tao-tai Hsia and Wendy Zeldin. They first consider the legislative history of emergency powers legislation in the Republic of China. In 1948 the National Assembly adopted the Temporary Provisions annexed to the 1947 Constitution granting extensive emergency powers to the president. It was on the basis of these Provisions that martial law was declared in Taiwan against an imminent threat of armed attack by the Communist forces of the People's Republic of China. In almost four decades, however, emergency powers have been invoked only on five occasions in Taiwan. Over the years, as noted by the authors, the military trial jurisdiction has gradually been reduced, and the number of persons charged and the number of detentions and prosecutions have also declined significantly. With time, Taiwan has emerged as an "economically strong, socially stable polity whose authoritarian cast has been tempered by the ruling party's steady, if grudging, attempts to edge closer to a system of full-fledged constitutional democracy."

The lifting of the decree on martial law in 1987 and the features of the new National Security Law in Taiwan are discussed in the last part of the chapter. Political and personal reasons are suggested for President Chiang Ching-kuo's decision to lift the martial law. The pros and cons for the new National Security Law are also presented. From a political perspective, the authors argue, there is a need for such a law as Taiwan still faces both internal and external threats. The challenge for Taiwan, in their words, lies in creating a successful balance between maintaining stability while introducing more democratic reforms.

From the careful examination of the five cases in this volume, one may ask what can be learned and what generalizations can be made about emergency powers. What do the cases have in common? How and why are they different? How should one evaluate the results of constitutional emergency powers? What constitutes success and what constitutes failure? How must a democratic polity act to achieve a balance between the demands for order and security on the one hand and the requirements of law and liberty on the other? These are the questions and issues to be addressed by Professor Inis Claude in the concluding chapter.

CHAPTER 1

Emergency Powers in Israel:
The Devaluation of Crisis*

ALAN DOWTY

On May 19, 1948, four days after the declaration of Israeli independence, the provisional government of the new state proclaimed a state of emergency. This state of emergency has been in force continuously ever since.

Since emergencies by definition involve unusual circumstances, comparing justifications for declared emergencies in different nations is at best a tricky task. But no one can dispute that Israel has contended with unusual pressures throughout its four decades of existence. When the emergency was first declared, the 650,000 Jews of Mandatory Palestine had already been engaged for almost six months in a civil war with 1.5 million Palestinian Arabs, and they faced an invasion by the regular armies of five Arab states with a total population of about 30 million. The new state survived by an effort of total mobilization, but about one percent of the population was killed—almost fifty times the American casualty rate in Vietnam.

After 1948 Israel remained, of necessity, on a permanent war-footing. Until 1967 the bulk of the population was within artillery range of hostile armies.

---

*I would like to thank Avraham Brichta, Menachem Hofnung, Nri Huppert, Yitzhak Hans Klinghoffer, Allan E. Shapiro, and Yael Yishai for reading and commenting on an earlier draft; special thanks go to Ari Rosenthal for his able research assistance.

1

With five subsequent wars, the Israeli public was never more than about five years from either the last conflict or the next one. Today the Arab world still outnumbers Israeli Jews by about 50/1, while Egypt, Syria, Jordan, and Iraq by themselves have an 18/1 margin. For these same four states, this translates into an advantage of almost 12/1 in regular armed forces, 5/1 with all reserves mobilized, 4/1 in both GNP and defense spending, 3/1 in major battle tanks, and 2.5/1 in combat aircraft.[1] Israel also faces a number of active terrorist organizations whose international support and sources of finance are without precedent. In addition, a growing international isolation has left the country increasingly dependent on a single major power for both vital military equipment and economic viability.

Like many new states, Israel often lacked established procedures for dealing with external and internal problems. The absence of a written constitution, for example, created more impetus for ad hoc measures. An Arab minority of between 12-18 percent, much of it concentrated in border areas, created a potential security problem with few parallels elsewhere.[2] Apart from this split, the often heated quarrels between religious and non-religious Jews, and the broad communal division between Jews of European background and those or Asian-African origin, also threatened internal unity.

The economic pressures have been enormous. The country tripled its population during the first decade, bearing an economic burden of staggering dimensions. In recent years defense spending as a proportion of GNP has hovered in the 25-30 percent range, against the 3-6 percent common in Western countries or the 12-17 percent in the Soviet Union. But with the highest per capita national debt in the world, debt service has topped even defense in the national budget, leading to an almost unbelievable level of total government spending: 60-80 percent of the GNP, depending on how it is measured.

All this falls on a population molded by the experience of disaster. From the first wave of immigrants fleeing the 1881 pogroms in Russia, most of the Jewish immigrants to Palestine or Israel were fleeing persecution elsewhere, whether from Tsarist Russia, Hitler's Europe, or Arab states after 1948. Most of Israel's population today are refugees or the children of refugees; any understanding of the country's political culture must incorporate this fact. A sense of insecurity and vulnerability, based on the assumption of a hostile environment, characterizes the national mood.

A protracted official state of emergency may, therefore, be more justifiable, or at least more understandable, for Israel than for almost any other contemporary state. But it is difficult to maintain the same sense of urgency for such an extended period of time. The protraction of the crisis leads, inevitably, to a routinization of crisis procedures, to a normalization of what were originally extraordinary measures. The crisis becomes devalued over time.

Even the broad use of police powers by Israel to put down the Arab "intifadah" in the occupied West Bank and Gaza, since December, 1987, has not reversed this general pattern, for two reasons: in the first place, most of the measures employed by the Israeli army fall under the international law of belligerent occupation, rather than emergency powers, and secondly, those emergency powers that have been employed do not represent new departures in scope or procedure, even though the numbers involved may have sharply increased.

Against the background of the intifadah, then, it may be useful to trace the patterns in the use of emergency powers generally in Israel, and to put current events into context. In this regard, the distinction between Israel and the occupied territories—Judea, Samaria, and the Gaza Strip—is crucial, and the latter will be dealt with separately.

The main characteristics of emergency legislation in Israel, over four decades of continuous use, reflect these overarching tendencies:

1. Emergency powers have not challenged the normal functioning of government. The Knesset (Parliament) has operated undisturbed, and has the formal power to change emergency measures as it sees fit (though the exercise of this right may admittedly depend on coalition politics); courts continue to function, and to review (within limits) the use of such powers. There is no general suspension of rights, even in wartime.

2. In practice, the use of emergency powers has fallen far short of what could be done, legally, under existing grants of authority. Many of the broad

powers available have not been utilized, and others have been moderated in usage by self-imposed administrative guidelines. This reverses the common pattern among many non-democratic governments which stretch their emergency authority in various ways; while the law in such cases is better than the practice, in Israel the practice is better than the law.

3. Over time, there has been a trend to greater regularity in use of emergency powers and greater reliance on legal and judicial procedures governing them. The role of judicial review, for example, has been expanded. In recent years there has been less automatic deference to security claims than in the early years of statehood. In recent years, a number of "Basic Laws," designed to be components of an eventual constitution, have included provisions preventing their alteration in any way by emergency measures.

Yet there is also a danger in the extension of a state of emergency over a long period of time. Measures conceived in time of war, or genuine crisis, can become so routinized that they continue unchallenged when any plausible connection to an emergency has passed. Questionable practices are perpetuated, rather than attenuated, by the passage of time. An example cited by one of Israel's leading legal scholars is the emergency power to open mail when necessary "for reasons of security and defense." While such authority might be arguably essential in wartime, it has apparently been used over the years to enforce economic and financial laws.[3] An even more egregious example, perhaps, has been the proliferation in the last few years of return-to-work orders in rather ordinary labor disputes, under emergency regulations justified as maintenance of "vital public services."

What is the solution when emergency becomes routine? How can a democratic government, under unceasing pressure, provide as far as possible for the normalization of its political life, while remaining prepared for sudden threats? One suggestion, made by another Israeli scholar, is to differentiate between a general state of emergency, for which measures can be routinized, and a "special" state of emergency that could be declared in time of actual hostilities or other grave threat requiring far-reaching, but temporary, steps.[4] We will return to this question after surveying Israeli law and practice on emergency powers in greater detail.

There are, in fact, three separate mechanisms for exercising emergency powers in Israel, and the issue of extended emergency has a different significance for each case.[5] These three types of emergency regulations are:

1. The Defence (Emergency) Regulations of 1945. Promulgated by the British Mandatory government, these are the most drastic and most controversial measures.

2. Emergency Regulations issued by government ministers under Section 9 of the Law and Administration Ordinance of 1948. These are, in other words, measures based on a grant of authority from the legislative branch, and they are not valid beyond three months unless extended by the Knesset.

3. Regular legislation whose period of validity is dependent on the existence of a state of emergency, or whose functioning is in some other way affected by the emergency. Such legislation may also give the government the right to carry out "emergency-type" measures, subject to review. The most important instance is the Emergency Powers (Detention) Law, 1979, which replaced the detention provisions of the 1945 British regulations.

THE BRITISH DEFENSE REGULATIONS

The 1945 Defence (Emergency) Regulations were a compilation of old and new Mandatory orders issued in response to the double threat of internal rebellion and world war. Following the Arab "revolt" in Palestine in 1936, the Privy Council in London adopted the Palestine (Defence) Order in Council 1937, authorizing the British High Commissioner in Palestine to enact such defense regulations "as to appear to him in his unfettered discretion to be necessary or expedient for securing public safety, the defence of Palestine, the maintenance of public order and the suppression of mutiny, rebellion, and riot and for maintaining supplies and services essential to the life of the community."[6] The subsequent regulations reflected the preoccupations of a colonial power facing widespread unrest and the threat of war; according to one British expert, they were "the type of regulations that came from the Boer War."[7]

In September, 1945, facing now the prospect of Jewish rebellion, the Mandate authorities published the collected set of regulations, including new measures on such subjects as illegal immigration.[8] The 147 regulations, covering 41 pages, establish a virtual regime of martial law. They include a military court system empowered to try all offenses against the regulations, with no writ of habeas corpus and no appeal. Broad powers of search and seizure were given to British soldiers. Other sections of the regulations severely circumscribe "unlawful" groups and permit long-term detention without trial—a provision under which thousands of Jews were held, some for up to five or six years. The regulations permit deportation of even native-born citizens, and establish prior censorship requiring a permit for any material of "political significance." Any area can be closed, with suspension of civil courts there, property can be requisitioned or destroyed, movement limited, mail opened, services suspended, or businesses closed—all by virtue of uncontestable military orders. Furthermore, the military is not even required to publish orders that it intends to enforce.

The Defence Regulations aroused a storm of protest from the Jewish population in Palestine. Richard Crossman, after hearing Jewish complaints as a visiting member of the Anglo-American Committee of Inquiry in early 1946, recorded in his diary that "I certainly had no idea of the severity of the Emergency Regulations. . . . there can be no doubt that Palestine today is a police state."[9] This opinion was shared by Bernard (Dov) Joseph, later Israeli Minister of Justice, who in 1948 published a critique of British rule in Palestine that also used the term "police state" in describing the Defence Regulations.[10]

As the state of Israel inherited all Mandatory legislation, unless explicitly annulled, this body of rules remained in force after May, 1948. Only the section restricting immigration was cancelled; the rest, despite previous criticism, remained on the books. As the Defence Regulations, and other emergency measures not collated into the 1945 enactment, had been promulgated unconditionally and with no terminal date, their validity was not even dependent on declaration of a state of emergency. Thus the new government found itself effortlessly in possession of a formidable apparatus of emergency powers for which the law-abiding British could be blamed.

There were some efforts to jettison this dubious colonial legacy, especially from the many Israeli leaders who had themselves been detained under the Defence Regulations. In the First Knesset the government proposed a bill that would replace the 1945 regulations, but it was not acted upon. In 1951, following the detention and alleged mistreatment of members of an ultra-Orthodox "underground," the Knesset condemned the Defence Regulations and called for a new law, but the issue was submerged in a governmental crisis that erupted that year. In 1962, Minister of Justice Pinhas Rosen offered a private bill which would have brought the 1945 regulations under Section 9 of the Law and Administration Ordinance, thus making them at least subject to declaration of an emergency and periodic Knesset review—again without success. Another Justice Minister, Yaakov Shimshon Shapiro, initiated another reform effort in 1966, but this work was cut short by the 1967 war.[11]

One notable opponent of the Defence Regulations was opposition leader Menachem Begin, who with his comrades in Etzel (National Military Organization) had been a prime target of the regulations under both the British and (briefly) the new Israeli government in 1948. During the 1951 debate Begin declared:

> The law that you used is Nazi, it is tyrannical, it is immoral; and an immoral law is also an illegal law. . . . You had no right to do this, when there is a Knesset, when there is a court, when you have at your disposal the entire investigative apparatus. . . . If these laws, terror laws of a repressive regime, remain in the State of Israel—the day will come when no group will remain unharmed by them. . . .[12]

But in time it became clear that there was no overwhelming impulse to revoke or replace the 1945 regulations. Apart from the convenience of being able to attribute these far-reaching powers to an impeccably democratic Western regime, the emergency conditions attending the state's birth did not prove, as originally expected, to be temporary. To the contrary, the continuing threat to national existence made retention of some extraordinary powers, beyond normal civil and judicial procedures, seem the better part of wisdom.[13] And it was unlikely that any subsequent Knesset legislation would provide the full range of measures fortuitously made available by the British.

Israeli courts have consistently upheld the use of the 1945 Defence Regulations, except where explicitly invalidated. Though it might be argued that the provision of a new mechanism for emergency regulations—through Section 9—ought to supersede any previous arrangements, the High Court of Justice has ruled only that no *new* regulations can be issued in the framework of the Defence Regulations. In other words, the empowering provisions in the 1945 regulations, which provide for enactment of additional regulations, have been frozen. Pre-1948 regulations remain valid, but any new measures must come through the channel provided, i.e., Section 9 (or the Knesset itself).[14]

With such wide powers available, the use of the Defence Regulations has been relatively limited (in the words of one observer, they have not been used "to any appreciable extent").[15] Whole sections of the regulations have hardly been utilized. Such measures as the death penalty and corporal punishment have never been invoked. The major use—and most controversy—involve a small number of the regulations: Regulations 86-101 on censorship; Regulations 109-112 on restriction, detention, and deportation; and Regulation 125 on closed areas.

The most broadly applied have been the censorship provisions, which still form the legal basis for control of the media. The regulations require the licensing of all media, and put the decision in the hands of Interior Ministry officials who need not justify their refusal to grant a license (an earlier 1933 Press Ordinance, not technically an emergency measure but still in force, also gives the Minister of Interior power to stop the publication of any newspaper for any period of time). The Defence Regulations also permit the censorship of any material "prejudicial to the defence of Palestine [Israel] or to the public safety or to public order."

These measures are potentially a most serious threat to freedom of speech; in practice, restrictions are usually limited to sensitive security information. In the case of the press, censorship is softened by a voluntary arrangement under which most newspapers submit military and political material for review, and excisions can be appealed to a committee of three representing the press, military, and the general public. Unanimous decisions of the committee are final, while majority decisions can be appealed to the Chief of Staff. This covers only the press; books are submitted directly to the censor for review if they "relate to state security," and some have been withheld from publication or censored, usually because of revelation of secrets. Censorship of movies and theater has usually, though not always, been limited to material that is offensive to religious or social mores—such as pornography—and a narrow appeal process is available.[16]

The major problem arises with the Arabic-language press, which is concentrated in East Jerusalem—thus falling under Israeli law rather than the military occupation regime—but which serves the West Bank and Gaza population as well as Israeli Arabs. Permits to publish a newspaper have been denied because of suspicion of links to hostile organizations, and there is little chance for an appellant to disprove the "security risk" label.[17] For example, on May 2, 1988, in the context of efforts to contain rioting on the West Bank and Gaza that had been taking place since the previous December, the Israeli government stopped publication of *Al Awdah*, a Jerusalem-based weekly said to have close ties to one of the more radical Palestinian organizations.

In addition, Arab newspapers do not benefit from the voluntary arrangement described above, but are required to submit all material for review, with no appeal process. Consequently there is continual disagreement over whether censored material is a threat to public order, or legitimate expression of political views; in some cases, even translated articles from the Hebrew press have been disallowed.[18] Newspapers that have tried to bypass the censor have sometimes been temporarily closed by military order. On the other hand, despite all these limitations, one of the newspapers published regularly in East Jerusalem is commonly regarded as spokesman for the Palestine Liberation Organization (PLO) position.

Even more than the censorship provisions, other Defence Regulations were aimed, by and large, at the Arab minority. From 1948 to 1966, many border areas, not coincidentally corresponding to most of the Arab-populated areas, were placed under a military government whose legal basis was the 1945 Defence Regulations. Though restrictions on movement were applied elsewhere as well, their main use was in the military government area. Under Regulation 125, these areas were declared "closed," and all entrance and exit required a permit—though in practice this was seldom required of Jews passing through such areas. Under Regulations 109 and 110, persons under special suspicion could be further restricted in their movements, to a particular town or even house arrest.[19]

Most serious, perhaps, was the way in which Regulation 125 could be used to create "uncultivated" or "abandoned" land that, in accord with Israeli legislation, became subject to expropriation by the state. Villagers who happened to be elsewhere could be kept there or prevented from entering their home village. In some cases—in at least 11 villages in the 1949-1950 period—Regulation 125 was used to evacuate entire villages of their existing populations, on security grounds. The courts interfered in these cases only on technical grounds, or when it seemed clear that the motivation was not security.[20]

Most of the land expropriations occurred in the early 1950s, and the military government in Arab areas ended in 1966. From that point, at least formally, emergency measures under the British regulations applied equally to all areas of the country and all sectors of the population. The most serious continuing controversy regarding the use of the Defence Regulations has been the matter of administrative detention.

Regulation 111 empowered "a military commander" to detain any person in any place of his choosing, for renewable periods of one year. In essence, this authority could mean indefinite imprisonment without trial, with no restrictions on the discretion of the commander, loose rules of evidence, and no judicial review (but only an "advisory committee" to make recommendations to the officer). As noted, this measure was used extensively by the British in the 1945-1948 period.

The use of this regulation in Israel was circumscribed by internal instructions issued by the Israel Defense Forces

(IDF) high command. Only high-level officers were allowed to order detention, and then only for a period of one month (three months in East Jerusalem) and only after the approval of a second advisory committee including non-military representatives. The Chief of Staff could order a detention of up to six months. All detentions were reviewed by the original advisory committee, chaired by a Supreme Court Justice, whose advice in practice became binding. Added to this were instructions of the Attorney General, stressing that detention must be preventive rather than punitive, that it must be the only available means of averting dangerous activity, and that it cannot be used to silence extreme opinions unless instigation of violence is likely.[21]

The argument is made that preventive detention may be the lesser of evils in dealing with the kinds of threats presented by terrorist organizations. The evidence available in such cases often cannot be used in a court of law: it is based on hearsay, or on intelligence sources that cannot be revealed, or on the testimony of informers whose identification would put them in jeopardy. Rather than changing the rules of the courtroom in order to obtain criminal convictions, it is preferable to adopt lesser measures, still subject to some form of review, that make it possible to act when a reasonable certainty of danger to society exists. Better this, it is argued, than to compromise the judicial system.[22]

There is, inevitably, controversy about whether those detained are actually threats to society. Alan Dershowitz, a strong critic of preventive detention who studied the cases of those detained in 1971, concluded "that virtually all of those detained had, in fact, been involved in terrorist activities; that the vast majority could not be tried under Israeli law; and that a considerable number would probably engage in future terrorism if released."[23] In any event, the number of those detained has never been great, and the overall trend has been to reduce the number. From the figures announced sporadically, it appears that around 315 detentions orders were issued in 1956-1957, but that the number of detainees fell to 23 in 1970 and 15 in 1971 (not including the West Bank and Gaza, where the number was much higher; see the following section). By 1978 the total, including the occupied territories, was 30; in 1979 (when Regulation 111 was replaced by regular legislation) there were 18; and by 1981 the number had dropped to 12 in the occupied territories and none in Israel.[24] Between 1982 and 1985 there were no administrative detainees. Since then, however, and especially since the unrest that began in December, 1987, wide use of administrative detention was reintroduced in the occupied territories, and the number of detainees reached record levels there (see below).

Like other emergency measures, however, administrative detention was directed primarily at the Arab population. In fact, after 1953 it was not used against Jews until the detention in 1980 of Rabbi Meir Kahane, leader of the ultra-nationalist Kach party, who was suspected of planning to instigate anti-Arab violence.

Moreover, the repeal of Regulation 111, if not all the 1945 Defence Regulations, was favored even by many who thought it had been applied judiciously. Dershowitz cited the dictum that such laws "lie about like a loaded weapon."[25] Finally, following the assumption of power by the right-wing Likud bloc in 1977, a law replacing Regulation 111 with more circumscribed procedures (and abolishing the deportation measures in Regulation 112) was enacted into law in 1979 (see "Knesset Legislation," below). The fact that many of the Likud leaders, including the Minister of Justice, had themselves been detained in the past, was of relevance to this result.

While this action moved one controversial aspect of the 1945 regulations into the realm of regular legislative and judicial procedures, it left other unresolved issues. The restriction of movement, for example, though applied sparingly, was not subject even to the kind of administrative review that had been applied to detention before 1979.[26] There was still no requirement for the publication of orders issued in the framework on the Defence Regulations, which could be a particular problem in the closure of areas under Regulation 125.[27] Finally, judicial review, though better than the British practice, was still somewhat limited in scope.

The incorporation of the Defence Regulations into Israeli law was challenged immediately after independence, and was upheld by the High Court of Justice (Leon vs. Gubernik, H.C. 5/48, 1 P.D. 58). In subsequent review of cases arising under the regulations, the courts have generally applied two criteria: whether the procedural requirements of the law have been followed, and whether substantively the authority has acted in good faith and in accord with the stated purposes of the regulation.[28]

The judicial review of formal legal requirements has been fairly thorough, and has led to the cancellation of Defence Regulation orders. For example, in the midst of the Israeli War of Independence, a detainee was ordered released because the statutory advisory committee had not been appointed (Al-Karbutli vs. Minister of Defence et al., H.C. 7/48, 2 P.D. 5). In another case, a detention order was annulled because it did not specify the place of detention (Al Khouri vs. Chief of Staff, H.C. 95/49, 4 P.D. 34). These interventions were reinforced by the Courts Law of 1957, which specifically empowered the High Court of Justice "to order the release of persons unlawfully detained or imprisoned."[29]

Regarding the merits of the case, however, the court has ordinarily declined to look at the content of orders under the Defence Regulations, beyond ascertaining that they were enacted in good faith and according to relevant considerations within the scope of the regulation (Alyubi vs. Minister of Defence, H.C. 46/50, 4 P.D. 222). In this the Israeli court was following the lead of the British House of Lords, which in a similar test of emergency detention declined to examine the reasonableness of such an order so long as the Secretary of State was convinced of its necessity (Liversidge vs. Anderson, 1942).[30]

The realistic possibility of reversing an order has also been limited by the refusal of authorities to divulge evidence or the reasons behind their actions. Such refusal, permissible under the regulations, can make it almost impossible to show that an authority has, in fact, acted in bad faith. This problem was alleviated to some degree by changes in the Law of Evidence, in 1968, which abolished absolute state privilege on disclosure of evidence and authorized courts to hear evidence *in camera* when state security was involved. Subsequently, judges on appeal have examined secret evidence to see if it really needed to be withheld from the defendant.[31]

In summary, the continuing existence of the 1945 British Defence (Emergency) Regulations raises serious problems from a civil liberties perspective, and hard questions can also be raised regarding some of the ways they have been applied. But at the same time, usage of the regulations has generally been selective and limited, considering the broad powers available, and has been softened in implementation by internal guidelines and court review that provide some protection against abuse. Critics ask why these guidelines, which actually define practice, could not be converted into laws that would remove the spectre of colonial police powers from the books. This has been done with administrative detention, perhaps the most controversial of the "emergency" measures; it would not be so revolutionary to apply the same treatment to the remaining regulations.

THE DEFENCE (EMERGENCY) REGULATIONS ON THE WEST BANK AND GAZA

The Israeli occupation of the West Bank and the Gaza strip in 1967 raised an interesting legal issue. As these areas had been part of Mandatory Palestine, were the 1945 Defence Regulations still in effect there, as they were deemed to be in Israel itself? The Jordanian government, and West Bank residents, have argued that they were implicitly annulled on the West Bank, first by a 1948 proclamation of the Jordanian military commander that cancelled any laws in conflict with the Jordanian Defence Law of 1935, and secondly by the Jordanian Arms and Ammunition Law and Explosives Law, both of which also invalidated any conflicting provisions.[32]

Israeli jurists reply that the conflict with these laws is non-existent, that the 1948 and other Jordanian proclamations all provided that existing regulations would remain in force, and that in the absence of explicit repeal they were therefore part of Jordanian law when Israel assumed control in 1967. In 1979 the Israeli High Court of Justice reviewed the arguments, and concluded that the Defence Regulations were indeed still in force. Among other things, the court cited two Jordanian court decisions that had upheld the validity both of the regulations and of detention orders issued under them.[33]

Of course even without the Defence Regulations, Israel would have grounds for using "emergency" powers in the occupied territories. The customary international law of military occupation allows a wide range of measures without legislative or judicial review, belligerent occupation might even be considered essentially as a type of emergency rule.

And although Israel maintains that the Defence Regulations already existed in the West Bank and Gaza, it has also restated them in the form of military orders as an occupying power. For example, Military Order 224 (1968) explicitly reaffirms the Defence Regulations, and Military Order 378 (1970) repeats the provisions on administrative detention.[34]

Explicit authority for particular measures might be drawn from the Hague Conventions and from the Fourth Geneva Convention of 1949. Israel does not recognize the applicability of the Geneva Convention since Jordanian sovereignty over the West Bank was never universally recognized (and Egypt never claimed sovereignty in Gaza). Therefore, it is argued, Israel is not occupying enemy territory in the sense of the convention. A second argument, accepted by the Israel High Court, is that Geneva is contractual rather than customary international law, binding on a country only with its consent. Nevertheless, the Israeli government has promised to observe the "humanitarian provisions" of Geneva, which raises the issue of compatibility with the security measures taken. As it happens, on such issues as detention, demolition of houses, and restricting free speech, the Geneva Convention gives the occupier almost as free a hand as the Defence Regulations. In fact, it is hard to see that shifting entirely to the Geneva Convention as a legal basis would significantly impinge on Israeli practices. Israeli courts ruling on appeals from the West Bank and Gaza have found these practices compatible with the Geneva Convention—even while denying its applicability.

Finally, even if both the Defence Regulations and the law of belligerent occupation were rejected as a basis for "emergency" measures in the West Bank, the latitude of Israeli authorities would hardly be reduced. Jordanian legislation would provide draconian measures against political unrest or opposition, including trials in military courts not bound by ordinary procedures and use of the death penalty. Jordan itself has been in a state of martial law since 1967, with 50 people in administrative detention at the end of 1985, many of them from previous years.[35]

Prior to the period of the "uprising" that began in December, 1987, the use of emergency regulations on the West Bank was most extensive in the period immediately after the 1967 war. In 1970 Defence Minister Moshe Dayan put the total number of administrative detainees at 1,131, all but 34 of them from the occupied territories. In later years this dropped to fewer than 100, and sometimes to fewer than 20. In the 1979 period, simultaneously with the introduction of the new law in Israel, the use of detention was phased out both in Israel and the territories, with the last detainee released in March, 1982.[36]

The procedures followed in detentions were basically the same as those followed in Israel itself, with allowance for organizational differences. The same criticisms were also heard: loose rules of evidence, withholding of evidence from the accused (who was sometimes even excluded from the hearings), and the unwillingness of courts to substitute their own judgment for that of the military officer on the merits of the case.[37] As within Israel, the detainee could appeal to the Israel High Court of Justice, though in the territories there was no court of appeals standing between the court of first instance and the High Court.

Much greater use was made on the West Bank of Regulation 112, providing for deportation, than had been in Israel. While deportation was not easily applicable to Israeli Arabs, the close ties between the West and East Banks of the Jordan made expulsion across the river a convenient way of dealing with problematic individuals. Attention was called to the prohibition, in Article 49 of the Geneva Convention, of "individual or mass forcible transfers, as well as deportations of protected persons from occupied territory to the territory of the Occupying Power or to that of any other country." Israeli authorities responded that, as Jordanian citizens, the deportees were not being transferred to the occupier's territory or to "another country," but merely to a different part of their own country. It was also argued that Article 49 had been aimed at the kinds of mass deportations, for purposes of forced labor or physical annihilation, that had taken place during World War II, and not at the expulsion of individuals acting as enemy agents to the territory of that enemy.[38]

During the 1967-1978 period, according to one compilation, 1,151 individuals were deported from the West Bank and the Gaza strip (an official Israeli source actually gave a slightly higher figure: 1,180).[39] Most of these deportations came in the first four years, with 406 in the peak year, 1970. By the end of the decade the figure had fallen to fewer than ten each year. While not contesting the overall number, Israeli authorities claim that the majority—whether originally from the area or not—had infiltrated back into Israeli-held territory after the 1967 war, and that some of the others chose deportation as an alternative to serving prison sentences.

The argument over expulsion was renewed following the outbreak of "intifadah" at the end of 1987, as the Israeli army sought to use it as a weapon against the presumed instigators of the unrest. Orders for the deportation of eight West Bank residents in April, 1988, aroused considerable international criticism, but were upheld by the Israeli High Court. By early 1989 the total number of deportations ordered since December, 1987, stood at 71.

Another controversial application of the Defence Regulations is the demolition of houses, or sealing of rooms, that military authorities consider to have been used for terrorist operations. These measures are based on Regulation 119, though—as in many other cases—they could also have been justified by a Jordanian ordinance that provides the same sanction. There is again argument over the compatibility with the Geneva Convention, which allows for destruction of property when "rendered absolutely necessary by military operations." An Israeli court case in 1979 upheld the legality of demolitions and sealings under the Defence Regulations, adding that the Geneva Convention was not relevant, but that even if it were, there would be no conflict. The number of demolitions carried out is estimated in the hundreds, with some 140 houses destroyed from December, 1987, the onset of the uprising, through mid-December, 1988.[40]

The censorship regulations have also been applied more strictly in the West Bank and Gaza than in Israel—which is one reason that Arab newspapers operate out of East Jerusalem despite the problems they face there, as already described. In theory, any printed matter requires a permit, and the occupation regime maintains a list of publications that are explicitly prohibited. In the control of printing and publishing most expressions of Palestinian nationalism are censored, though considerable material of a like nature finds its way into circulation. In fact, given the free movement across the Jordan River, as well as constant penetration of radio and television from neighboring countries and even the relatively freer press of East

Jerusalem, it might be asked whether censorship efforts on the West Bank are not an exercise in futility.[41]

The Defence Regulations have also been used on the West Bank, as they were in Israel, to requisition land "for military purposes" and to make it available for Jewish civilian settlement. One such expropriation, at Beth-El (near Ramallah) was upheld by the Israeli High Court of Justice, which accepted the claims of military necessity. But in a subsequent case, involving land at Elon Moreh, near Nablus, the court ruled otherwise. Reviewing the security claims made by the Chief of Staff, the judges concluded that the motives were primarily ideological rather than military, and ruled the requisition illegal. Of some importance was the fact that the Minister of Defence did not back the Chief of Staff, and that prominent former military commanders disputed the claims of military necessity before the court. In any event, the decision indicated that the court, in reviewing the use of emergency regulations, assumed the right to check the way in which a military officer's discretionary powers were used under those regulations.[42]

Following the enactment of the 1979 Israeli law that replaced Regulation 111 on administrative detention in Israel, changes were also made in the West Bank and Gaza. A new military order brought practice there into line with the reforms of the 1979 law: more limited authority for issuing orders, the requirement of approval by a qualified judge at the time of detention, and expanded judicial review of detention orders (see "Knesset Legislation," below).[43]

As noted, these changes occurred simultaneously with an overall phasing out of administrative detention in Israel and the territories. However, a series of events in late 1985 led to its reintroduction, after a lull of over three years. A controversial prisoner exchange in mid-year, in which 1,150 security offenders were released in return for two Israeli soldiers captured in Lebanon, put the government on the spot to show that security had not been impaired. As many of those released remained on the West Bank, there was apprehension of a renewal of terrorist activities. Consequently a series of incidents, and especially the murder of two Israeli teachers at the end of July, triggered a wave of detentions. By year's end 131 people had been detained, and in the year that ended on July 31, 1986, a West Bank human rights organization recorded 145 detentions, as well

as 35 restriction orders, 35 deportations, and 65 demolitions
or sealings of houses—though no deportations had occurred
after February, and most of those initially detained were
released at the end of the initial six-month period, in
February and March.[44]

The unrest that erupted in the occupied territories in
December, 1987, however, brought a sharp upsurge in these
measures. By April, 1988, the Israeli government revealed
that it was holding some 1,700 West Bank and Gazan
residents in administrative detention, and by early July the
total had increased to over 2,500.[45] These numbers put an
unaccustomed strain on the procedures designed to guarantee
legal review, and in addition the Israeli army had detained
several thousand prisoners, arrested in violent demonstrations, who were not covered by the detention guidelines
and whose processing for release or trial was protracted at
best.

However, while the 1987-1988 "uprising" was the most
serious challenge to Israeli occupation since its inception,
most of the measures employed to contain it fell under the
customary powers of an occupying power, rather than the
emergency regulations. Under these customary powers, an
occupier may use reasonable force to disperse an unlicensed
demonstration, provided that force not be used punitively
without judicial procedure, and that no punishment be
collective—and on these latter two points, the Israeli
Attorney General issued a statement declaring any such
actions to be illegal and subject to prosecution.

Therefore, despite the tremendous increase in army
activity on the West Bank and Gaza, and the vast increase
in the number of detainees, even the unprecedented unrest
of early 1988 did not reverse the overall trend to declining
use of the 1945 Defence Regulations. In fact, for the
occupied territories, the need to employ special "emergency"
regulations, even if legally justifiable, was questionable.
The latitude allowed by customary international law in
dealing with threats to security—reinforced if necessary by
circumspect use of already existing Jordanian laws—would
seem adequate to any occasion. Since the Israeli government maintains that its actions are compatible with the
Geneva Convention, why not actually apply this universally
accepted instrument?

EMERGENCY REGULATIONS UNDER SECTION 9

The first law passed by the Provisional State Council of the new state of Israel, on May 19, 1948—the Law and Administration Ordinance—provides in Section 9:

(A) If the Provisional State Council finds it advisable, it may declare that a state of emergency exists in the state, and when this declaration is published in the Official Gazette, the Provisional Government may authorize the Prime Minister or any other Minister to promulgate emergency regulations at his discretion for the defense of the state, the public safety, and the maintenance of essential supplies and services.

(B) Emergency regulations may alter, temporarily suspend, or add conditions to any law, and may also impose or increase taxes or other compulsory payments.

(C) Emergency regulations will expire three months from the date of their promulgation, unless they are extended or cancelled before that time by an order of the Provisional State Council, or cancelled by the regulatory authority.

(D) When the Provisional State Authority finds it advisable, it will declare the end of the state of emergency, and when this declaration is published in the Official Gazette, the validity of the emergency regulations will expire at a date or dates specified in the declaration.[46]

As noted, the required state of emergency was declared on the same day that the Ordinance was enacted, and has been in continuous existence since.

The purposes for which regulations might be issued—"defense of the state, the public safety, and the maintenance of essential supplies and services"—was borrowed directly from British practice (see above, p. 5). The powers are given to individual ministers, rather than the government (i.e., the Cabinet) as a whole, and, at least on a literal reading, the minister's powers are not even limited to his normal area of responsibility. But there are also important limitations in comparison to the British regulations: first, the requirement of a declared state of emergency by the legislative branch (Provisional State

Council, later the Knesset); second, the requirement of prior
authorization of the minister's powers by the government;
third, and most important, the limitation of regulations to
three months without action of the legislature.

The Knesset can extend an emergency regulation for
any additional period of time that it chooses, or—as it has
often done—for the duration of the state of emergency. In
the second case, the regulation begins to look like ordinary
legislation, given the permanence of the emergency. In
fact, one of the questions regarding such extensions is
whether they are to be regarded as laws, since they are the
result of a legislative process, or merely as extended
regulations. The question is of more than academic interest;
for one thing, in cases where the Knesset acts only after
the expiration of three months, a renewed regulation would
be retroactively valid for the interim period only if it is
considered to be a law. Secondly, in Israel regular Knesset
laws are not subject to judicial review in the same way that
administrative regulations are.[47]

It has been suggested by a leading legal scholar that
regulations extended by the Knesset are in fact laws, but of
a lesser stature than ordinary legislation. This is
demonstrated by the fact that the Knesset can, and often
has, chosen to renew the regulations in the form of a
regular law rather than in the form of extending the
existing regulations. This being the case, courts should be
able to review extended regulations as regulations, rather
than as laws.[48] The High Court, however, has ruled (Bialar
vs. Minister of Finance, H.C. 243/52, 7(2) P.D. 424) that
Knesset extensions are laws in both senses, being extendable
after the expiration of three months and, like other Knesset
laws, not subject to judicial veto.

Once the Knesset has extended an emergency regulation, it may even be superior to other Knesset laws in one
respect. While other laws are subject to modification by
new emergency regulations, it is somewhat illogical to allow
a minister to make new modifications in regulations that
have just, as required, been acted upon by the Knesset.
Otherwise the substantive consideration of the regulations
by the Knesset has no meaning. Nevertheless, there have
been a few cases where ministers have made changes *after*
Knesset action, though usually in non-controversial matters
and sometimes with retroactive approval by the Knesset.[49]

A more serious threat is that the minister may simply reissue emergency regulations at the end of three months—and so on indefinitely—if the Knesset does *not* vote to extend them. Such a procedure would place permanent legislative power in the minister's hands, and eliminate the Knesset supervision clearly intended by the Ordinance. On the other hand, it would also not be reasonable to forbid a minister from ever again issuing emergency regulations in an area where he had once acted, even if similar circumstances should recur at some time in the future. Klinghoffer suggests a double test for such cases: either that the new regulations differ substantially from the previous ones, or that there has been a significant passage of time before the "recreation" of the circumstances necessitating the emergency measures.[50] The Directives of the Attorney General also explicitly forbid ministers from simply reissuing regulations not extended by the Knesset.

Until recent years, there were few attempts to circumvent the Knesset in this fashion. The major case occurred in January, 1957, when Prime Minister David Ben-Gurion issued regulations on goods and services nearly identical to some imposed three months earlier, at the onset of the Suez campaign, which the Knesset had not managed to act upon. These regulations were, however, subsequently renewed twice by the Knesset, and were eventually replaced by a permanent law on the subject.[51]

As will be seen below, the major use of Section 9 emergency regulations in the last decade has been in authorizing return-to-work orders to employees providing "vital public services." With the increase of such orders has also come a number of instances in which ministers have reissued emergency regulations, without Knesset action, in order to keep a particular group of employees working. In the 1977-1982 period, ten such renewed regulations were issued either before the end of the three month period, or within three months after its expiration. In one of these cases, involving workers in the Ministry of Education, the reissue of the regulation without Knesset approval was successfully challenged in a district labor court.[52]

Court review of emergency regulations under Section 9 (before they become laws) is similar to that of the Defence Regulations. That is, the courts will ascertain that the formal requirements of law were met, and that the minister acted in good faith and for relevant considerations, but do not rule on the merits of the case. One Israel High Court ruling (Kardosh vs. Registrar of Companies, H.C. 241/60, 15 P.D. 1151), dealing with a minister's discretionary authority in a non-emergency context but applicable to also to emergency powers, suggests that the court can also rule on whether the minister is acting within the stated purposes of the authority granted to him. In another case, the High Court threw out an emergency regulation on grounds that it must be "able to be seen as essential in the eyes of the Minister," even though the court would not rule on whether it was actually essential (Paka Investment Company vs. Minister of Agriculture, H.C. 269/67, unpublished).[53]

Like the 1945 British Regulations, the Section 9 powers have been criticized for the broad scope allowed for administrative action in the name of emergency. Substantively, use of Section 9 is limited only by very broadly-defined purposes; it can be, and has been, used in situations where the element of urgency is remote at best, as in the return-to-work orders issued to striking workers. The High Court has often criticized the use of emergency regulations in economic matters that could easily be covered by ordinary legislation, even while it upheld the minister's authority to use them. Emergency regulations were even used once, in 1952, to limit Sabbath driving for motives entirely unrelated to any state of emergency.[54]

Other criticisms involve the way in which hastily-drafted regulations often clash with existing emergency arrangements and with each other. Since Section 9 does not furnish guidelines or define areas of authority, as did the 1937 British Order-in-Council, examples of such conflicts abound.[55] Above all, it is questionable that the drafters of Section 9 envisioned a permanent state of emergency, with these exceptional grants of authority available to Cabinet ministers as everyday alternatives; otherwise, they would not have required a Knesset declaration of emergency. As Ben-Gurion explained when Section 9 was approved by the Provisional State Council, "This is not a constitution for regular periods. This is a constitution for time of emergency."[56]

Outside of their recent use in labor disputes, the Section 9 powers have been used primarily in time of war, with the heaviest usage coming in the first decade of the state's existence. This is explained by the self-restraint of ministers who have been authorized to issue regulations, by the effect of alert supervision by the Knesset, and by the fact that ordinary legislation has given many ministers extensive powers to issue regulations anyway.[57] In addition, the Cabinet has required ministers to obtain its consent for any specific regulations they wish to enact, going beyond the wording of Section 9 which defines the Cabinet's role as granting overall authority to the minister. This requirement, which developed as a custom, is now embodied in the Attorney General's Directives and in internal government rules-of-order.[58] Finally, most of the Basic Laws—legislation designed to form part of an eventual written constitution—contain provisions that they cannot be altered or superseded by emergency regulations.

To date, the Cabinet has given 14 ministers general authority to enact emergency regulations under Section 9. Eight of these authorizations came already in 1948: the Ministers of Defense, Finance, Commerce and Industry, Agriculture, Transportation, Interior, and Immigration, and the Prime Minister. The Minister of Labor was added in 1952, and the Minister of Posts (later Communications) in 1956. The 1967 war triggered the addition of the Ministers of Development and Justice. The only ones added since then are the Minister of Health (in 1976) and of Energy and Infrastructure (in 1979).[59]

The trend in recent years, when emergency rules seemed needed, has been to grant the minister limited, one-time authority covering the matter at hand. Though there is no specific provision for this in the 1948 Ordinance, there is also nothing to prevent it, and it avoids giving a blanket authority to ministers whose role in genuine emergencies may be marginal. Such specific authorizations were made to both the Minister of Health (in 1976) and the Minister of Energy and Infrastructure (twice in 1978) before these officials were given general authority; four such grants of power (in 1977, 1979, 1982, and 1984) have been made to the Minister of Education and Culture (who still lacks a general authorization).[60] Altogether at least seven ministers in the usual Cabinet—Foreign Affairs, Police, Housing and Construction, Education and Culture, Religious Affairs, Economics and Planning, and Tourism, plus Ministers without Portfolios (of whom there have been from two to five in recent governments)—lack general authority to issue emergency regulations under Section 9.

Up to 1962, 79 emergency regulations had been enacted (as opposed to about 1,000 regular laws by the Knesset). Forty-four of these regulations came during the 1948-1949 war, and another ten at the time of the 1956 Suez campaign. Only 11 of the regulations were still in effect in 1962, all by virtue of extensions by the Knesset (only three new regulations had been enacted since 1958). Many of the regulations were never extended beyond the original few months, and many others were replaced by regular laws (not extensions)—suggesting that, in addition to its wartime use, Section 9 was being employed in part to bridge gaps until laws could be passed.[61]

This pattern remained consistent until after the 1973 war. Apart from waves of regulations accompanying the wars of 1967 and 1973, the number of new regulations each year ranged from zero to five, and most of these regulations were not extended by the Knesset.[62]

This pattern seems, at first glance, to change radically in the mid-1970s. The number of new regulations jumps to an annual average of nearly 20 after this date, where it remains today. Most of this quantitative leap, however, is a result of an explosion of regulations authorizing return-to-work orders for striking public employees. Of the 144 new regulations in the 1975-1982 period, 124 were of this type, meaning that the underlying pattern had not significantly altered. At the rate of two to three a year, non-work-related emergency regulations were being enacted *less* frequently than during the first fifteen years of the state's existence, and a large proportion of these came during the 1982 Lebanese War.[63]

The first case of the use of emergency regulations to authorize return-to-work orders was in 1960, against striking pilots of the El Al airline. Until the mid-1970s such use remained sporadic, with only 13 cases total by the end of 1974. But beginning then, and especially after the assumption of power by the less pro-labor Likud bloc in 1977, the use of Section 9 to force public employees back to work became almost routine in labor disputes. By the early 1980s, such regulations were being issued at the rate of almost two per month, against public employees in all categories. Nor was this a reflection of increased striking by public workers; while the number of strikes remained fairly constant, nearly a third of them, by the early 1980s, triggered the use of Section 9 regulations by the government. Such broad use of Section 9 authority during peacetime, going apparently far beyond the original intention of the drafters, aroused strong criticism from some quarters.[64]

Most of the regulations authorizing return-to-work orders were, in the nature of things, temporary. A full 42 percent were cancelled even before the end of three months—usually because the labor dispute was resolved—and nearly all the rest were allowed to expire without renewal. Only two of the return-to-work regulations, one directed at X-ray technicians in 1980 and another at health service physicians in 1983, were extended by the Knesset beyond the original three months. There have also been, as mentioned, about ten cases of ministers, under dubious authority, reissuing similar or identical regulations without action by the Knesset.[65]

The fact remains that, of the over 300 emergency regulations enacted from under Section 9 from 1948 to the end of 1985, only ten were still in force by virtue of extension by the Knesset. Of these, six were enacted initially in the first year of statehood, and then extended by the Knesset until the end of the emergency. This would suggest that a periodic review of such measures, and their replacement by regular legislation, would be a logical step. The most controversial of the early regulations were the Emergency (Security Zones) Regulations of 1949, which empowered the Minister of Defense, with the approval of the Knesset Foreign Affairs and Security Committee, to declare broad areas as security zones and, if necessary, evacuate the inhabitants. This regulation, which went beyond even Regulation 125 of the Defence Regulations, was used to evacuate a small number of villages, including the famous cases of Birim and Ikrit. However, after several extensions by the Knesset, it was allowed to lapse in 1972.[66]

In 1985 Section 9 was used by the National Unity government—a wall-to-wall coalition that followed the 1984 elections—to enact a broad-ranging and drastic Economic Recovery Program. The emergency regulations, signed by both Shimon Peres of Labor as Prime Minister and Yitzhak Modai of Likud as Minister of Finance, established strict controls on wages, prices, conditions of employment, taxes, welfare, and number of public employees, superseding all previous laws and agreements. Leaders of both major parties defended the unusual use of emergency powers on grounds that the economic crisis was threatening imminent disaster, and that getting such a program through the Knesset expeditiously was a practical impossibility, given the range and importance of interests affected. Nevertheless, there were strong reactions from many sources, including condemnation by a former Minister of Justice and some calls for resignation of the Attorney General, who had approved the use of Section 9.[67]

In 1975 a proposed Basic Law legislation was tabled and referred to committee, where it languishes to this day. The proposed wording of the Basic Law included provisions on emergency regulations that would replace those in the 1948 law. The differences between the two documents are slight, though the new wording would clarify the procedure for ending an emergency, and provides explicitly for making Basic Laws (including itself) unalterable by emergency rules. On the other hand, it adds a provision against protecting regular laws, and some other minor reductions in the Knesset role, that have aroused criticism.[68]

On the whole, the use of Emergency Regulations under Section 9 has been relatively non-controversial, despite the broad wording of the statute, and has tended to decline over time. Apart from the recent (numerically important) use in labor disputes, their major use has been in wartime, which probably reflects the initial intention as well as the need, even under conditions of permanent crisis, to reserve some measures for the most threatening occasions only. It is interesting to note that during the 1982 Lebanese War, for example, the government made use of Section 9 to authorize the detention of non-Israeli citizens, but in doing so proclaimed a "special" state of emergency whose legal provenance was uncertain.[69] The need to have exceptional measures during actual wartime could be meet, presumably, by reserving Section 9 for that purpose—that is, by ending the state of emergency during peacetime and providing through regular Knesset laws for any necessary secondary legislation by Ministers now covered by permanent "emergency" regulations. To a certain extent, such arrangements already exist.

KNESSET LEGISLATION

Since it is the act of a deliberative legislative body, Knesset "emergency" legislation represents the greatest degree of normalization in adjustment to permanent crisis. When a declared state of emergency is a permanent fixture, laws whose operation is dependent on its existence are difficult to distinguish from other laws. A number of Israeli laws fit this description, as do emergency regulations under Section 9 that were simply extended by the Knesset until the end of the state of emergency.[70] Many of these laws are "emergency" measures in name only, since in scope, procedure, reviewability in court, and other respects, they do not differ from ordinary legislation.

There are, on the other hand, laws specially relevant to emergencies either because they give a minister emergency rule-making power, or because they involve subjects (such as preventive detention) linked to security. But even laws giving ministers broad powers to make "emergency" regulations may not differ that much from ordinary legislation granting extensive powers of secondary legislation to the minister, of which there are many examples. Labelling such regulatory authority as "emergency" powers may be good politics in the Knesset, but may be misleading. The Israel High Court of Justice has, for example, criticized the use of "emergency" regulatory power, under the 1957 Supervision of Goods and Services Act, to cover such matters as animal slaughter houses or delivery to bread shops.[71] Presumably the Knesset does not wish to concern itself with the details of animal slaughter or bread delivery, but labelling the delegated authority as "emergency" powers only adds needless confusion and controversy.

An example of delegated powers that are genuinely emergency-related is the authority given the Minister of Defence, in the Law of Military Service, to order a mobilization and take other appropriate military measures in the face of an imminent threat. As befits genuine emergencies, these powers are limited to fourteen days without Knesset approval.[72]

The most important legislation whose *content* is emergency-oriented is the Emergency Powers (Detention)

Law of 1979. This act, also operative only during a declared state of emergency, replaces the British Defence Regulations on detention and deportation. In contrast to the British regulations, it requires judicial approval of any detention within 48 hours (as with ordinary police arrests). The detention is limited to six months, with a review of the case after three months. The detainee must be present at hearings, but it may still be closed and evidence can still be withheld (though not from the judge). Judicial review explicitly includes examination of the "objective reasons of state security" that justify the detention. The law also abolished the deportation provisions of Defence Regulation 112, eliminating that particular emergency measure in Israel (though not in the occupied territories). Rubinstein, who had been among the leading critics of previous arrangements called the new law a "most liberal arrangement—almost without precedent in countries facing emergency situations and war. . . ."[73]

As it turned out, the first detention to be challenged in court under the new law involved the first Jewish detainee in decades, Rabbi Meir Kahane, the leader of the vehemently anti-Arab Kach party. Kahane was believed to be planning acts of violence aimed at encouraging Arab emigration, and was therefore ordered detained in May, 1980. After the order was upheld in the normal review process, Kahane appealed to the Supreme Court, which also upheld the order in an opinion that seemed to limit the scope of judicial review. Despite the broader wording of the new act, the court decided that the detention, though subject to judicial review, was "still an administrative detention." Consequently, it declined to "substitute its own considerations for those of the Minister of Defense."[74] Some observers felt the court had unnecessarily limited itself, as the law required it to check the "objective reasons of state security" underlying the order, which it could hardly do without examining the minister's judgement. If the court was going to accept any order that was "legal" in form, it was argued, then the language of the 1979 law was emptied of content.[75]

In 1982, however, the High Court set aside a detention order that it felt had been issued not for legitimate security reasons, but in order to hold a prisoner, whose conviction had been overturned, until the state's appeal could be heard.[76] The same year another detention order was annulled on grounds that the acts of the detainee had consisted primarily of expressions of opinion and did not constitute the "objective reasons" that would justify his detention.[77]

Insofar as it functions as ordinary legislation and involves standard judicial procedures, the 1979 Emergency Detention Law can even be judged by normal human rights standards rather than as emergency legislation. The International Covenant of Civil and Political Rights, which Israel has signed but not ratified, provides (Article 9) that "no one shall be subjected to arbitrary arrest or detention. . . ." Insofar as Israeli procedures guarantee against arbitrariness, they meet this standard. Shetreet also makes a strong case that they meet the International Law Association standards on administrative detention: procedures set by law, the right to be informed of grounds for detention, the right to consult a lawyer, judicial review, limited duration, and humane treatment. Only on publication of the names of the detainees is Israeli practice remiss.[78]

It is also argued that Israeli practice compares favorably to other countries. According to the International Commission of Jurists, at least 85 countries have laws permitting preventive detention and have used such laws in recent years.[79] Compared even to such nations as Great Britain (especially in Northern Ireland), Canada (where 450 French Canadians were detained in 1970), or the United States in its treatment of the Japanese during World War II, the 1979 Israeli law, as applied, seems unexceptional. This, however, raises another question: if this most problematic part of the 1945 British Defence Regulations can be successfully replaced by "ordinary" legislation, then why are the rest of them still on the books?

CONCLUSIONS

As shown, there has been movement over time from the more drastic forms of emergency powers to the more regularized forms. In terms of our categories, Section 9 has in some cases replaced the use of 1945 British Defence Regulations, and Knesset legislation has expanded at the expense of both. Related to this are the three patterns described at the outset:

First, government institutions have functioned normally throughout Israel's history, despite recurrent wars and continuous tension. The Knesset has asserted its role vigorously, often challenging the use of emergency powers and expanding the range of subjects covered by regular legislation. The obvious example is the 1979 law on detention that replaced more drastic British regulations, but other parts of the Defence Regulations have also become dead letters in the light of Israeli legislation. The major exception to normal government functioning (apart from the occupied territories) was the military government in Arab-inhabited border areas, which ended in 1966. The use of Regulation 125 and other emergency measures to expropriate Arab land also took place primarily in the earlier period. In fact, since the events of "Land Day" in 1976, in which the country was rocked by violent Israeli Arab demonstrations, expropriation of Arab land has halted and some previous confiscations have even been reversed (notably the controversial "Area 9" in 1986).

Second, many emergency powers on paper were not utilized in practice, or when used were moderated by stricter internal guidelines. The censorship arrangements inherited by the Mandate remain formidable in theory, but are mitigated in reality by voluntary arrangements that do not appear in the statute books.[80] Likewise the application of Regulation 111 on detention was severely circumscribed by administrative guidelines, in the period before it was superseded by legislation. The authority given ministers under Section 9 has been tempered by the practice of requiring Cabinet consent for specific regulations, and by the recent tendency to make one-time specific grants of authority—neither procedure being drawn from the original statute (on the other hand, the increased use of Section 9 in labor disputes represents a step in the other direction).

Third, the balance between security considerations and the regular processes of law and justice has tipped more in the direction of the latter. Apart from the passage of regular legislation, the role of the courts has been modestly expanded. Judges may now see secret evidence and can order it disclosed to the defendant. Judicial review of the procedures in the use of emergency regulations has usually been strong—legal and judicial institutions being generally a strong point of the Israeli system—and in recent years there has also been greater willingness by the courts to question the substantive judgments in emergency orders, especially in the important areas of detention and land confiscation. There is no longer an automatic deference to security claims, a development that may also reflect the damage done to the prestige of the security establishment by mistakes in the wars of 1973 and 1982.[81]

Considering the amount of discretion available, and the absence of firm institutional obstacles in a system without a written constitution or bill of rights, the use of emergency powers in Israel has been modest. The same might be said in comparison to other nations; for example, the British Emergency Powers (Defence) Acts of 1939 and 1940 (in Britain itself) went much further than Israeli laws or practice, and many of its provisions were continued after the war, until as late as 1959.[82] Nevertheless, an alert civil libertarian could easily identify several areas of weakness in the application of Israeli emergency powers. Among these would be the use of emergency regulations in non-emergency situations, the remaining limitations on judicial review, defective safeguards in the administrative process itself, the unequal application of emergency rules, and the use of measures questionable in themselves.

Despite efforts to legislate, there is still continuing use of emergency powers in areas of questionable urgency, such as economic regulations and return-to-work orders. The use of emergency authority to enact the Economic Recovery Program in 1985 demonstrates the continuing temptation to take the shortcut through normal procedures when it is available.

Judicial review was expanded in the 1979 detention law to cover the "objective reasons" behind a detention order, but in other issues involving emergency regulations the courts continue to exercise restraint in challenging the content of a minister's or military officer's judgment.

Administrative procedures do not always provide for internal review, as they do in the case of detention. For example, orders restricting an individual's movements, or confining him to his town or residence, are not reviewed. In addition, there is continuing complaint about the lack of a requirement that orders under the Defence Regulations be published.

The fact that emergency regulations impinge dispropor-tionately on the Arab population of Israel is to some degree inevitable under current political and military conditions.

The targeting of the Arab population has also decreased somewhat over time, especially with the abolition of military government in 1966. But the continued existence of different arrangements for newspaper censorship, for example, raises the question of equality before the law.

Whether they are based on the Defence Regulations or on some other source, such practices as deportation and demolition of houses can be challenged. Deportation, still used in the West Bank and Gaza, is very difficult to justify in international law except under exceptional circumstances. Even the argument that Jordanian citizens are merely being deported to Jordan is undercut when deportees are sent across the Lebanese or other borders. The demolition of houses is a punitive measure—unlike detention, which is considered preventive—and therefore raises the issue of punishment without trial in a way that detention does not.

Despite these problems, however, the main problem is not as much the actual exercise of emergency powers as the continued existence of a broad range of potentially usable powers in a climate where emergency has become routine. The logical answer would be to bring law into accord with practice, by eliminating the "loaded weapons" that are still lying around, and by continuing the process of regularizing and domesticating those measures that are used. Basically, this would mean eliminating the remainder of the British Defence Regulations, a step favored—as seen—by many Israelis. There is also Shetreet's suggestion, mentioned above, to differentiate between two levels of emergency: a general level necessitating only minimal measures, and a special level for wartime and other moments when exceptional steps are justified. The need to distinguish these two situations was clearly felt by the Israeli government during the Lebanese War, when it conjured up the concept of a "special" state of emergency to fit its needs of the moment.

The emergency regulatory powers under Section 9 of the Law and Administration Ordinance might be best suited for such "special" conditions. In any event these powers have been used mainly in wartime, when there was no time for Knesset action, and are of a temporary character unless extended by the Knesset. Their use during other periods, when the Knesset is able to act, has never had a clear logical basis. If it were decided to limit their activation to a "special" period of emergency, declared either by the

Cabinet or the Knesset, it would not impede the ability to act in time of crisis.

More general measures that reflect more urgency can be embodied in legislation whose duration is dependent on a general state of emergency, as is increasingly being done anyway. One logical step would be to provide legislation governing the issuance of return-to-work orders for public employees so that these orders—when and if needed—do not fall under provisions intended for wartime. At the same time, the regulations that originated from Section 9 authority, but which have been indefinitely extended by the Knesset, could also be transferred to the status of regular legislation, with no real change in their operation but greater clarity in their status.

To complete this scenario, the 1945 Defence Regulations could be replaced either by regular legislation, on matters requiring ongoing supervision, or Section 9 authority, for measures reserved for wartime. A model for the former is the Emergency Powers (Detention) Law of 1979, which replaced draconian British regulations with more circumscribed procedures. A natural candidate for such treatment is press censorship, where the law would only have to be changed to reflect an informal, and less drastic, arrangement that already exists.

As for the West Bank and Gaza, since Israel usually goes to the trouble of arguing the compatibility of its measures there with the Geneva Convention, there would be little to lose in recognizing the applicability of that convention.[83] There would then be little need to cling to the dubious authority of the Defence Regulations in the occupied territories either. Other improvements that could be made would include establishment of a military court of appeal, in order to make the situation more parallel to that existing in Israel, and the termination of censorship efforts that seem doomed to futility in any event.

In conclusion, the balance between the demands of security (and consequently emergency powers), and those of law and liberty, is at least as problematic in Israel as in any other democratic state. Given the circumstances, Israel may even represent the extreme test case of such balancing. In the event, there are good arguments for criticizing the weight assigned to emergency powers, and for wishing the balance moved somewhat in the opposite direction. But it is important to bear in mind that an act of balancing is taking place. Despite extraordinary pressures, and whatever the blemishes, Israel has managed to maintain the rule of law.

ENDNOTES

1. *The Military Balance 1986-1987* (London: The International Institute for Strategic Studies, 1986), pp. 92-112, 213.

2. Cases of minorities identified with an "enemy" state include Greeks in Turkey and Turks in Greece; Moslems in India and Hindus in Pakistan; Somalis in Ethiopia; and (during World War II) Germans in the Soviet Union and Japanese in the United States and Canada. None of these models is particularly auspicious; consider, for the sake of comparison, the "emergency measures" taken against the North American Japanese.

3. Amnon Rubinstein, *The Constitutional Law of the State of Israel* (Tel Aviv: Schocken, 1980), p. 224 (Hebrew).

4. Shimon Shetreet, "A Contemporary Model of Emergency Detention Law: An Assessment of the Israel Law," *Israel Yearbook on Human Rights*, 14 (1984a): 195.

5. For an overview of the three mechanisms of emergency legislation, see *ibid.*, pp. 187-196, and Baruch Bracha, "Addendum: Some Remarks on Israeli Law Regarding National Security," *Israel Yearbook on Human Rights*, 10 (1980):295-297.

6. Bracha, "Restriction of Personal Freedom Without Due Process of Law According to the Defence (Emergency) Regulations, 1945," *Israel Yearbook on Human Rights*, 8 (1978):299.

7. Professor G.I.A.D. Draper, in "Symposium on Human Rights," *Israel Yearbook on Human Rights*, 1 (1971): 383. Draper adds that he and others dissuaded the British Secretary of State for War from applying similar regulations later on in Cyprus, on the grounds that "they were thoroughly bad regulations."

8. *The Palestine Gazette*, No. 1422, Supplement No. 2, September 27, 1945, pp. 1055-1098.

9. Richard Crossman, *Palestine Mission: A Personal Record* (New York and London: Harper and Brothers, 1947), p. 129.

10. Bernard Joseph, *British Rule in Palestine* (Washington: Public Affairs Press, 1948), pp. 218-230. For severe critiques at the time by Jewish legal scholars, see M. Friedman, "Detainees under the Emergency Regulation," *Hapraklit*, 2 (August 1945): 242-243 (Hebrew); and R. Nuchimowski, "Deportations under the Defence Regulations," *Hapraklit*, 3 (April, 1946): 104-109, and 3 (May, 1946): 134-140 (Hebrew).

11. Rubinstein, pp. 219-220 (see also Rubinstein, "Need for Amendment of Defence Regulations," *Hapraklit*, 38 (July, 1973): 486-499); Yitzhak Hans Klinghoffer, "On Emergency Regulations in Israel," in Haim Kohn, ed., *Jubilee Book for Pinhas Rosen* (Jerusalem: Mifal Hashichpul, 1962), p. 121 (Hebrew).

12. *Divrei Haknesset* (Knesset Proceedings), May 21, 1951 (Hebrew).

13. Bracha, 1978, p. 318. However, those parts of the *1939* British Defence Regulations that were *not* incorporated into the 1945 edition were explicitly repealed by Prime Minister David Ben-Gurion by the Emergency Regulations issued, under Section 9, at the time of the Suez Campaign (October 31, 1956). These provisions, involving the regulation of goods and services, were superseded by similar provisions in the new emergency regulations, which were subsequently enacted into regular legislation.

14. *Ibid.*, p. 303. The relevant court case is Ziv vs. Gubernik, H.C. (High Court) 10/48, 1 P.D. (Piskei Din) 85, from 1948. Klinghoffer, pp. 119-121, cites a 1950 case that seems to show that Mandatory authority for new regulations is sometimes valid, and suggests that the proper interpretation is that British regulations cannot be the source of new rules that change existing laws or regulations.

15. Bracha, 1980, p. 296.

16. Asher Arian, *Politics in Israel: The Second Generation* (Chatham, NJ: Chatham House Publishers, 1985), p. 254; U.S. Department of State, *Country Reports on Human Rights Practices for 1985* (Washington: U.S. Government Printing Office, 1986), p. 1260. It should be kept in mind that articles and books published abroad can usually be reprinted or quoted in the Israeli press, thus providing a convenient method of circumventing controls; in other words, blocked material finds its way into Israeli newspapers via the European or American press. Sometimes, however—as during the famous Lavon affair—this method is also blocked on grounds that the reprint of a news item in Israel would constitute a form of "confirmation" for its truth.

17. Edi Retig, "The Sting: Secret Evidence, the Burden of Proof, and Freedom of Expression," *Mishpatim*, 14 (1984): 118-120, 125-126 (Hebrew).

18. Virgil Falloon, *Excessive Secrecy, Lack of Guidelines: A Report on the Military Censorship in the West Bank* (Ramallah: Law in the Service of Man, 1986), pp. 5-8.

19. Michael Saltman, "The Use of the Mandatory Emergency Laws by the Israeli Government," *International Journal of the Sociology of Law*, 10 (November, 1982): 385-394 (Hebrew version: *Machberet L'mechkar U'lbikoret*, 9 (1984): 55-63); Sabri Jiryis, *The Arabs in Israel* (New York: Monthly Review Press, 1976), pp. 16-18, 26.

20. Saltman, 1984, 58-61; Avraham Poyastro, *Land as a Mechanism of Control: Israel's Policy towards the Arab Minority 1948-1966*, (Master's Thesis, Department of Political Science, University of Haifa, 1985), pp. 19-22, 37-42 (Hebrew).

21. Alan Dersohwitz, "Preventive Detention of Citizens During a National Emergency—A Comparison between Israel and the United States," *Israel Yearbook on Human Rights*, 1 (1971): 316-317; Bracha, 1978, 306-308.

22. Dershowitz, p. 303.

23. *Ibid.*, pp. 316-317.

24. Based on official figures collected by Jiryis, p. 30; Dershowitz, pp. 310-311, and Shetreet, 1984a, p. 187.

25. Dershowitz, p. 321.

26. Rubinstein, in "Symposium on Human Rights," p. 384.

27. Rubinstein, 1980, pp. 223-224.

28. Bracha, 1978, p. 309.

29. Rubinstein, 1971, p. 384; Shetreet, 1984a, p. 185; Harold Rudolph, "The Judicial Review of Administrative Detention Orders in Israel," *Israel Yearbook on Human Rights*, 14 (1984): 150.

30. Bracha, 1978, pp. 311, 313; Shetreet, 1984a, p. 185.

31. Bracha, 1978, pp. 316-317; Rubinstein, 1971, p. 384; "Human Rights in Time of Emergency (Symposium)," *Z'chuyot Haezrach* (The Association for Civil Rights in Israel), 5 (1983): 13-17 (Hebrew).

32. Michael Goldstein, "Israeli Security Measures in the Occupied Territories: Administrative Detention," *Middle East Journal*, 32 (Winter, 1978): 37 (summarizing the claims made by the United Nations Special Committee to Investigate Israeli Practices Affecting Human Rights of the Population of the Occupied Territories). The

applicability of the Defence Regulations to the Golan Heights or Sinai would seem altogether dubious, as neither had been part of Palestine, but in both cases the affected population was small and the question has become moot (in Sinai by the return to Egyptian sovereignty, and on the Golan by the extension of municipal Israeli law).

33. Dov Shefi, "The Protection of Human Rights in Areas Administered by Israel: United Nations Findings and Reality," *Israel Yearbook on Human Rights*, 3 (1973): 344-345; Fania Domb, "Judicial Decisions: Supreme Court of Israel," *Israel Yearbook on Human Rights*, 9 (1979): 343-344; Israel National Section of the International Commission of Jurists, *The Rule of Law in the Areas Administered by Israel* (Tel Aviv, 1981), pp. 68 (includes citations of the Jordanian court cases).

34. Emma Playfair, *Administrative Detention in the Occupied West Bank* (Ramallah: Law in the Service of Man, 1986), p. 11.

35. *Amnesty International Report 1986* (London: Amnesty International Publications, 1986), pp. 338-340.

36. Playfair, pp. 3-5; Goldstein, p. 44.

37. Thomas S. Kuttner, "Israel and the West Bank: Aspects of the Law of Belligerent Occupation," *Israel Yearbook on Human Rights*, 7 (1977): 211-212; Playfair, pp. 14-15, 19.

38. Attorney General Meir Shamgar, "The Observance of International Law in the Administered Territories," *Israel Yearbook on Human Rights*, 9 (1971): 274-275; Shefi, pp. 348-349; Kuttner, p. 216.

39. Ann M. Lesch, "Israeli Deportation of Palestinians from the West Bank and the Gaza Strip, 1967-1978," *Journal of Palestine Studies*, 8 (Winter, 1979): 102-103; the Israeli figure is given in *Financial Times*, December 9, 1977.

40. The court case is Sakhwil et al. vs. Commander of the Judea and Samaria Region, H.C. 434/79, 34 (1) P.D. 464; see Domb, "Judicial Decisions: Judgments of the Supreme Court of Israel Relating to the Administered Territories," *Israel Yearbook on Human Rights*, 10 (1980): 345-346. See also Kuttner, p. 218, and Shamgar, pp. 275-276. On statistics during the uprising since December, 1987, see *Jerusalem Post International Edition*, December 17, 1988.

41. Falloon, pp. 8-18.

42. The Beit El case is Ayub vs. Minister of Defence, H.C. 606/78, 33(2) P.D. 113; Elon Moreh is Dweikat et al. vs. the Government of Israel et al., H.C. 390/79, 34(1) P.D. 1; see Domb, 1979, pp. 345-349.

43. Itzak Zamir, "Directives of the Attorney General on the Matter of the Emergency Powers (Detention) Law, 5739-1979," *Israel Law Review*, 18 (Winter, 1983); 157-158; Shetreet, pp. 186-187.

44. *Amnesty International Report 1986*, pp. 336-337; Playfair, p. 5; *Newsletter*, Law in the Service of Man, No. 14 (July-August, 1986): 6, supplemented by other information supplied by Law in the Service of Man.

45. *New York Times*, April 25, 1988; *Jerusalem Post International Edition*, July 2, 1988.

46. *Iton Rishmi* (Official Gazette), 1948, No. 2, Supp. A, 1 (Hebrew).

47. Rubinstein, 1980, pp. 385-388, provides a definitive discussion of this point. It has also been argued that a regular law cancelled by an emergency regulation does not automatically become valid again when the emergency regulation expires; see Yitzhak Vines, "The Authority of an Emergency Regulation to Cancel Any Law," *Hapraklit*, 15 (July, 1959): 380-381.

48. Klinghoffer, pp. 107-110.

49. Klinghoffer, pp. 102-104, gives as examples the extended regulations on ship regulation and mobilization (both approved by the Knesset in 1948, and changed by the minister in 1957), on registration and mobilization (Knesset approval 1950, changed 1956), compulsory payments (Knesset approval 1952, changed 1953), and departure abroad (Knesset approval 1949, changed 1953, but an identical law was quickly passed).

50. Klinghoffer, pp. 96-99.

51. *Ibid.*, pp. 100-102; Rubinstein, 1980, pp. 388-389.

52. Mordechai Mironi, *Return-To-Work Orders: Government Intervention in Labor Disputes Through Emergency Regulations and Work Injunctions* (Tel Aviv: The Institute for Social and Labor Research, University of Tel Aviv, 1983), pp. 26-27 (Hebrew).

53. Rubinstein, 1980, pp. 381-385.

54. Klinghoffer, pp. 86-89; Shetreet, 1984a, pp. 192-193; Rubinstein, 1980, pp. 382-385.

55. Several cases are described by Hannah Avnur, "Emergency Legislative Policy," *Hapraklit*, 23 (October, 1967): 528-533 (Hebrew).

56. Quoted by Mironi, p. 40.

57. Klinghoffer, pp. 118-119.

58. Shetreet, 1984a, pp. 189-189; Mironi, p. 9.

59. *Iton Rishmi*, 1947-1948: 16, 70; 1948-1949: 82; *Yalkut Hapirsumim* (Collected Publications), 1951-1952: 779; 1955-1956: 474; 1966-1967: 1618, 1830; 1976-1977: 908; 1978-1979: 908 (Hebrew); information on this topic has been collected by Meroni, p. 7.

60. *Yalkut Hapirsumim*, 1976-1977: 262, 281; 1977-1978: 1520, 1707; 1978-1979: 908; 1981-1982: 1318; 1983-1984: 2730; Mironi, pp. 8-9.

61.   Klinghoffer, 92-93, 107, 115-118.

62.   Based on a survey of the *Kovetz Takanot* (Collected Regulations, Hebrew) for the years involved.

63.   Mironi, pp. 17-18; *Kovetz Hatakanot* for the years involved.

64.   A full analysis of this new pattern is provided by Mironi, especially pp. 17-19, 23, 25, and 39-54. The operation of a National Unity government since late 1984 has not significantly reduced the recourse to this weapon in labor disputes, to judge from the figures available to the end of September, 1985.

65.   Mironi, pp. 25-27.

66.   Poyastro, pp. 22-25; Jiryis, pp. 90-91; *Sefer Hahokim* (Collected Laws, Hebrew), various years.

67.   The emergency regulations were published in the Israel press on July 8, 1985; see, for example, *Ma'ariv* and *Yediot Ahronot* of that date. The interview with the former Justice Minister, Haim Tsadok, is in *Davar*, July 8, 1985.

68.   A full critique is provided in Bracha, "The Emergency Regulation Provisions in Basic Law: Legislation," *Hapraklit*, 31 (1977): 491-511 (Hebrew).

69.   Shetreet, 1984a, pp. 191-192.

70.   Klinghoffer, p. 90, provides a list of laws whose duration or functioning is dependent on the existence of a state of emergency. These include the Prevention of Terrorism Ordinance, 1948; the Absentee Property Act, 1950; the Prevention of Infiltration Act, 1954; the Supervision of Goods and Services Act, 1957; and a number of labor laws.

71.   Shetreet, 1984a, pp. 188-189, 192-193.

72. Shetreet, "Democracy in Wartime in Israel—The Legal Framework in Practical Perspective," *Skira Hodshit* (Monthly Survey) (August-September, 1984b): 48, 51 (Hebrew).

73. Rubinstein, 1980, p. 220; see analysis of law, pp. 220-223. Also, Shetreet, 1984b, especially p. 186; and Klinghoffer, "Preventive Detention for Reasons of Security," *Mishpatim*, 11 (1981): 286-289 (Hebrew).

74. Rabbi Kahane et al. vs. Minister of Defense, A.A.D. (Appeal Against Administrative Detention) 1/80, 35(2) P.D. 253.

75. Rudolph, pp. 155, 158, 178; Klinghoffer, 1981, pp. 289-293.

76. Qawasma vs. Minister of Defense, A.A.D. 1/82, 36(1), P.D. 666. This case, involving a Hazem Mahmud Qawasma, should not be confused with the better known court case involving the 1980 deportation of Hebron Mayor Fahd El-Qawasma.

77. Bathish vs. Minister of Defense, A.A.D. 18/82, unpublished; Rudolph, pp. 167-170, 173-174.

78. Shetreet, 1984a, pp. 218-219.

79. Niall MacDermot, "Draft Intervention on Administrative Detention to the U.N. Commission on Human Rights," *ICJ Newsletter*, No. 24 (January/March, 1985): 53.

80. Rubinstein, 1971, p. 385.

81. Shetreet, 1984b, pp. 55-56.

82. Rubinstein, 1980, p. 219.

83. Arie Pach, "Human Rights in West Bank Military Courts," *Israel Yearbook on Human Rights*, 7 (1977): 252.

CHAPTER 2

Emergency Powers in Northern Ireland

J. C. GARNETT

It is both commonplace and true to claim that the problems of Northern Ireland can only be solved by a *political* settlement, for which, at minimum, there must be a grudging acquiescence on the part of the warring factions and the other participants to the conflict. Unfortunately, though various possible solutions have been canvassed during the last fifteen years, no consensus on any of them has emerged, and the province today is as divided as ever. My impression is that the record of failure so far is not a result of any lack of imagination, will, or creative effort on the part of those concerned, but an inevitable consequence of trying to reconcile the irreconcilable. The plain fact of the matter is that so long as the participants in the conflict continue to think as they do, no "political" solution is possible.

In short, so long as the Protestant and Catholic communities in Northern Ireland continue to hate and mistrust each other, so long as the British government remains committed to the wishes of the majority in Northern Ireland, so long as the IRA practices violence, so long as the Dublin government seeks to resolve the issue in the context of a "United Ireland"—so long as these fundamental attitudes and postures set the parameters for debate, no political solution can ever be devised. The Irish question is at least as intractable as the Palestinian issue, and the basic problem facing the British government is not how to solve it, but how to contain, manage, and live with it for the foreseeable future.

This fairly bleak assessment means that whatever the long term future of the province turns out to be, the British government faces the immediate problem of governing a part of the realm which is wracked with violence and where the prospect of major civil war is never far beneath the surface of every day events. Though it is undoubtedly interested in pursuing measures to reconcile the embittered communities within the province, the immediate prerequisite is the maintenance of law and order. As W. Whitelaw put it at the beginning of the 1972 Green Paper "The British government have a clear objective in Northern Ireland. It is to deliver its people from the violence and fear in which they live today and to set them free to realize their great potential to the full."[1]   Perhaps the Westminister government can be criticized for the bankruptcy of its ideas for a long term solution to the problem of Ireland, but its short term objective is surely right.

In the pursuit of this short term objective it has been necessary to amend the constitution of Northern Ireland in fairly fundamental ways.   Until 1972, a good deal of government in the province was devolved to the Stormont parliament in Belfast, but when this became unworkable, it became necessary to rule the Province directly from Westminister.   Today, Northern Ireland is ruled on much the same basis as Scotland and Wales, and the measure of devolution traditionally enjoyed by Stormont is in abeyance. This is not regarded as a satisfactory arrangement by anyone—least of all by the British government—but it is a solution which is tolerable to both communities in the province, and, from their point of view, preferable to any of the alternative "power sharing" models that have been suggested so far.   It is not a particularly "democratic" arrangement in that it clearly diminishes the role of the Irish people in running their own affairs, but it removes the accusation of "unfairness" which is inevitably leveled by either the Protestant or Catholic community at every suggested alternative.   I believe that for the foreseeable future "direct rule" is the least risky pattern of government for Northern Ireland, and there is more than a possibility that it may become—largely through default—a permanent pattern of government.

EMERGENCY LEGISLATION

Of course, what makes Northern Ireland constitutionally different from the United Kingdom is not "direct rule" but the gamut of emergency powers legislation which, over the years, has been enacted to enable the British to combat terrorism and civil disorder within the province, and enhance the role of the British army in enforcing this legislation. From the moment when Northern Ireland was created in 1922, right up to 1984, a variety of statutes and statutory instruments have provided a complicated and frequently overlapping web of laws and regulations designed to increase the powers of both the government of Northern Ireland (when it existed) and the British government to control political violence within that troubled community.

It is difficult to be precise about what is meant by the phrase "emergency powers." To simply argue, as some have done, that emergency powers are those which are enacted to deal with emergencies threatening the vital interests of states, is not very satisfactory, if only because a good deal of "normal" law is applicable to such emergencies. But though difficult to define precisely, it seems sensible to agree with David Bonner that emergency powers usually share the following three characteristics. First, they are conceived by those who wield them to be extraordinary in the sense that in the absence of emergency they would not normally be available; second, they tend to confer on the government wide discretionary powers which are unfettered by normal constitutional constraints; third, they are usually considered to be of a temporary nature.[2]

Normally this emergency legislation, like the rest of British law, is enforced by the police authorities in Northern Ireland. But on a number of occasions, and continuously since 1969, the responsibility for law enforcement within the province has been shared with the British army. And during the early 1970s it was the army which played the dominant role, particularly in the most sensitive Catholic areas of the province. This highly visible and active role for the military in the security affairs of the province has given Northern Ireland a distinctive flavor, quite unlike the rest of the United Kingdom.

The emergency legislation began with the Civil Authorities (Special Powers) Act of 1922. This act was originally intended as a purely temporary measure to be dispensed with as soon as normality returned to the province. However, it was found necessary to reenact this legislation annually until 1928 when it was further extended for a period of five years. In 1933 it was thought necessary to make the act permanent, and between that date and 1973, when it was replaced by the Emergency Provisions Act, it was supplemented by numerous statutory instruments made by the Northern Ireland prime minister under powers conferred on him by the Act.

The "Special Powers" Act was particularly sweeping in the powers which it conferred. Amongst other things, it empowered the government of Northern Ireland to impose curfews, internment without trial, arrest and search without warrant, and detention for up to 48 hours for interrogation. In addition, any assembly of three or more persons could be ordered to disperse if an officer making the demand believed that the assembly might lead to a breach of the peace. The Minister for Home Affairs could, under Section I, "take all such steps and issue all such orders as may be necessary for preserving the peace and maintaining order."[3] He could prohibit the publication and distribution of any newspaper or periodical. He could outlaw various associations, impose the death penalty for certain "explosives" offenses and order floggings for lesser offenses. And under Section II (4) there was a remarkable "catch all" provision:

> If any person does any act of such a nature as to be calculated to be prejudicial to the preservation of the peace or maintenance of order in Northern Ireland and not specially provided for in the regulations, he shall be deemed guilty of an offence against the regulations.[4]

Other security legislation in the province includes the Flags and Emblems Act (1954), the Criminal Justice (Temporary Provisions) Act (1970), and amended in 1971, the Firearms Act (1969) and amended in 1971, the Northern Ireland (Emergency Provisions) Act (1973), the Prevention of Terrorism (Temporary Provisions) Acts (1974 and 1976), and the Prevention of Terrorism Act (1984).

Taken together these acts enormously increase the power of the security forces in their battle against terrorism and in their efforts to maintain law and order. In general terms, this legislation severely limits the activities of organizations connected with terrorism by making it impossible for them to operate within the law; it extends the substantive criminal law to encompass any activity which may be supportive of terrorist activity; it curtails the procedural "due process" protection afforded to defendants charged with "scheduled" offenses; it authorizes searches without warrant, expands powers of seizure, arrest, and detention by the police and security forces; it permits the secretary of state to exclude suspected terrorists from British territory; it empowers the secretary of state for Northern Ireland to issue detention orders of unlimited duration for suspected terrorists.

In more detail, this body of special legislation proscribes the IRA, the INLA, and certain Protestant paramilitary organizations, and prohibits both membership and support of them. It limits the availability of bail to those arrested for certain offenses; it abolishes the requirement of jury trials, permits the admissability of "confessions" as evidence, limits the need for witnesses, and establishes a "reverse onus of proof" for the crimes of possession of firearms, munitions, and explosives. Furthermore, these various acts give substantial powers of entry to security forces, permitting them to enter private property without warrant in their search for terrorists and their weapons. Those arrested can be detained for up to 72 hours before being brought before a magistrate. The security forces are permitted to arrest without warrant those suspected of committing, or of having committed, or of being about to commit, an offense under the Prevention of Terrorism Act and detain them for 48 hours. Members of the armed forces are empowered to arrest a suspect without warrant and to hold him for up to four hours without stating the grounds for arrest.

This legislation is clearly controversial and has attracted hostile comment from those who are worried by its impact on civil liberties in Northern Ireland. Theirs is an important perspective from which to examine emergency legislation, but it is not the only viewpoint—and in terms of making an overall assessment of the value of this legislation it is inadequate. An equally valid approach, and arguably a more important one, is one which looks at the legislation in terms of its effectiveness in combatting terrorism and civil disorder.

I would argue that judging emergency legislation solely in terms of its side effects on civil rights is as absurd as judging a new highway on the basis of its aesthetic appeal—without considering the contribution which it makes to alleviating the traffic problem. Equally, to evaluate a new highway without paying some attention to the environmental damage which its construction caused would be shortsighted.

The rest of this chapter examines the emergency legislation enacted for Northern Ireland in terms of its military and political effectiveness, but it also pays due regard to the implications of this legislation for democratic values in the province. Though the two perspectives clash rather than coincide, an examination of both is a necessary prerequisite for proper judgment of the legislation.

INTELLIGENCE GATHERING AND INTERNMENT

To contain terrorism it is necessary first to identify those who are engaged in it, and second, to remove them from the body politic. Much of the emergency powers legislation outlined above is designed to facilitate these tasks by making it easier for the security forces to collect intelligence and by streamlining the process by which suspects are "put away."

In any counter-insurgency campaign, intelligence gathering is of crucial importance, and the British army, through the street patrols, house searches, "head counts," arrests, "screening procedures," and interrogation techniques made legal by the security legislation, were able to build up a detailed picture of day-to-day life in Catholic communities in which terrorists operated. Hundreds of properties were searched and thousands of people screened. In 1973, for example, 75,000 houses, almost one-fifth of the total number of houses in Northern Ireland, were searched, and some of them were searched many times.[5] Very few Catholic males over the age of sixteen in Belfast and Londonderry have not been picked up at one time or another for routine questioning.[6] Through this low level intelligence gathering the army acquired a mass of information about Republican activities and those who sympathized with them.

In the early 1970s army and police intelligence assessments tended to be of very poor quality—witness the odd list of candidates for internment arrested on 9 August 1971. These included a suspect in his late 70s, a blind man, a man who had been dead for four years, and many others with very tenuous connections with the IRA.[7] But despite mistakes and a longstanding inability to cooperate and share information with the Royal Ulster Constabulary (RUC), the army began to get its act together. Brigadier Frank Kitson, a specialist in low intensity operations, was only one of those in Northern Ireland who allocated high priority to intelligence collection. A comprehensive data bank was built up. Detailed dossiers were compiled on large numbers of people. New computer and surveillance equipment was introduced. By 1974 the Provisionals were finding it increasingly difficult to operate on the streets.

The army's success in this field was particularly remarkable because intelligence gathering in a community which is at best neutral and at worst downright hostile to the security forces is quite a different operation from normal police work where public cooperation can be taken for granted. Inevitably, success had to be paid for—in terms of further alienation of the Catholic community whose lives were seriously disrupted by the constant searches, arrests, and interrogations which were vital to the intelligence operation.

Capturing a terrorist is difficult enough, but it is only the first step in a process of incarcerating him. Here again the emergency legislation proved to be critically important, because it was under powers conferred on it by the "Special Powers" Act that the Northern Ireland government was able—at various times—to resort to its controversial policy of detention and internment of terrorist suspects without trial. Until 1971 internment was usually employed against suspected members of the IRA—as it was in 1921-22, 1938-39, 1956-62, and 1969. Occasionally it was used against Republican politicians as, for example, when some leading Republican politicians were interned for one week during a Royal visit to the province in 1951.[8] But in 1971, against the advice of the British army, it was used in a massive and spectacular way. On August 9, British troops suddenly "lifted" 342 suspects who were detained indefinitely and without trial. During the next six months of internment 2,375 people were arrested, although it is only fair to point out that many were quickly released after interrogation.

In Britain most people had serious reservations about the policy. The Home Secretary Reginald Maudling readily admitted that "internment is a very ugly thing," but he believed that "political murder is even uglier."[9] The Northern Ireland Prime Minister Brian Faulkner justified his decision on the grounds that "the ordinary law cannot deal comprehensively or quickly enough with such ruthless viciousness as the terrorists displayed."[10]

In one sense, internment was a success. It undoubtedly removed many dangerous men from the community, and the intelligence community learned a good deal from the interrogation of detainees in the newly created interrogation centers at Palace Barracks, Castlereagh and Gough Barracks, Armagh. But if its aim was to stop the violence it was a miserable failure. On this the statistics are clear. In 1970, the year before internment was introduced, 25 people lost their lives in communal violence. In 1971, the figure rose to 173, and more than four-fifths of these happened after 9 August.[11] We ought not, of course, to read too much into those figures for two reasons. First, the security situation in Northern Ireland was deteriorating anyway and a rise in violence was in the cards whether or not internment was introduced. Second, we have no way of knowing how many more deaths might have occurred if internment had not been introduced.

The benefits of internment are largely imponderable; the costs were real. First, because of the insensitivity with which it was pursued, a large number of innocent men were locked up without redress. Second, because the initial swoop was confined to Catholics, and because some of them were ill treated, the effect of internment was to unite the Catholic community against the security forces who were perceived, perhaps wrongly, to be siding with the Protestants. Third, internment, which clearly involved a suspension of "habeas corpus," provided the IRA with a perfect propaganda weapon for exposing British tyranny. Fourth, the detention centres became training centres for terrorist tactics and ideology. As one staff officer put it, "detention becomes a kind of staff college for terrorists."[12] Fifth, detention without trial gave the terrorists a *political* rather than a criminal label, thereby enhancing their status both within the United Kingdom and abroad. Detainees were given "special category" status, were allowed to wear civilian clothes, and were permitted to live in self-organizing compounds with members of their own organizations. In effect they were treated more like prisoners of war than common criminals.[13] Finally, the Compton Report and the adverse publicity associated with the "in-depth" interrogation which accompanied internment and the notorious "five techniques" severely damaged Britain's reputation, both at home and abroad.

For all these reasons, when direct rule was introduced in 1972, the British government began to examine ways in which internment could be phased out. Once the no-jury "Diplock" courts[14] were established it became clear that terrorists could in fact be brought to justice through the courts. The Diplock courts were themselves contro-versial, but they were undoubtedly an improvement on internment which was finally abolished in 1975 when all internees were released. For all their vices, the Diplock courts moved Northern Ireland one step closer towards a restoration of trial by "due process of law."

CIVIL LIBERTIES AND EMERGENCY LEGISLATION

It should be clear from the foregoing that under the emergency legislation some important individual liberties were no longer adequately protected by the law, but were more or less at the mercy of the Executive. The National Council for Civil Liberties has, for many years now, drawn attention to the dangers inherent in this legislation. The Council, with the support of the Cobden Trust, has carefully documented numerous instances when these special powers have been abused.[15] The Council's unease is surely understandable. In Northern Ireland there has been a substantial erosion of individual freedom and liberty, so much so that for some people the quality of life available in the province has been significantly diminished. There is something insidiously corrupting about wide-ranging legislation which vests the police and armed forces with powers that are unchallengeable in the courts and which whittles away the normal standards of justice. Dermot Walsh has drawn our attention to the curious submissiveness of the people of Ulster to restrictions on their freedom. He argues that the absence of any consciousness of the civil liberties problem in the province bodes ill for democracy.[16] But in this he may be too pessimistic. Acquiescence in the erosion of their liberties may simply reflect the fact that when the citizens of Northern Ireland face civil war they instinctively allocate a higher priority to "security" and "order" than they do to "justice" and "freedom."

It has been suggested that a "Bill of Rights" might be a sensible way of providing the population of Northern Ireland with a measure of protection against the loss of their civil rights. However, the Standing Advisory Committee on Human Rights, which examined the idea, came out against it in 1977. This may seem odd to those American readers who are shocked to discover that the United Kingdom has no "bill of rights," but they must understand that the basis of civil rights in the United Kingdom is quite different from that in the United States. In the British situation two facts are critically important. First, in Britain everything is permitted except what is expressly forbidden; second, Parliament has absolute powers to enact any law and change any previous law. It follows from this that whatever freedoms are enjoyed by citizens of Britain and Northern Ireland are entirely at the discretion of a Parliament which, at the stroke of a pen, is legally empowered to restrict their freedom in whatever way it pleases. Clearly, a bill of rights which put certain rights beyond the reach of Parliament has its attractions, particularly in an age in which the state has become very intrusive, but bringing it into effect in the United Kingdom would require fundamental constitutional changes.[17]

Despite the threats to liberty inherent in emergency powers legislation, it is difficult to see how else a responsible government could have reacted when faced with a serious challenge to its authority in part of the United Kingdom. Merlyn Rees, secretary of state for Northern Ireland (1974-1976), summarized most people's feelings about this legislation when he introduced the Emergency Provisions Act to parliament in 1975. "I never acquired a taste for special laws but I could not dismiss the activities of paramilitary murderers able to use modern machine guns and explosives. As long as violence was there, the state had the right to react and I could not ignore reality by sitting in my office as if it were an ivory tower from which I could occasionally descend to make elegant speeches in the Commons."[18] The British government could, of course, have reacted to the violence in a more extreme way by imposing a state of "martial law" on the province. However, though

Ulster was sometimes disorderly and violent it was never near being out of control. To allow the military to take over completely the entire machinery of government in Northern Ireland would have been a disproportionate response. From the outset of the "troubles" it made much better sense to try to maintain the authority of the civil government, but to supplement its powers in a manner which would give teeth to the security forces in dealing with terrorism and civil disorder. All the emergency legislation has been designed with that in mind.

I have already hinted that order is a more basic value than justice, and when the smell of insurrection is in the air it is perhaps inevitable that justice is pushed into the background. When the state totters toward the "war of every man against every man," the Hobbesian preference for security and order over freedom and justice is a natural response. Civil liberties, government by debate, constitutionalism—all are luxuries when the viability of the state itself is threatened. No one should be surprised, therefore, that both Parliament and the British public have unquestioningly accepted that the fight against terrorism has required some curtailment of their traditional freedoms. Indeed, even the European Convention of Human Rights recognizes the right of any society threatened by violent upheaval to protect itself by "derogating" from most of its provisions during an emergency.

The hard, paradoxical truth is that, when threatened by insurrection, no democratic government can survive unless it considers undemocratic measures to save itself. Clinton Rossiter has described how all democracies, in conditions of crisis, have to turn themselves into "constitutional dictatorships."[19] In doing this, the government gathers new powers to itself. The people enjoy fewer rights and freedoms, and power that is usually vested in the legislature is delegated to the Executive. In practice, emergency legislation the world over manifests similar characteristics—a *concentration* of power, an *expansion* of power, and a *liberation* of power from constitutional control.[20]

Inevitably, legislation which embodies these characteristics generates fears for democracy. The powers necessary to suppress riot, insurrection, and revolution can easily be used to overturn democracy. The history of the Weimar Republic provides a classic example of emergency powers subverting the democracy they were designed to protect.[21] Article 48 of the Weimar Constitution gave the president of the Reich powers which were not very different from those contained in the Northern Ireland Emergency Powers Act. Those powers, when added to the president's power to dissolve the Reichstag—whose oversight was the major safeguard against the abuse of Article 48—easily led to despotism, and eventually to Adolf Hitler.

Despite the dangers of abuse which are inherent in emergency legislation, we have to agree with F. M. Watkins that "the need for emergency powers is implicit in the very nature of constitutional government."[22] The need for some procedures for the suspension of normal political procedures in the face of crisis is universally recognized. To save democracy it is sometimes necessary to run the risk of losing it. But whenever a "constitutional dictatorship" is created to protect democratic values, society is confronted with the classical dilemma brilliantly expressed by Abraham Lincoln's question, "Must a government of necessity be too *strong* for the liberties of its people, or too *weak* to maintain its own existence?"[23] In modern parlance, is it possible for a state to combat terrorism and remain a democracy?" I do not profess to know the answer to these questions. In terms of their Northern Ireland policy, both Labour and Conservative governments would, no doubt, like to answer the former question negatively and the latter positively. Whether the record justifies their optimism is perhaps debatable, but both political parties can claim to have wrestled with the problem.

PERMANENT EMERGENCY

In normal usage the term "emergency" has a temporary connotation suggesting a sudden and transient crisis; but in Northern Ireland, as we have seen, the terrorist threat is "structural"—built into the situation by the existence of irreconcilable communities juxtaposed within the same province. The "emergency" has existed virtually since the creation of Northern Ireland in 1920, and it is unlikely to disappear in the foreseeable future. Despite the honest intention of various governments to repeal its emergency legislation at the first possible opportunity, the sad reality is that it has become a permanent feature of the legal

landscape in Northern Ireland. A virtually permanent
"emergency" is undoubtedly a very peculiar state of affairs,
but it corresponds very closely to the Northern Ireland
situation.

One of the consequences of this is that citizens in the
province are deprived of important rights and privileges
more or less permanently, and have had to adjust themselves
to living under an abnormally harsh legal regime in some
ways analogous to a state of martial law. It is tempting to
believe that emergency powers legislation only affects the
terrorists and criminals it is directed against; but this is not
the case. This legislation touches the lives of almost
everyone in the province.

Outsiders, particularly Americans, find it difficult to
understand why these repressive measures are necessary.
That is because they cannot imagine what it is like to live
in conditions of intimidation and violence such as those
which prevail in both Catholic and Protestant working class
communities. In a culture where bombing and violence have
become an accepted way of life, even among young children,
and where tribal hatred is a dominant emotion, random
sectarian murder is commonplace. The IRA has had a
Mafia-like grip on Catholic ghettos where extortion and
intimidation stretch into every corner of life, and where
threats of "knee-capping," tar-and-feathering, or worse,
guarantee compliance. Protestant para-military forces,
mainly in the form of the Ulster Defence Organisation and
the Ulster Volunteer Force, pursue equally ruthless
techniques of persuasion in Protestant strongholds, and it is
clear that inside this murder culture the normal processes of
law simply cannot work. This is a world in which witnesses
to violence can never be found, jurors are intimidated and
probably biased anyway, and judges threatened. Under
ordinary criminal procedures it is simply impossible to obtain
convictions even against known terrorists. Lord Diplock
made the point like this:

> The minimum requirements are based upon
> the assumption that witnesses to a crime will be
> able to give evidence in a court of law without
> risk to their lives, their families or their
> property. Unless the State can ensure their
> safety, then it would be unreasonable to expect

them to testify voluntarily and morally wrong to try to compel them to do so.

This assumption, basic to the very functioning of courts of law, cannot be made today in Northern Ireland as respects most of those who would be able, if they dared, to give evidence in court on the trial of offenses committed by members of terrorist organizations. . . .

We are thus driven inescapably to the conclusion that until the current terrorism by the extremist organizations of both factions in Northern Ireland can be eradicated, there will continue to be some dangerous terrorists against whom it will not be possible to obtain convictions by any form of criminal trial which we regard as appropriate to a court of law; and these will include many of those who plan and organize terrorist acts by other members of the organization in which they take no first-hand part themselves. We are also driven inescapably to the conclusion that so long as these remain at liberty to operate in Northern Ireland, it will not be possible to find witnesses prepared to testify against them in the criminal courts, except those serving in the army or the police, for whom effective protection can be provided. The dilemma is complete. The only hope of restoring the efficiency of criminal courts of law in Northern Ireland to deal with terrorist crimes is by using an extra-judicial process to deprive of their ability to operate in Northern Ireland, those terrorists whose activities result in the intimidation of witnesses. With an easily penetrable border to the south and west the only way of doing this is to put them in detention by an executive act and to keep them confined, until they can be released without danger to the public safety and to the administration of criminal justice.[24]

Few objective observers would query the need for emergency powers to deal with the breakdown of law and order which Lord Diplock has so graphically described. Extraordinary conditions require extraordinary legislation, and even though that legislation causes a good deal of unease among those concerned to protect democratic values, the worries tend to focus on the *extent* of the legislation and the *manner in which it is enforced* rather than on the fact of the legislation itself.

CRITICISMS OF GOVERNMENT POLICY

It is not absolutely clear that *all* of the draconian powers now vested in the secretary of state are necessary, either for the successful prosecution of an anti-terrorist strategy by the security forces, or for the restoration of a measure of justice to the civil community. After all, the ordinary criminal law gives the police wide powers to arrest and detain anyone suspected of a terrorist offense.[25] Nor is it clear that the emergency legislation has been enforced in an unambiguously fair way. Indeed, there is evidence of malpractice, particularly in respect of the way in which the law has been applied to the Catholic community. For example, it has been argued that Catholics have been charged with more serious offenses than Protestants when they have been engaging in comparable behavior; that in some instances Protestants have escaped scot-free while Catholics have been charged; and that even when charged with similar offenses, Catholics tend to be sentenced to heavier punishments than their Protestant counterparts.[26]

One of the most persistent criticisms of the manner in which the emergency legislation is applied has focused on the behavior of the security forces. Over the years they have been criticized for the brutal and careless way in which they have carried out their duties under the emergency legislation. Accusations have varied from rough and insensitive treatment to physical assaults, beatings, and even complaints of unlawful shootings by British soldiers. It is difficult to assess the extent to which the security forces have abused their powers in the execution of their duties. Certainly the number of successful actions against individual soldiers and policemen has been small; but given the difficulty of collecting evidence in this kind of case, it would be unwise to read too much into this fact.

What is clear is that abuse has occurred. A variety of independent investigators have produced clear evidence of malpractice which may have been more widespread than the authorities are willing to admit.[27]   But though there can be no excuses on the part of the security forces, we need to remember the endless provocations and dangers to which they were constantly exposed.   It is not easy to police coolly and calmly in the face of hatred and hostility.   Any army is a blunt instrument in an internal security role, but the record in Northern Ireland surely suggests that the British army is less blunt than most.   In the words of one well known commentator, "It is doubtful whether any other army in the world could have performed the internal security role in Northern Ireland with such humanity, restraint and effectiveness."[28]

In any democracy, emergency powers legislation highlights the difficulty of reconciling the need to restore order with the requirement to preserve individual rights and freedoms.   The dilemma facing a democratic society is, as we have seen, that "the means needed to defeat terrorism and suppress insurrection are the very ones needed to enforce a tyranny."[29]   There is inevitable tension between the individual desire for liberty and the constraints required by a society to enable that desire to be satisfied.   What this means is that overreaction by a government facing terrorism or insurrection can be as dangerous as under-reaction.   In protecting society from those who would destroy it, we need to ensure that defensive measures do not undermine democratic values to the point where the quality of life for individual citizens is so diminished that the society in which they live is no longer worth protecting.

In Northern Ireland the problem of "injustice" surfaced in its most acute form when the Diplock courts were created.   Because they relied heavily on confessions by those who were accused of terrorist offenses, these courts created a certain pressure within the police force to obtain confessions by bending or stretching the rules relating to the proper treatment of suspects under interrogation.   In any society the desire to convict generates understandable (but certainly not condonable) frustration with legal niceties.   Indeed, a *strict* application of the "Judges' Rules"[30] would probably make questioning a futile activity.   Since guilty men almost invariably prefer not to confess or talk about their crimes, an interrogation cannot be conducted as a friendly discussion over tea and biscuits.   As the Diplock Report makes clear, the whole point of the exercise is to build up "a psychological atmosphere in which the initial desire of the person being questioned to remain silent is replaced by an urge to confide in the questioner."[31] For that to happen a degree of intimidation and fear has to be induced. In the extraordinary circumstances of Northern Ireland, Lord Diplock believed that the threshold of permissible intimidation, pressure, and fear had to be raised if justice was to prevail and terrorists were to be effectively tried an punished; hence his recommendation to abandon the common law rules relating to the admissibility of inculpatory statements by the accused and to replace them with the controversial Section 6 of the Emergency Provisions Act 1973.[32]

Section 6 refers to the admissibility of statements made by suspects under interrogation. It permits the Court to accept these statements provided it is satisfied that they have not been extracted by "torture" or "inhuman" or "degrading" treatment. But Section 6 does not define these terms, and there is therefore uncertainty about the whereabouts of the line which distinguishes what is euphemistically called "interrogation in depth" from torture and inhuman or degrading treatment.

Now the European Commission on Human Rights has defined inhuman treatment as that which "deliberately causes *severe* suffering, mental or physical"; torture as "an *aggravated* form of inhuman treatment"; and degrading treatment as "punishment . . . which *grossly* humiliates."[33] (my italics) Using these interpretations a certain rough treatment and physical pressure is clearly permitted under Section 6. The question is how *much* rough treatment is permitted? Can the suspect be slapped, punched, or kicked? If so, how hard and how often can this be done before the adjectives "severe" and "aggravated" apply? Similarly, how much humiliation can a prisoner be subjected to before he is "*grossly*" humiliated?

It is probably impossible to *eliminate* injustice from any legal system, but when the law is as ambiguously drafted as this, abuse is very likely. Indeed, its occurrence in Northern Ireland has been proved on numerous occasions. And even on occasions when those accused were not able to prove maltreatment one is left with an uneasy feeling that it might nevertheless have taken place. Of course, we need to remember that many of those who complained of brutality were vicious, dangerous men seeking to discredit the security forces. What is more, they may have inflicted wounds upon themselves in order to justify their confessions to their own henchmen. But at the end of the day, there remain justifiable doubts about the way in which suspects were treated under the Diplock procedure. The high conviction rate (94%) and the fact that between 70% and 90% of those convictions depended on admissions made under interrogation inevitably raised eyebrows.[34] Any system of justice which in effect shifts the focus of determining guilt away from what happens in the Court towards what takes place in the police station is undoubtedly moving in a dangerous direction.

SAFEGUARDING CITIZENS RIGHTS

And yet, despite these worrying aspects of the emergency powers legislation, it cannot be reiterated too strongly that Northern Ireland is not a police state in the grip of some totalitarian regime. Despite the curtailment of individual rights and clear evidence of a degree of police and army brutality, the province remains an essentially "open" society. And because it is an "open society" it has built into it a number of safeguards which reduce the dangers of emergency powers legislation designed to combat terrorism.

First, Northern Ireland and the United Kingdom enjoy the benefits of a free press experienced in investigative journalism. The media generally is anxious to publicize any derelictions of duty on the part of the military and civil authorities tasked with enforcing the emergency legislation, and it is equally anxious to criticize those aspects of the legislation which seem unduly oppressive. The glare of publicity is a powerful constraint on those who may be tempted either to break the law or interpret it too harshly. Police and security officials are held in check by the possibility of exposure, criminal charges, and dismissal from their jobs. There are numerous examples of successful actions against the security forces—though perhaps not as many as the National Council for Civil Liberties would like.

But it is perhaps worth adding that although publicity is a powerful safeguard against illegal or overzealous behavior on the part of security forces, it can also inhibit their enthusiasm for quite legitimate anti-terrorist measures. When, as has sometimes happened in Northern Ireland, soldiers stand idly by while people and property are criminally attacked, one of the reasons is their fear of adverse publicity and accusations of brutality in the press. This cost has to be weighed against the very real benefits of a free and critical press.

A second safeguard against government brutality is to be found in the various public enquiries which, from time to time, have investigated events and official behavior within the province. All major cities in Northern Ireland, from the first major disorders in 1969 right through to the present day, have been the subject of investigation and report. Typical examples of this sort of inquiry are the Scarman Report (which examined the initial outbreak of violence) and the Widgery Report (which examined the events of "Bloody Sunday" in January 1972).

Over the years, a variety of government-sponsored enquiries have looked into the working of the emergency powers legislation, and none of them can be regarded as "whitewash" investigations.[35] In 1969 the Cameron Commission reported on "Disturbances in Northern Ireland" and commented critically on the workings of the Special Powers Act. In 1971, a three-man enquiry chaired by Sir Edmund Compton investigated allegations of brutality on the part of the security forces in respect of their interrogation techniques. "Interrogation in depth" was criticized as physical ill treatment. In 1973 the government appointed a "Standing Advisory Commission on Human Rights" to advise on the effectiveness of the law in preventing discrimination on the grounds of religious or political belief. In 1977 Judge Harry Bennett presented his report on "Police Interrogation Procedures in Northern Ireland"—and the British government accepted its broad conclusions. In the same year a completely independent enquiry into interrogation techniques was conducted by Amnesty International. In 1978 Lord Shackleton reviewed the operation of the "Prevention of Terrorism Acts of 1974 and 1976"—and again the British government accepted most of his proposals for reform.

All the evidence suggests that the British government, far from riding roughshod over its critics, is sensitive to their fears and anxious to do all that it can to minimize the dangers to democracy which are inherent in the legislation it has thought necessary to enact. If Britain is an oppressor, she is a reluctant oppressor. Both Labour and

Conservative governments have understood very clearly that their judicial policies in Northern Ireland must enjoy the confidence of the majority of people in the United Kingdom if they are to work. Their willingness to conduct public enquiries in controversial areas and their general responsiveness to the findings of these enquiries are part of the process by which the British public is reassured that what happens in Northern Ireland is critically monitored.

Of course, public enquiries are not infallible.[36] Their terms of reference may be inadequate (this was the criticism levelled at the Widgery Tribunal); their conclusions may not be closely related to their findings (this accusation was levelled at the Compton Report); those who carry them out may be denied access to important information (this was the complaint voiced by Amnesty International); the enquiry may be so protracted that its impact is dramatically reduced (this accusation was levelled at the Scarman Tribunal which did not report until nearly three years after the events it was examining had occurred); finally, some of the recommendations suggested by an enquiry may not be implemented by the government (this was the case with both the Gardiner Committee's report and the report of the Standing Advisory Commission on Human Rights on "The Protection of Human Rights in Northern Ireland").[37] Nevertheless, despite these criticisms, it remains true that these various public enquiries have gone a long way towards reassuring the British people that although there may be instances of injustice and brutality on the part of the security forces they are not widespread, and the government is trying to reduce them.

A third safeguard against illegal and excessively brutal behavior by government forces is to be found in the right of every individual citizen with a grievance to complain either to the European Court of Human Rights or to the civil courts or to the police or military authorities themselves. Any complaint against a soldier has to be fully investigated; and non-frivolous complaint against a police officer has to be examined. In 1978 the European Court of Human Rights ruled that the techniques used in "interrogation in depth" (hooding, sleep deprivation, noise, etc.) constituted "inhuman and degrading treatment,"[38] and that by using these techniques Britain was in violation of Article 3 of the European Human Rights Convention of 1950. The British government accepted the finding and agreed not to use them again in the United Kingdom. Over the years, lawyers acting on behalf of those claiming to have suffered injustice or injury have mustered procedural and technical defenses based on misconduct by the security forces. They have also sought redress in both the civil and criminal courts. In general, satisfaction has more easily been achieved in the civil rather than the criminal courts;[39] but in 1984 a British soldier was convicted of murder while on duty in Northern Ireland and given a life sentence. No one can pretend that the procedures for legal redress are perfect, but, again, their existence helps to reassure an uneasy British public that avenues of justice are available to those who have been wronged.

Finally, the watchful eye of the British parliament provides a vitally important safeguard against any abuse of emergency powers in Northern Ireland. Apart from the fact that emergency legislation has to be renewed by parliament at frequent intervals (every year in the case of the 1984 Prevention of Terrorism Act), the House of Commons always contains enough enemies of the government of the day to seek to discomfort it at the first sign of any abuse of its powers. The possibility of an awkward parliamentary question is usually enough to keep most ministers constantly alerted to their responsibilities.

THE ROLE OF THE ARMY

Besides the distinctiveness of special powers legislation which, in various forms, has been in force since 1922, Northern Ireland can be distinguished from the rest of the United Kingdom by the role which the British army has played in enforcing that legislation within the province since 1969. In Britain, the traditional role of the armed forces is to combat external aggression; the maintenance of public order and the containment of terrorism falls within the mandate of the police. Nevertheless, "aid to the civil power" has always been one of the residual roles expected of the armed forces whenever it has become manifestly clear that the police are unable either to uphold the law or preserve public order.

Over the years there have been numerous instances when the British army has been called out of its barracks to perform this, its most unpopular, task. Ireland is simply the most recent and protracted instance of a well-established role. In 1969, when the Stormont government lost control of a civil rights demonstration and an exhausted police force was unable to cope with the rioting which ensued, the army was called in, first to restore order, but later, when IRA pressure mounted, to counter terrorist activity within the province. Without the policy decision being taken, the army slid from one role to the other.

In pursuing these twin tasks as many as 22,000 troops have, on occasion, been deployed in Ulster, and in times of tension their presence has been felt on almost every street corner. For years on end it was the army and not the police who enforced the law in Catholic strongholds in Belfast. As one who was intimately involved in the security operations put it, "The Army was a heavy, brooding presence over the city. . . . Sandbagged sangars guarded the police stations, and patrols were everywhere. The Army ran everything in the Catholic areas. The RUC was still struggling to recover from the body blows of the past few years."[40] Indeed, it was not until 1976 that the army began to take a back seat, and the RUC, under Kenneth Newman, was back in the driving seat in matters of law enforcement and policing.

Today the British army is still pursuing its thankless task of combatting terrorism, and, though the visibility and scope of its activities have declined in recent years, there are no immediate prospects that its current "low profile" role will diminish to the point where soldiers can return to their garrisons. Those well-meaning individuals who sometimes call for the total withdrawal of the British army, on the grounds that its presence aggravates the communal conflict, simply do not appreciate that its presence, however unwelcome, was, for many years, the only guarantee against civil war in the province.

In coming to the assistance of the civil power, the British army was not responding to any emergency powers legislation. But once it moved away from the restoration of law and order and became involved in an anti-terrorist campaign, then it operated under the complicated web of emergency regulations which prevail in Northern Ireland.

In theory, when the armed forces of the United Kingdom are assisting the civil authorities to suppress disorder, their sole, common law, responsibility is to uphold the law of the land. Contrary to popular opinion in this matter, they are not answerable to ministers of the Crown, and the government of the day has no constitutional power to tell them how to enforce the law. Nor are they under the jurisdiction of the police who may have requested their assistance and with whom they may be cooperating. In this respect, like magistrates and chief constables, the military is responsible solely to the Courts for their behavior.[41]

But in practice, Westminster politicians exercise considerable influence over both the decision to deploy troops in the first instance and over the day-to-day way in which those troops carry out their duties—even to the extent of determining whether, in a particular situation, the law should or should not be upheld.

When, for instance, in August 1969, troops were finally deployed to quell the riots between the Republican population of the Falls Road area and the Protestants of the Shankhill Road, it was not a consequence of any decision by any military or police authority in Northern Ireland but a result of a political decision in London in response to a request for military assistance from the Stormont government. Similarly, on the many occasions during the emergency when the law has deliberately *not* been enforced, this too has been a result of political decisions in Westminster.

Many citizens of the United Kingdom were genuinely puzzled and upset by the existence of "No Go" areas in Catholic strongholds which were controlled entirely by armed IRA terrorists, and where no attempt was made to enforce the law of the land. They were equally outraged by TV news pictures showing soldiers standing by doing nothing while manifestly illegal activities were taking place. Viewers were shocked by illegal marches and funerals at which armed and hooded men fired armalite rifles over terrorist graves. It needs to be made clear that these flagrant breaches of the emergency powers legislation were permitted on the express authority of a central government which, rightly or wrongly, judged the consequences of strict law enforcement by whatever military means were necessary to be potentially worse than the certain consequences of appearing to condone lawbreaking by failing to act.[42]

From one perspective, the unevenness with which the emergency powers legislation has been enforced in respect of marches, demonstrations, arrests, "No Go" areas, etc., demonstrates government sensitivity to a constantly changing political situation. But from another perspective, a high price has to be paid for this kind of flexibility. First, the population of Northern Ireland is genuinely uncertain about whether or not, in a particular situation, it is going to enjoy the protection of the law. If Catholics cannot rely on the British army to enforce the law on their streets who can blame them from turning to the IRA to protect them from Protestant gangs? Whenever the law is deliberately not enforced the power of the U.K. government to handle the Northern Ireland problem is called into question, and encouragement is given to men of violence and their supporters.

In addition, when an offense is openly condoned on one occasion and penalized on another, the average citizen does not know where he stands or whether his behavior is likely to result in prosecution or not. If some marches are permitted and others stopped on the basis of some fine political calculation in Whitehall—a calculation which is completely incomprehensible on the streets of Londonderry— then an impression is created that the enforcement of law is a matter of political will rather than something which is axiomatic.

Finally, this flexibility in law enforcement seriously damages morale in the security forces. Neither soldiers nor policemen have a clear idea of their role. Inevitably, they become obsessively concerned with not falling foul of politicians in London either by policing too aggressively or too softly in ambiguous situations. Conceivably, for all these reasons, in the long run the price that is paid for flexible law enforcement may exceed the undoubted short-term political benefits of maintaining a low profile.

THE EFFECTIVENESS OF EMERGENCY LEGISLATION

It is very difficult to assess the effectiveness of any anti-terrorist legislation if only because it is impossible to know how much more or less terrorism there would have been in its absence. However much the social scientist might regret the fact, it is impossible to experiment by re-running history with one of the variables changed. But we can make a number of observations.

First, it is quite clear that the emergency legislation has not enabled the British army either to destroy the IRA, or to prevent sectarian violence, or to free the province from terrorist activity. If that was the aim of the legislation it was completely unrealistic. Terrorism is the outward manifestation of a serious disease of the body politic, and its elimination invariably requires substantial economic, social, and political reforms. Every writer on the subject of counterinsurgency is at pains to emphasize that suppressing terrorism is fundamentally a "political" rather than a "security" problem. Security forces operating under emergency powers may be necessary to control and limit terrorist activity, but its permanent elimination requires an attack on those social and political evils on which it feeds.

This should not be taken to mean that, given *carte blanche* instructions to wipe out the IRA in Ulster the army could not have done it. At a price, it clearly could—and probably easily and within a matter of days; but this ambitious goal could certainly not be achieved within the framework of the emergency powers legislation enacted for Northern Ireland. This legislation may have gone too far for those obsessively interested in civil liberties, but it did not go nearly far enough for those who wanted the army to eliminate terrorism at any price. To destroy the IRA by the ruthless use of military power requires a quite different political and legal framework from the one implicit in British anti-terrorist legislation, and one which can probably only be provided by a totalitarian state. For example, it might require strict censorship, a willingness to shoot suspected terrorists on sight, and an attempt to remove the "sanctuary" south of the border.

Quite rightly in my judgment, successive British governments have decided that the price of outright military victory against the IRA is too high for any democratic society. Pussyfooting around with wicked and dangerous men is bound to cause irritation and accusations of "softness"; but the alternative is so damaging to democratic values that it is unlikely to be contemplated except in the direst circumstances. In practice there is a level of violence which democratic societies find acceptable and can live with even in the long run. Northern Ireland provides a good example of a society where below a certain threshold, violence is an acceptable feature of the political scene.

Notwithstanding its failure to eliminate terrorism, common sense suggests that the emergency legislation has contributed significantly to its management and reduction to tolerable levels. The emergency legislation enabled the "No Go" areas to be eliminated in a single military operation on 1972; over the years it facilitated the location and seizure of large stockpiles of weapons and ammunition; it helped put many of the most important terrorists behind bars, and controlled the movement of others; and by the late 1970s it had put the security forces in a dominant position. Ulster has never erupted into civil war or a full-fledged insurgency, and the violence which does exist has not precluded the possibility of fruitful and happy lives for most of its citizens. Those whose knowledge of "the troubles" is gleaned almost entirely from television shows, with its inevitable emphasis on crisis and violence, may be forgiven for believing that Northern Ireland is in a state of permanent uproar. They perhaps need reminding that much of the province is quite untouched by killings and explosions. It is worth remembering that at the height of the violence the murder rate in Belfast was 18.8 per 100,000; that figure includes both IRA men who were shot by the security forces or who blew themselves up as a result of their own incompetence, and the soldiers and policemen who were killed by the IRA. "At that time . . . the murder rate in Cleveland, Ohio, was 35.6 per 100,000 and . . . in twenty-five of America's major cities the murder rate was higher than Belfast."[43]

Of course, this statistic provides no grounds for complacency, but it does help to put the violence in Northern Ireland in perspective, and it provides some evidence that the British army, acting under the emergency powers legislation, was having some success in containing the IRA in general, even if it was unable to prevent some spectacular atrocities—such as the murder of Lord Mountbatten, and on the same summer day in 1979, the killing of eighteen British soldiers in an ambush at Warrenpoint. But I think we must also recognize that the emergency powers legislation was not ideal for combatting terrorism. Certainly it is possible to imagine different laws having a greater effect. One of the weaknesses of the emergency legislation was that it concerned itself more with the treatment of terrorist suspects once they were captured than it did with finding and arresting them in the first place. In a peaceful, normal, democratic society, the police can count on public support to help them locate criminals and those who break the law; but in any society which is alienated from the forces of law and order by intimidation and a resentment of the status quo, security forces cannot rely on any public help whatsoever. In these conditions, rooting out terrorists is extremely difficult, if not impossible.

To make it possible, what is required is a sophisticated intelligence gathering system capable of providing comprehensive surveillance of the entire population. Security forces need to be able to identify "who is who, what they look like and where they live,"[44] so that they can monitor individual behavior and recognize when it is unusual or suspicious. Elements of this kind of comprehensive surveillance system would inevitably include the introduction of identity cards, fingerprinting, photographing, and interviewing the entire population. Clearly, it has "Big Brother" overtones reminiscent of Orwell's *1984*, and it would certainly outrage those who jealously guard civil liberties; but the kind of intelligence that could be obtained from this sort of population surveillance would have paid real dividends in identifying and capturing terrorists.

Unfortunately, the anti-terrorist legislation in Northern Ireland did not permit this kind of operation. What is even more bizarre, the security forces were denied access to all kinds of information which was readily available to other departments of government. The army was not able to examine driving license records, health and social security records, or census details.[45] As a result, the security forces were compelled to build up their own "card index" of intelligence records—later computerized. And the only way of doing this was by painstaking observation and questioning by foot patrols, "p-tests,"[46] searches, head counts, screening, interrogations, and more or less random trawls through the population in search of terrorists. In Robin Evelegh's words, "no system could have been more futile, more ineffective, or better calculated to alienate the mass of the people."[47] Adequate intelligence is probably the single most important key to successful anti-terrorist campaigns, and failure to provide for its acquisition was a major defect in the Northern Ireland emergency legislation.

Not only was comprehensive surveillance ruled out, but the emergency legislation gave little encouragement to security forces interested in gathering intelligence either through the infiltration of terrorist organizations or through the persuasion of known terrorists to become informers. All information is power, but of special significance is inside information gleaned from informers or infiltrators who are in a position to supply details of names, meeting places, ammunition stores, and terrorist plans. "Inside informers to a terrorist movement are like an internal hemorrhage to a human body."[48]   Without something to go on, searches for individual terrorists and their weapons are a time-consuming, wasteful, hit-and-miss business; but with proper intelligence they can be transformed into highly effective and rewarding operations.

To facilitate the acquisition of "inside information" it is clearly necessary to provide those who undertake the dangerous task of infiltrating terrorist organizations with immunity from prosecution for any offence committed in that role.   Obviously, no one who has successfully penetrated the IRA or INLA should be encouraged to pursue his membership to the point of becoming an "agent provocateur."   But to maintain credibility with his fellow conspirators he obviously has to display a degree of involvement, even enthusiasm, for terrorist activity. Without some guarantee of indemnity against prosecution, security forces are unlikely to be very enthusiastic about this activity.   And yet the British government and judiciary has been very reluctant to encourage infiltration by introducing an unequivocal policy of indemnifying security forces risking their lives in this way.

In a similar vein, the government has been equally reluctant to encourage inside information by rewarding known terrorists turned informer either by granting them indemnity—perhaps through Royal Pardon—for past terrorist crimes, or by rewarding them financially for valuable information.   However distasteful it may be to allow guilty men to go free, even to be rewarded for their misdeeds, the kind of intelligence gleaned from those within a terrorist organization is usually of such a high order that this policy has to be taken seriously, despite the difficult moral choice it implies.   Again, the anti-terrorist legislation in Northern Ireland can be faulted for not taking it seriously.   Many of those struggling to get to grips with terrorism on the streets of Belfast would have willingly traded such cosmetic laws as those proscribing the IRA or even the highly disruptive laws which permitted large-scale internment for some important concessions in the field of intelligence gathering.

TWO EMERGENCIES

A further weakness in the Northern Ireland anti-terrorist legislation is that it failed to recognize that there are *two* distinct, though related, emergencies in Ulster. First, there is the perennial conflict between the Protestant majority and the Catholic minority communities. It was this deep-seated, bitter intra-communal antagonism which exploded in the civil rights issue of 1969 and brought the army into action as a weapon of last resort for the civil power. In this war the role of the army has primarily been that of a peacekeeper, anxious to restrain both sides and prevent them from killing each other. Those who break the law in this conflict are best regarded as common criminals.

The second emergency is more serious; it is the war between the United Kingdom and the IRA which seeks to usurp the power of the British government in Northern Ireland by terrorist acts. In this war the role of the army is quite different, and has nothing to do with "holding the ring." Here, the function of the military is to defend the realm by defeating the terrorists through the exercise of whatever armed force is required. Those who break the law in this conflict are not common criminals; they are enemies of the state.

Arguably, the two "wars" needed different kinds of emergency legislation instead of the blanket legislation which was applied to both. It is possible to argue that the Northern Ireland legislation was too tough for the intra-communal conflict and not tough enough for the war against the IRA. Of course, in practice the two conflicts are inextricably entwined; the main purpose of separating them in this way is to show that the emergency legislation had to be applied to very different situations and was not ideally suited to either of them.

Regarding the Ulster conflict as two separate but connected emergencies is helpful in a slightly different context. It makes it clear to everyone that when the British government poured money and effort into the province in an attempt to promote much-needed reforms and to reduce injustice, it was tackling the war between the two communities, not the war against terrorism. Sometimes even the British authorities have been confused on this point; but as Enoch Powell has reminded us, " . . . to imagine that the fixed and settled interest of those whose purpose is to use violence and terror to annex Northern Ireland could be deflected or appeased by 'reforms' was from the start a belief so patently childish as to raise doubts whether those who professed it could really be in earnest."[49]   Against the IRA, political, economic, and social reform in Northern Ireland is a waste of effort, though if it was successful in drawing the two communities closer together and giving working-class Catholics more of a stake in the system, then it might make it more difficult for the IRA to operate within the province.

So far, there are not many signs that the British government's vigorous attempts to improve housing conditions, end discrimination, generate employment, etc., have had much impact on life within the disadvantaged Catholic communities.   At least one writer concluded (in 1980) that " . . . in comparison with Protestants, working class Catholics in Northern Ireland are no better off under direct rule from Westminster than they were under the Unionist regime.   Many are worse off in both relative and absolute terms."[50]   Severe economic recession has not helped, and with the best will in the world and despite a good deal of financial support (currently running at about 600 million pounds per annum), the British government has not been able to create the conditions for growth which are a prerequisite for prosperity in the province.

But the most intractable problem of intra-communal violence is not economic at all; it is social—the problem of changing the deeply ingrained bitter hatreds which are embedded in both communities.   To date very little progress has been made in this direction, and Catholics and Protestants are as far apart as ever.   Indeed, in some ways the emergency legislation has contributed to the division by appearing to operate mainly against the Catholic community. It was in the Catholic areas where the heavy hand of the British army was most felt.   (In 1974, for example, twelve of the eighteen operational army battalions were in militant Republican areas.)[51]   And it was members of the Catholic community who, in the main, ended up in detention centres. (In 1974, for example, there were five hundred Republican detainees and only fifty Loyalists).[52]

This one-sided pattern of law enforcement was probably unavoidable, since security measures were concentrated on suppressing IRA terrorists who survived and operated from within the Catholic ghettoes; but one of its effects has been to reinforce feelings of discrimination and alienation in the Catholic community, where lives were often turned upside down by soldiers searching, sometimes none too gently, for terrorists and their weapons. (In 1974, 71,914 houses were searched).[53] In a sense, therefore, it has actually fed the conflict it was intended to control by further embittering citizens on one side of the divide.

Fundamental reforms are as far away as ever. One of the most obvious is the creation of shared or integrated schools within the province which would bring Catholic and Protestant children together during their formative years; but this idea has been bitterly resisted. Merlyn Rees has described Catholic hostility even to the idea of discussing it. "In his summary, Cardinal (Conway) said that the Catholic Church would not attend an open conference to discuss the subject and would wage a campaign to fight any proposals which set out to relax the hold of the Church on the education of its children."[54] Given the sharpness of the religious divide and the intensity of sectarian hatred in Northern Ireland, it is difficult to envisage any short- or medium-term improvement in the relationship between the two communities. Ending the internecine strife is going to be a long business, and we can see the need for "emergency powers" stretching away into the future.

The gist of the argument so far is to suggest that from the perspective of those for whom the highest priority was the defeat of terrorism rather than the maintenance of civil rights, the emergency legislation failed to give the security forces the power they needed to carry out their task effectively, and quickly. Apart from the examples of inadequacy already quoted, soldiers were not permitted to operate in civilian clothes or to use civilian vehicles—even though these measures would have enormously improved their chances of survival; their use of firearms was hemmed about with legislation which stacked the cards against them;[55] in checking vehicles they were not even allowed to insist on the production of driving licenses and vehicle documents. In many circumstances soldiers were unsure of the law and uncertain whether they were operating within it. Inevitably their confidence was undermined by the fear that their duties might land them in court.

THE ABSENCE OF AN OVERALL STRATEGY

But those who framed the security legislation can be criticized, not only for failing to do properly what they sought to do, but also for failing to legislate at all in areas of crucial importance to an internal security campaign. For example, they did not consider the security problem in any kind of wider context than that of extending the power of the executive at the expense of citizen rights. The legislation is oblivious to the fundamental problem of coordinating political, military, and economic policies into some sort of cohesive strategy. In particular, it failed to spell out the relationship between the two bodies responsible for operating the emergency legislation—the army and the police. No new administrative structure was legislated into existence and the two organizations tended to compete rather than cooperate in the war against terrorism.

The basic problem here was that there was no proper division of labor between the two forces. In theory, of course, the army's role in coming to the aid of the civil power was simply to restore order by the effective use of military force, and then to promptly hand back authority to the police who would resume their traditional function of upholding the law of the land. But in Northern Ireland this could not happen, largely because, in the early years of the emergency, the police were incapable of policing the province without continuous military back-up. Indeed, in the early 1970s in Catholic areas, the law was upheld almost entirely by soldiers who were performing a policing rather than a military role. This was a role for which they were not trained and one which many found bewildering, but it was a role which was forced upon them by the simple fact that the RUC was not able to undertake it and it had to be undertaken. In an important sense, the army was not aiding the civil power; it had *become* the civil power. What this meant in practice was that the police and army had overlapping functions, and this was a cause of perennial friction between them.

Mutual mistrust and differing perspectives on how the campaign should be fought were translated into serious failures of collaboration in the field of intelligence gathering and sharing, and inadequately coordinated operations. Even in the late 1970s, when "police primacy" was the agreed policy and a revitalized, thoroughly modern and professional RUC was anxious to take the lead in policing the province, disagreements continued to surface.

On several occasions the army found it necessary to remind the police that "police primacy" meant only that the police would determine what needed to be done, not that they would tell the army how to do it. In the words of one general officer commanding Northern Ireland forces, "The army do not stand in front of the police, nor do we stand behind them and certainly we do not stand in their way."[56] Perhaps it was inevitable that the army, after so many years of intense activity, would find it difficult to adjust to a low profile on the streets and a role which involved concentration on "covert" operations and policing the bandit country of South Armagh. But there is no doubt that coordination between the army and the police could have been much improved by legislating new arrangements into existence in the early days of the conflict.

The emergency legislation enacted for Northern Ireland has come into existence piecemeal, and there is a suspicion that some of it was drafted and legislated in haste. For example, the 1974 Prevention of Terrorism (Temporary Provisions) Act was passed only eight days after a serious bomb attack which killed twenty-one people in two bars in Birmingham, and it was put before the House of Commons after only eight hours of discussion at the committee stage. The National Council for Civil Liberties complained that "the 1974 bill was rushed through all its Parliamentary stages in two days without any pretence of any thorough scrutiny of its provisions."[57]

There may, therefore, be a case for conducting a more leisurely and systematic examination into the requirements of effective emergency legislation. In the words of Lord MacDermott, former Lord Chief Justice of Northern Ireland, "Instead of meeting the problems I have mentioned piecemeal, it would be better and more effectual to enact an emergency code for the United Kingdom which would be applicable, as events warranted, to the whole or part thereof and be operative only in times of crisis."[58] In other words, it might make sense for Parliament to bring into existence new comprehensive anti-terrorist legislation which would simply be dormant until such time as the government felt the need to invoke all, or part, of it to deal with a particular contingency. Hopefully, this new emergency powers legislation would be clearer and more comprehensive than its current counterpart. It might pay more attention to the fears of those seeking to protect individual freedom as well as to the requirements of the security forces; but in the nature of things, it cannot completely satisfy both, and even if it is well-conceived it is quite likely to satisfy neither.

When the foundations of civilized life are threatened by insurrection and terror, it is virtually impossible to reconcile the continuing need for freedom and justice with the emergency requirements for force. But although security forces and civil libertarians judge emergency powers legislation from incompatible perspectives, democratic governments cannot afford the narrow vision of either. Somehow they have to be mindful of *both* perspectives, and hence, in the legislation which they enact, they have to balance the risk of ineffectiveness in dealing with terrorism and disorder with the risk of destroying the democracy they are trying to preserve. It is not an easy balancing act, and no state can feel confident of getting it right. Perhaps the British in Northern Ireland have got it less wrong than most.

ENDNOTES

1.   Quoted by Martin Wallace in his *British Government in Northern Ireland: From Devolution to Direct Rule* (David and Charles, Newton Abbot, London, North Promfret, 1982), p. 177. This is a very balanced, sane account of events in Northern Ireland between 1968 and 1981.

2.   See D. Bonner, *Emergency Powers in Peacetime* (Sweet & Maxwell, London, 1985), pp. 7-8.

3.   Details of the act are to be found in *Halsbury's Statutes of England* (2nd Edition), Vol. 17 (Butterworth, London, 1950), pp. 167-173. This

quotation is to be found on p. 168.

4. *Ibid.*, p. 170.

5. Details of army intelligence gathering techniques are to be found in K. Boyle, T. Hadden & P. Hillyard, *Ten Years on in Northern Ireland: The Legal Control of Political Violence* (The Cobden Trust, 1980), pp. 25-29. The authors are very much concerned to preserve civil liberties in Northern Ireland and the book is written from this perspective.

6. Another useful account of army intelligence gathering—written from the same "civil rights" perspective—is to be found in P. Hain, ed., D. Humphry & B. Rose-Smith, *Policing the Police, Vol. I, the Complaints System: Police Powers and Terrorism Legislation* (John Calder, London, 1979), pp. 138-142.

7. An interesting account of "Operation Demetrius" is to be found in D. Hamil, *Pig in the Middle: The Army in Northern Ireland 1969-1984* (Methuen, London, 1985), pp. 57-61.

8. See K. Boyle, T. Hadden & P. Hillyard, *Law and State: The Case of Northern Ireland* (Robertson, London; University of Massachusetts Press, Amherst, 1975), pp. 55-56.

9. Quoted by P. Taylor, *Beating the Terrorist? Interrogation in Omagh, Gough and Castlereagh* (Penguin Books, Harmondsworth Middlesex, 1980), p. 20.

10. M. Wallace, *op. cit.*, p. 48.

11. D. Watt, ed., *The Constitution of Northern Ireland: Problems and Prospects* (Heinemann, London, 1977), p. 126.

12. Quoted by P. Wilkinson in *Terrorism and the Liberal State* (John Wiley & Sons, New York; Macmillan, London, 1977), p. 161.

13.   The Gardiner Report recommended the ending of "special category" status, and the British government began to phase it out on March 1, 1976. Many people felt, as Merlyn Rees did, that it had been a mistake from the outset, and that to treat cold-blooded killers as "specially motivated people was morally and legally wrong; they were plain murderers." While sharing this natural revulsion for the wicked acts perpetrated by the IRA, and understanding the government's desire to brand members of the IRA as common criminals, I have never understood how it could be argued that their terrorist acts were not politically motivated. The IRA is manifestly a political organization pursuing political goals.
        Like Enoch Powell I have no objection to granting the IRA combattant rights under the Geneva Convention provided—and here is the rub—*that they are pursued with the same ruthlessness as a war-time enemy.* But so long as that condition is not met, so long, that is to say, as they are pursued as *criminals* rather than *enemies*, then there is no *moral* justification for treating them as prisoners of war. (The European Commission on Human Rights decided in 1980 that there were no *legal* grounds for treating them as prisoners of war.)

14.   "Diplock" courts take their name from Lord Diplock, a lord of appeal who was the chairman of a committee to consider legal procedures to deal with terrorist activities in Northern Ireland. The terms of reference for this committee required it to consider arrangements for the administration of justice to deal with terrorism other than by internment. In view of jury and witness intimidation Diplock recommended "no jury" trials for cases involving terrorist offenses, and this recommendation was accepted by the British government and incorporated into the Emergency Powers Act 1973.

15.   See, for example, the Cobden Trust publications, K. Boyle, T. Hadden & P. Hillyard, *Ten Years on in Northern Ireland*, 1980; T. Hadden & P. Hillyard, *Justice in Northern Ireland: A Study in Social Confidence*, 1973; in addition the following pamphlets from the National Council for Civil Liberties, Catherine

Scorer, *The Prevention of Terrorism Acts 1974 and 1976*, 1976, and C. Scorer, S. Spencer & P. Hewitt, *The New Prevention of Terrorism Act: the Case for Repeal*, 1985. Further evidence of the erosion of individual liberties in Northern Ireland is to be found in P. Taylor *op cit.*, D. Korff, *The Diplock Courts in Northern Ireland: A Fair Trial?* (Netherlands Institute of Human Rights, 1984); B. Rose-Smith, *Politics, Power and Terrorism Legislation*, in P. Hain, ed., *op. cit.* See also the Compton Report entitled *Report on the Enquiry into Allegations Against the Security Forces of Physical Brutality in Northern Ireland Arising out of Events on the 9th of August 1971*, Cmnd. 4823, London, 1971; the Gardiner Report entitled *Report of a Committee to consider, in the context of civil liberties and human rights, measures to deal with terrorism in Northern Ireland*, Cmnd. 5847, 1975; the Bennett Report entitled *Report of the Committee of Inquiry into Police Interrogation Procedures in Northern Ireland*, Cmnd. 7497, 1979; The Shackleton Report entitled *Review of the operation of the prevention of Terrorism (Temporary Provisions) Acts 1974 and 1976*, Cmnd. 7324, 1978; *The protection of human rights by law in Northern Ireland*, Cmnd. 7009, 1977.

16.   D. Walsh, "Civil Liberties in Northern Ireland," in P. Wallington, ed., *Civil Liberties 1984* (Martin Robertson, Oxford, 1984), pp. 343-344.

17.   The problem is one of "entrenchment"—arranging things in such a way that a Bill of Rights could be permanently protected against repeal or amendment by an act of Parliament. It is extraordinarily difficult to do this in a country where there is no written constitution. A useful brief discussion of this problem is to be found in I. N. Stevens & D. C. M. Yardley, *The Protection of Liberty* (Blackwell, Oxford, 1982), pp. 173-182. The usefulness of a Bill of Rights to enhance civil liberties is also discussed in D. Bonner, *op. cit.*, pp. 274-287.

18.   M. Rees, *Northern Ireland: A Personal Perspective* (Methuen, London, 1985), p. 333.

19. See C. L. Rossiter, *Constitutional Dictatorship: Crisis Government in the Modern Democracies* (Princeton University Press, Princeton, 1948).

20. *Ibid.*, pp. 288-290.

21. A full account of what went wrong in Germany is to be found in F. M. Watkins, *The Failure of Constitutional Emergency Powers under the German Republic* (Harvard University Press, Cambridge, Mass., 1939).

22. *Ibid.*, p. 135.

23. Quoted by Rossiter, *op. cit.*, p. 3.

24. The Diplock Report, *Report of the Commission to consider legal procedures to deal with terrorist activities in Northern Ireland*, Cmnd. 5185, 1972, p. 9 and p. 14.

25. C. Scorer, S. Spencer, & P. Hewitt, *op. cit.*, p. 11.

26. K. Boyle, T. Hadden & P. Hillyard, *op. cit.*, pp. 123-125.

27. See, for example, the Bennett Report, *op. cit.*, which concluded, "Our examination of medical evidence reveals cases in which injuries, whatever their precise cause, were not self inflicted and were sustained in police custody" (p. 136). Paragraph 164 (p. 55) of the report also hinted at "the possibility of ill treatment which leaves no marks."

28. P. Wilkinson, *op. cit.*, p. 153.

29. R. Evelegh, *Peacekeeping in a Democratic Society: the Lessons of Northern Ireland* (McGill-Queens University Press, Montreal, 1978), p. 60.

30. The "Judges' Rules" are a code of practice drawn up to govern police procedure in questioning subject. Originally devised in 1912 they have been revised several times by the judges and the Home Office. The full title of these rules is the *Judges' Rules and*

Administration Directions to the Police and the version which has been applicable in Northern Ireland since 1976 is the version which was introduced in England in 1964. These rules spell out clearly the way in which suspects are to be treated in police stations, their rights to remain silent, their rights of access to a solicitor, etc. There is some debate about how generally the "Judges' Rules" have been applied in Northern Ireland.

31. The Diplock Report, *op. cit.*, p. 32, (para. 90).

32. See *ibid.*, p. 32 (para. 89)

33. These distinctions were first made by the Commission when it examined the case filed in 1967 by the Netherlands, Norway, and Sweden against Greece alleging violations of human rights (for details see *Yearbook of the European Convention on Human Rights*, Vol. 12, p. 186). Details of the way these distinctions were applied by the Commission to the Northern Ireland case are to be found in *Yearbook of the European Convention on Human Rights*, Vol. 19, p. 748. In applying these distinctions to the "five techniques" of interrogation, the Commission felt that if they had been used separately none of these techniques would have violated Article III of the Convention, but their simultaneous application certainly did constitute a violation. The Commission judged the techniques, taken together, to be not only inhuman and degrading, but also torture within the meaning of Article III. See *Yearbook of the European Convention on Human Rights*, Vol. 19, pp. 792-794.

34. See M. Wallace, *op. cit.*, p. 140.

35. Apart from those enquiries already mentioned in footnote 15 there was:
    a) The Cameron Report, *Disturbances in Northern Ireland*, N.I. Cmnd. 532, 1969.
    b) The Hunt Report, *Report of the Advisory Committee on Police in Northern Ireland*, N.I. Cmnd. 535, 1969.
    c) The Parker Report, *Report of the Committee of*

Privy Counsellors appointed to consider authorized procedures for the interrogation of persons suspected of terrorism, U.K. Cmnd. 4901, 1972.
d) The Widgery Report, *Report of the Tribunal appointed to enquire into the events on Sunday, 30 January 1972, which led to loss of life in connection with the procession in Londonderry on that day*. UK, HL 101, HC 220, 1972.
e) The Black Report, *The handling of complaints against the police: Report of the Working Party for Northern Ireland*, UK Cmnd. 6475, 1976.

36.   For a harshly critical assessment of the value of the various official enquiries held into allegations of misconduct in Northern Ireland, see K. Boyle, T. Hadden & P. Hillyard, *op. cit.*, pp. 126-130.

37.   For an elaboration of these points see M. Wallace, *op. cit.*, pp. 120 and 175.

38.   This was a majority ruling (16 to 1) of the Court. Though the court also held (13 to 4) that the "five techniques" did not constitute torture, it unanimously regarded them as inhuman treatment. For details of this judgment see *Publications of the European Court of Human Rights, Series A: Judgments and Decisions*, Vol. 25, Case of Ireland v. The United Kingdom, p. 94.

39.   See K. Boyle, T. Hadden & P. Hillyard, *op. cit.*, pp. 130-143 for a discussion of the various ways in which those who have suffered injury or injustice at the hands of the security forces may pursue their grievances legally.

40.   D. Hamil, *op. cit.*, p. 136. The term "sangar" in this quotation refers to some kind of construction to give cover to a firing position.

41.   These points are nicely made by R. Evelegh, *op. cit.*, pp. 8-11. His book, *Peacekeeping in a Democratic Society*, is an excellent, tightly-argued analysis of the inadequacies of the law in providing a framework within which the military can effectively combat terrorism. I have relied heavily on his ideas for many

points in the following pages.

42. See *ibid.*, pp. 17-23 for a full discussion of "flexible law enforcement" and its problems.

43. Quoted by D. Hamil, *op. cit.*, p. 171.

44. R. Evelegh, *op. cit.*, p. 119.

45. *Ibid.*, p. 66.

46. P-tests are random personnel checks carried out by the security forces on the citizens of Northern Ireland which make use of computerized data to verify their identity.

47. R. Evelegh, *op. cit.*, p. 65.

48. *Ibid.*, p. 68.

49. J. Wood, ed., *J. Enoch Powell: Still to Decide* (B.T. Batsford, London, 1972), pp. 180-181.

50. K. Boyle, T. Hadden & P. Hillyard, *op. cit.*, p. 12.

51. *Ibid.*, p. 47.

52. *Ibid.*, p. 48.

53. P. Wilkinson, *op. cit.*, p. 154.

54. Quoted by M. Rees, *op. cit.*, p. 332.

55. Bearing in mind that they were involved in a "shooting war" it may be argued that the circumstances in which British soldiers were permitted to open fire were ludicrously restricted. For his legal protection each soldier was issued with a "yellow card" which explained to him that he could only shoot someone who was actually killing or causing serious injury to another or looked as if he was immediately about to do so. In effect, soldiers were only permitted to open fire against a specific enemy carrying a firearm, and then "only if you have reason to think that he is about to

use it for offensive purposes and if he refuses to halt when called upon to do so," or "if there is no other way to protect yourself or those whom it is your duty to protect from the danger of being killed or seriously injured." Actually the restraints described on the yellow card were greater than the law demanded. This meant that the soldier could exceed the instructions without necessarily breaking the law, but if he kept within the instructions he would certainly be within the law. The main weakness of British policy was that it handed over the "shooting first" initiative to the enemy and exposed soldiers to fearful risks.

56.   Quoted by D. Hamil, *op. cit.*, p. 262.

57.   C. Scorer, S. Spencer, & P. Hewitt, *op. cit.*, p. 7.

58.   Rt. Hon. Lord MacDermott, "Law and Order in Times of Emergency," *Juridical Review*, 1972, p. 21. Lord MacDermott's lecture, reproduced in the above journal, reviews the problem of maintaining public order in a free society. His conclusion that a new code for the whole of the United Kingdom is required is echoed by W. Twining, "Emergency Powers: A Fresh Start," *Fabian Tract*, No. 416, 1972, p. 29.

CHAPTER 3

Terrorism and Subversion of the State:
Italian Legal Responses

ROBERT H. EVANS

On February 12, 1987 the Italian Parliament approved a law which, in the minds of its sponsors, was to signal the end of the period of emergency provoked by the terrorist activities which had racked the country since the late 1960s. The law offered jailed terrorists substantial reduction of sentence in exchange for a declaration of dissociation from terrorism and the repudiation of violence as a method of politics. It was to be the final law on the *pentiti*, the repentants, those who had a change of heart. Within forty-eight hours, in via dei Prati del Papa in Rome, the Red Brigades robbed an armed postal truck of one billion lire; willfully and carefully, two policemen in the escort car were assassinated. Overly confident, they were not wearing the bullet-proof jackets or carrying the guns that were in their cars, as required. At least ten terrorists were involved in the operation. It confirmed that the State once again had become the Red Brigades' primary objective, and that they remained the most dangerous national terrorist group. Though seriously disorganized after 1982, the terrorists committed several killings every year (notably General Leamont R. Hunt in February 1984) and continued recruiting inside and out of Italian jails. Today their effectives number about 290 members, of which 160 are in France; with a declining number of supporters, they can no more hold the State to ransom now than they could fifteen years ago.

Prime Minister Bettino Craxi, in a speech to the lower house of Parliament on February 18, the day the law on dissociation was published in the *Gazzetta Ufficiale* and became effective, recognized that "Well founded fears may also be nurtured . . . in connection with the activities of terrorists still at large . . . [who] appear able to constitute a substantial rallying point for relaunching the armed struggle. . . . [Our] information confirms the existence of a specific plan to reorganize terrorism on a larger scale. . . . These plans will inevitably come up against the response of a country where there is no longer room for large scale organized extremism, for the diffusion and glorification of the mentality of violence, or for the wholesale brandishing of revolutionary or pseudo revolutionary myths."[1] On March 20, General Licio Giorgieri was assassinated. The Red Brigades claimed "the execution of the highest official in the construction of arms and of aeronautic and space weapons."

These tragic events and Craxi's speech are symbolic of Italy's plight in dealing with terrorism. The Prime Minister is undoubtedly correct in recognizing that it is "extremely difficult to guarantee comprehensive preventive defense" against terrorism though it is no longer a serious threat to the country today. However, the major objective of his speech, in which discussion of the government's actions against terrorism occupied less than 15 percent of the time, was to allude to the forthcoming governmental crisis and prospective collapse, fruit of a year of near paralysis, of the near total political immobilism which has characterized the country for several decades.

Eppur si muove. Galileo's assertion remains popular and reality often belies appearances.[2] The economic situation of the country has improved radically, and Craxi's lengthy term as prime minister undoubtedly has been a contributing factor, but the political system seems incapable of following the lead. The rhetoric is abundant, the action infrequent or repetitive. Yet terrorism has declined.

How such a seemingly weak political system has dealt successfully with violence poses interesting questions which will occupy us for the bulk of this essay. The Italians, more often than not, advance conspiratorial explanations and theories. *Dietrologi* (specialists of behind-the-scene analysis), speculate on how the consummation of the historic compromise—the effective association of the PCI [Italian

Communist Party] with the DC [Christian Democracy] in government—was prevented, and correspondingly on how the historic compromise was one of the root causes, if not the root cause, of terrorist activity in Italy. Gianfianco Sanguinetti argues that all terrorism is orchestrated by elements of the Italian secret services who oppose the PCI-DC *rapprochement* and see in terrorism the opportunity to move towards an authoritarian regime.[3] Giorgio Galli in his chronicle of violence that covers the period 1968-82 (and that is used extensively in this paper),[4] provides a different and more reasonable explanation even if it is not entirely convincing. The absence of alternation between parties, which is a partial cause for social tensions, has allowed the ruling parties to exploit the terrorist threat to curb social protest. Italian security forces, rather than break the back of terrorism early, deliberately provided it with enough rein to discredit the left and aggregate moderate political opinions behind the ruling DC-dominated coalition. Thus terrorist cycles of violence coincide with electoral periods, or with moments foreboding governmental crisis. One may retort that, independently of government wishes and of the activities of the secret services, which might have brought terrorism to a halt, had they been effectively organized in the first half of the seventies, the terrorists, naturally and independently of DC wishes, would seek to strike Party and State, when and where they appeared most vulnerable. An even more accurate description and simple explanation may be that until the elections of 1972, the early years of terrorist activity were exploited for short-term political gains by all Italian governments, which chose to ignore the involvement of their secret services in illicit activities. At the very least we can say that the governments of the day did not react vigorously to the so called "strategy of tension," which they viewed as only mildly threatening, and even beneficial, both to the DC and to the minor parties of the democratic coalition. The State "failed to take seriously the intentions of the terrorists to pursue to the bitter end their choice of clandestinity and terrorist violence."[5] Only after 1974 would a series of tentative responses, products of political compromises and of the "traditional immobilism of the Italian State [which] is not easily changed,"[6] come forth. The new legislation increasing police powers would contribute to the destruction of the Red Brigades and of the multiple groups that flourished after 1974. But these measures were only partially instrumental in the final victory. Above all else, Italian civil society, strongly committed to the democratic choice, would grant the terrorists minimal levels of support while engineering an economic recovery that would offer little fertile breeding ground to any but the most extreme ideologues, and leaving little room for fellow travelers.

It is useful briefly to consider the development of terrorism in Italy, to examine its causes, types, phases, linkages, to assess the instruments available to the State to combat it, especially the police forces and the judiciary. Because the issue goes deeper than the parameters we have set, we shall be led to look at the decision-making mechanisms of the democratic state, when it is confronted by violence. Then, as the central focus of this essay, we shall turn to the legal response to internal terrorism and subversion, focusing on legislative provisions and changes in the Italian penal code, before we consider Italian legal responses to international terrorism.

I. TERRORISM AND THE STATE

Italy has been at the center of terrorist attacks in Western Europe, subject to over 14,000 episodes of violence between 1969 and 1987, to 414 deaths and some 1,400 injuries. Forty-four percent of these occurred between 1978 and 1980, with 6,394 attacks, 391 people injured, 184 killed, among which are the 85 victims of the central station in Bologna and the statesman Aldo Moro. Nowhere else in continental Europe did the attack on the State reach such proportions, and nowhere else in Western Europe would the State offer so mild a deterrence to terrorist attacks. For some, the State sought to preserve fundamental rights and liberties, for others it was incapable of acting resolutely.

Wounding, killing, and destruction are the basic means of influence used by terrorists,[7] whose purpose it is, indeed, to terrorize. Terrorists therefore select victims whose value is symbolic in the wider community. Terrorism relies on unexpectedness, rather than unpredictability, and on the eruption of violence in environments that normally are not subject to it.[8] Seldom does it involve large numbers of participants—its strength comes from stealth and from blind commitment to a cause; the cause must be one for which the government and its supporters are judged responsible. "Terrorism per se is not usually a reflection of mass discontent or deep cleavages in society. More often, it represents the disaffection of a fragment of the elite, who may take it upon themselves to act on behalf of the majority, unaware of its plight."[9] To attain its aims, contemporary national terrorism engages in criminal activities (kidnapping, bank robberies) to keep its cadres on a payroll and finance the organization attacking the State.

Italian jurists define terrorism as "a form of political struggle which, by means of attacks on persons and things, seeks to create terror in the population, creating panic and a lack of confidence in the institutions, and to call attention to specific ideologies, programs, associations."[10] The definition is clear. Regrettably the substance of terrorism is complicated by Law 191 of May 18, 1978 (written in reaction to the Moro kidnapping), which distinguishes between terrorist intent *and* intent to overthrow the democratic order, introducing in the penal code article 289: "Kidnapping persons to further terrorist aims *or* to overthrow the democratic order." Two years later, Law 15 of February 6, 1980 introduced a new article 270 into the penal code, "Associations whose purpose is terrorism *and* the overthrow of the democratic order." In brief the legislator introduced ambiguity, especially in 1978, as if he were anticipating revelations about the Masonic Lodge P2 affair, or secret connections between politicians and mafia.[11] Furthermore the concept of "democratic order," no better defined until 1987, was introduced into the penal code and it is clearly a political rather than a juridical concept, over the content of which legal commentators note that Italian political parties disagree (formal vs. substantive democracy), while terrorist organizations often claim "democratic order" as their final goal.

The point is that Italy in fact rapidly provided a strong and emotional response to the Moro kidnapping, seeking to distinguish between terrorist aims and the overthrow of democratic order. The distinction may have been rhetorically satisfying but it was politically imprudent and juridically indefensible. Hasty and imperfect drafting, often the result of many compromises among parties, characterizes much of Italian legislation, including this law.

The development of the Italian State, its political
parties, the divisions in the political culture, combined with
economic and social problems of the sixties and seventies—
these factors go far in explaining the violence that would
rock the peninsula for nearly two decades. The 19th
century liberal state established itself by force, and
especially in the south, where it did so at the cost of
untold numbers of deaths. Those who opposed it—anonymous
southern peasants in revolt, Romagnoli anarchists, Emilian
and Lombard socialists—recognized the value of political
violence, and in success or in failure they were glorified for
their actions. Fascism added its unfortunate contribution,
only to confront after 1943, with its German ally, the
Resistenza. Partisans became a symbol of regeneration, of
the second, democratic *Risorgimento* endorsed by the long
established democracies, thus the critical symbol for all
Italian democratic parties ranging from liberal to communist.
Their noble task was fulfilled with arms and sanctified by
blood; honoring their mission and accomplishments regularly
helped maintain the idea that force often provided the
proper solutions: many a terrorist group would pattern itself
on models of the Resistance (e.g. Gruppi Azione Partigiana,
or GAP and Nuclei Azione Proletaria, or NAP).

Violence remained a reality in Italy in the years
immediately after the war. In the red triangle of Emilia,
several thousand people disappeared between 1945 and
1946.[12] In Sicily, separatism and banditism became one, and
the saga of bandit Giuliano continued through 1949. In
Alto-Adige South Tyrol, terrorist activities would bring
bloodshed and property destruction that the De Gasperi-
Gruber agreements of 1947 and the granting of regional
autonomy would not quell. This violence would peak in the
1960s and is not completely stilled. In Sardinia, separatists,
leftists and bandits have recently combined in the MAS, the
Sardinian Armed Movement, and claimed six assassinations
and several kidnappings; the Sardinian Action Party, which
seeks independence from Italy, received over 91,000 votes at
the parliamentary elections of 1983.[13]

It is impossible to ignore the criminal violence in
Southern Italy, which the State seems unable to contain.
The very violence of mafia can also breed terrorism because
it gives no importance to human life. Since 1970, in the
south, over 500 deaths per year have been ordered by the
mafia, the camorra, or the 'ndrangheta. Gang wars in

Palermo alone have provoked in excess of 200 murders per year in the 1980s. In Calabria "for a time, the homicide rate in Gioia Tauro—population 17,000—exceeded that of New York City."[14] The daily presence and actuality of violence can make terrorism seem less of a threat.

The immediate causes of terrorism are to be found in the rapid and radical transformation of Italian society in the wake of the "economic miracle" of the late 1950s. In two decades the country jumped from a barely removed peasant society into the post-industrial age. While the economy took off, slowed down, and accelerated again, the political world was grinding to a standstill. Administered by a virtual gerontocracy of revolving politicians, Italy was challenged by a left which, for international reasons, was deemed unfit to rule. That very lack of alternation, of any new solution, made the country fertile for terrorism. Political immobilism was a contributing cause of the near-collapse of an over-burdened educational system, which continued to admit increasing numbers of students, many of whom would not graduate, while many of those who did graduated into unemployment as the economy slowed down, a consequence of the "hot autumn" of 1969 and of the several oil crises of the 1970s.

The sociologist Sabino Acquaviva[15] has documented what he terms the disaggregation of the Italian value system, the collapse of the traditional values of the family, the decline of religion and formal religious values, and the exaltation of new sexual values. With 1968 came the slogan "to be personal is to be political." Leftist culture became all-encompassing and pervasive, and soon one would talk of a "cathocommunist" mold of revolt.[16] Intellectuals were directly involved in society life, sharing the lives of the *emarginati*, the marginalized groups, aggregating their forces in the "collectives" (which often began with squatters), and constantly harping on the theme of freedom and liberation. The media exalted distant guerilla wars and revolutions.[17] Soon, to shoot would become a symbol of liberation. Young middle- and working-class Italians of Catholic, communist and lay extraction sought change in a political world that was incapable of providing it, or even of offering new symbols or apparently, new men. As Paul Furlong writes:

> So the preconditions of political terrorism may be clearly perceived in Italy: an economic crisis

producing unemployment particularly among the younger age groups, political parties that are unable to agree on appropriate measures, a social fabric severely threatened by the industrial mobilization of the immediate postwar period, and not least a political culture that supports radical expectations and gives legitimacy to the unsatisfied hopes and programmes of the postwar political reconstruction.[18]

Terrorism of both right and left profoundly affected the country, though it is now clear that no more than 3,500 people have been actively engaged in such activities. They benefitted from adherents to and supporters of similar ideological persuasions, many of whom cannot be considered *stricto sensu* terrorists. Terrorists of the right,[19] who represent the smallest fraction (at their peak, perhaps 200 or so), hover on the margins of the neo-fascist MSI (Italian Social Movement); they are as well, in most cases, on the margins of society. Suffering from severe identity problems and prone to heavy drug use, they live in a world of fantasy, striving to establish a strong authoritarian state, cleansed of communist enemies who are viewed as "useless worms in a putrid society."[20] Proponents of a "strategy of tension," they would like to be the creators of a new state emerging resplendent from social disorder.

On the left, the primary revolutionary aim was to provoke sufficient instability to force an authoritarian reaction by the State which, in turn, would lead the proletariat to revolt. The Red Brigades sought to create "a party of armed cadres, distinct from the class movement, but in dialectic relationship to it,"[21] an avant garde that would strike at the heart of the imperialist state. Originating in Milan and Turin they expanded to the major Italian cities, notably Genoa, Naples, and Rome. Organized on the basis of a classic Leninist matrix, living essentially underground, this perilous organization would begin to unravel along with its clandestine links, as members fell into police hands.

More complex are the organizations that stem from *Autonomia* and the Armed Movement, and their very complexity has given them better chances of survival.[22] Originating in groups concerned with post-material values (ecologists, anti-technology groups), suspicious of capitalism,

they emphasize proletarian self-improvement ("a radically
different alternative from the total process of capitalist
production and reproduction"), the discovery of "the
personal as political," and "the refusal of capitalistic labor,
that is to say of exploitation in general."[23] Self-
improvement first led to sabotage and then to armed revolt.
By the early 1980s both groups were practically destroyed
and the Brigades sought survival by establishing links with
organized crime, the mafia in particular, and with foreign
terrorist elements.[24]

Terrorism of the right, which started in the mid-1960s,
strikes indiscriminately and has sought to influence society
by maximizing the number of its victims. In December 1969,
a bomb at the Banco dell' Agricoltura, Piazza Fontana in
Milan, left 16 dead and 90 injured. In 1974, bombs planted
at a political rally in Brescia and on a train, the Italicus,
travelling from Rome to Milan, caused 20 deaths. In August
of 1980, 85 people were slaughtered and 200 injured in an
explosion at the central station in Bologna while the same
year the Armed Revolutionary Nuclei (NAR) fire-bombed
some 90 buildings in Rome and claimed several assassinations. There seem to be few patterns, beyond the common
use of time-controlled explosives which seek to provoke
massive destruction. For many, this "strategy of tension"
would become the detonator of leftist violence.

The left started organizing in 1969 in Milan, in the
colettivo politico metropolitano. Through 1971 various
groups sought to penetrate the factory world, in Milan (Sit-
Siemens, Pirelli), in Turin (Fiat), and Genoa. Their actions
consisted of carefully planned fire-bombings and the
distribution of manifestoes. In March 1972 Giacomo
Feltrinelli, the Milan publisher, operating on the fringe of
the Red Brigades, was killed while seeking to plant
explosives on a high-tension power line. From 1972 to 1974
the Brigades kidnapped and submitted to "people's courts"
four well-known citizens, including the deputy state
attorney for Genoa, eventually releasing them unharmed.
The Red Brigades were not at the center of attention, but
were also successfully infiltrated by the police and quickly
lost their top leadership. From 1976 to 1980 they entered
their phase of greatest activity, *gli anni di piombo*, the
leaden years, assassinating the state prosecutor of Genoa in
1976, murdering 16 in 1978, 24 in 1979, and 29 in 1980.[25]
In 1978, Aldo Moro, the leading proponent of the

compromesso storico, was kidnapped, held captive in Rome for 54 days, then murdered, his body being left close to the headquarters of both the DC and the PCI. The state seemed incapable of breaking the cycle of violence. Yet three years later, with increased powers and hard-driving leadership, the police had destroyed most of the terrorist ring. The kidnapping of the American general Dozier in December 1981 was the last Red Brigade operation of any magnitude; his liberation by the police was symbolic of the great progress achieved.

For years, Italian terrorists of the right benefited from important protection inside the secret services, while the State, notably through the minister of the Interior, was well informed of activities of the Red Brigades.[26]   At a time when the secret services were covering up rightist coups d'etat (DiLorenzo, 1964; Prince Borghese, 1970), they were also covering up the Piazza Fontana bombing, which they had inspired.[27] "When it comes to fascist terrorism, Italian authorities seem to be a bit blind in the right eye."[28]   In Rome, a politicized police and judiciary have often refused categorical evidence presented by prosecutors; in one case this resulted in the death of one of them.[29]   "Far-right activities remain enshrouded in an obscurity that can be only likened to products of neorealist Italian cinema, where the boundary between fact and fantasy, dream and reality is so shadowy and indistinct as to produce a sense of near hallucination."[30]   The statement could well be a definition of the P2 affair.

On the other side of the political spectrum, the situation is not totally different. Consider for example the destiny of certain letters written by Moro in captivity and recovered by the *carabinieri*, only to disappear under a clause of state secrecy; the letters would have proved particulary embarrassing to politicians in power, especially Andreotti.[31]   And what is one to say of Prime Minister Cossiga, now president of the Republic, who in 1980 is said to have urged his colleague Senator Carlo Donat Cattin, vice secretary of the DC, to advise his son Marco to seek refuge in France rather than risk arrest in Italy, since his leadership role in the *Prima Linea*, a position he had held from 1977 to 1979 probably in full knowledge of the police, had now been exposed?[32]   Marco Donat Cattin would eventually escape, return, and be confined to house arrest.

Under such conditions, it is indeed remarkable that the police managed to operate at all.

The history of the Italian police forces precedes the unification of the country. That fact and the subsequent development of the police explain many of the oddities that still are extant in the police today. The *carabinieri* were created by Piedmont in 1814; the Corps of Public Security dates to 1848; and the Finance Police were established in 1862. In different incarnations, all three subsist today, the Republican founding fathers having failed to unify them. Municipal police and forest guards can also be considered as police forces, though their jurisdiction is extremely limited, and they too extend back to early Italian history.[33]

About two hundred thousand people make up the Italian police forces. The Corps of Public Safety takes orders from the minister of the interior; the *carabinieri* are an integral part of the armed forces, in fact one of their most revered bodies, and depend on the minister of defense; the task of the Finance Police is to seek out fiscal and financial fraud; subject to the minister of finance, it is also charged with the maintenance of order and public safety. The police are exclusively a state police, organized on military principles. Only in 1981 did legislation, inspired by the terrorist events of the time (Law 1 April 1981, no. 121), demilitarize and return the police to civil administration under the coordinating powers and direction of the minister of the interior, who is in charge of what is called *polizia di stato*, the state police—which embraces all three corps.

Organized on a territorial base and extending to the smallest administrative unit of the state, the *comune*, the components of the state police do not necessarily follow the regular administrative divisions of the state (20 regions, 90 provinces, 8,000 *comunes*). This is particularly true for the *carabinieri*, present in the smallest villages but reporting to territorial commanders whose jurisdiction covers several regions, while public safety corps report to the prefects who head the provinces.

The distinction between prevention and repression remains in the organization of the police. Article 109 of the Constitution is categorical: "The judiciary authority disposes directly of the judiciary police." In brief the State police exercise a safety function under the minister of the interior and a judiciary function subjected to the judiciary. At the levels of the court of appeals, the tribunals and the local magistrate courts, select representatives of the three police corps are detached and constitute "nuclei" of judiciary police. These policemen are functionally dependent on the magistrates, yet hierarchically they are subject to the commanders of their various corps. Members of the judiciary police thus follow a career in which their future and advancement is subject to a magistrate, often politicized, while they can be recalled at all times by their hierarchical superior; both facts can seriously damage their careers.

The final group to consider is the secret services. They have had a checkered history in republican Italy, under control of the Ministry of Defense until 1977. The Armed Forces Information Services (SIFAR), which became Defense Information System (SID) in 1965, engaged in political maneuvering and parliamentary espionage, in flagrant contradiction of several governments' efforts to establish a center-left government. For all practical purposes, they became sponsors of terrorism of the right. By 1963, thousands of dossiers had been established, all with blackmail potential over the political, parliamentary, and union elites. By 1964 the possibility of a military coup was being considered. The former head of SIFAR, commanding general of the *carabinieri* Giovanni di Lorenzo, was responsible. In 1965 he became army chief of staff and was elected as a neo-fascist to Parliament, thus enjoying immunity from prosecution. In 1970 the head of the reformed SID, General Vito Miceli, was implicated in another coup, to be led by Prince Valerio Borghese. Arrested, he too would be elected an MSI parliamentarian.

An apparently radical purge ensued, and the services were re-organized in 1977 (Law 24 October 1977, no. 801). The Service for Information and Security (SIS) is now directly dependent on the prime minister and on an interministerial committee which includes Interior and Defense. It is divided into two branches, one dealing with external security (SISMI), the other with internal security. The latter, the Service for Information and Democratic Security (SISDE) is charged with gathering information and maintaining security to ensure "the defense of the Democratic State and of its institutions for which the Constitution provides the foundation, against whoever may attack them and seek their overthrow." In March 1981 the

P2 scandal exploded: the heads of both branches of the secret services were members!

While it is correct to note that law enforcement is "ill equipped to deal with the unprobable and unusual character of terrorism,"[34] it is reasonable to advance that in Italy the decks were stacked against the State. The secret services have consistently been supportive of the right and have systematically sought to prevent any evolution of the parliamentary world towards the left. In the 1970s as in the 1940s, their objective has always been to undermine the Socialist and Communist lists. During the entire terrorist emergency, they have either been actively plotting or in the process of "reorganization." At the time of the Moro kidnapping, their entire leadership belonged to P2. The consequent cleansing operations—assuming they were successful—created a serious vacuum at the very height of the terrorist emergency. Their accountability to Parliament and to the judiciary is already tenuous: the prime minister provides a bi-annual written report on the services' activities, but the Constitutional Court in 1977 recognized the prime minister's right to invoke a State-secret clause to prevent the judiciary from inquiring into matters pursued by the services, since its members, unlike other police forces, escape judiciary jurisdiction.

The many branches of the regular state police, each with its own independent intelligence gathering operation, are symptomatic of the lack of coordination (exercised in theory at the highest levels) and of the jealousies that exist between the services. Such coordination as exists is further weakened by the different territorial jurisdictions each branch covers, while the ambiguous status of the police members belonging to the nuclei of judiciary police does not facilitate the development of inquiries in a world where the judiciary is radically politicized. Finally, like the secret services, the state police has its own collection of files and this has had a clearly negative impact on parliamentary oversight of its activities.

Even under such circumstances Italy has defeated terrorism, and that may go down as another Italian miracle. But it may also indicate how superficial the influence of terrorism was in the society at large in the first instance. Alberto Ronchey remarks that "the inefficiency of the public powers certainly did not lie in the size of the Italian police force . . . but rather in the fact that a police force of peasant extraction was left to fend for itself in the face of an uprising of well-trained groups of armed intellectuals. . . ."[35] Yet, starting in 1971 and more effectively by 1974, the various intelligence services had infiltrated the Red Brigades with informers; they could continue to do so as the bands dissolved and reconstituted themselves; by 1979 the first terrorists would start talking, revealing information which would allow the police to decapitate the terrorist organizations. The *carabinieri* would be in the forefront of the battle, leading the offensive, and often not coordinating with the judiciary nuclei, considered too politically "engaged." In December 1970, head of the *carabinieri* General Corrado di San Giorgio launched the first offensive; in October 1973 General Carlo Alberto Dalla Chiesa established the first anti-terrorist nucleus in Turin; in May 1974 he would lead the assault on the prison of Alessandria, where the Brigade prisoners had revolted and taken hostages; in 1975 he established and was put in charge of special high security prisons for terrorists; in 1978, following Moro's death, he would coordinate all anti-terrorist forces. By 1981 the Brigades were defeated, and arrested leaders and troops were talking, to earn shorter sentences. Dalla Chiesa was named Prefect of Palermo in 1982. The lower levels of all the police forces, the "peasant police," had performed their duty and rejected political engagement. The *carabinieri*, also a peasant police, provided most of the troops. Most importantly the leadership performed the task it was entrusted with rather than play politics, carefully separating itself from the magistracy, deemed unreliable because it was too politicized. An infrastructure was in place when the terrorists struck the hardest after 1976; there was also a clear will to use it in the police and in the government, which saw its future threatened by further inertia. Constrained to act, the government acted. And the "people's police" did its job.

The proverbial slowness of justice is reaffirmed in Italy, where in 1986 the courts were still dealing with the Piazza Fontana massacre of 1969, first brought to trial in 1972: seven years for the first trial, three in appeal—all quite within the norm. Simple cases handled by one judge take around 500 days; 900 days, if they are considered by a tribunal. The court of appeals should take another two years, and recourse to the court of cassation, three more. Appeal is normally exercised as the courts treat the case *ab imis,* reviewing the record, seeking new testimony, reconsidering the facts. Every year the court dockets are fuller, the judges fewer, the trials slower. The courts are forced to deal "with a crazy-quilt of judicial and legislative accretions,"[36] while both the civil and penal codes date from the Fascist period and are being constantly modified by the Constitutional Court and Parliament, in response to challenges and to events, but in a topsy-turvy way which considerably complicates the work of the judiciary.

The Italian magistrate is completely independent, and his independence is established by the Constitution (art. 104). He is also thoroughly politicized. By the end of the 1960s, younger magistrates were challenging their superiors' authority and their theory of law. While conservative and right-wing judges endorsed a restrictive view of the judicial role, their leftist colleagues invoked ideology and envisioned the courts as an instrument of the class struggle. The *pretori d'assalto,* the fighting judges, were on the bench, some becoming involved with the Red Brigades. Split into three different factions, "independents" (37 percent), center-left "unity for the Constitution" (45 percent), and "democratic" (18 percent), the judiciary was open to political influence.[37] Cooperation with the police forces, via the judiciary police nuclei, became difficult and occasionally problematic when the two sides divided politically. For the Red Brigades, the judges were symbols of the State and most of them defended it strenuously. In April 1974 the deputy state attorney in Genoa, Mario Sossi, was kidnapped. In June 1976 Francesco Coco, state prosecutor in Genoa, would be the first magistrate to be gunned down. In June 1980 Judge Mario Amato was assassinated by rightist terrorists in Rome. With up to 30,000 people in jail awaiting trial, presumed guilty rather than innocent, the judicial system of Italy is overloaded and cracking at the seams. It was already so by 1970 when the terrorists struck. Today 3,013 of them are involved in 141 penal trials. Like the codes the magistracy seeks to apply, the judicial and penal systems are in need of a radical overhaul which can only come from the political authorities.

The terrorists were extreme manifestations of changes that were sweeping Italian society while Parliament remained immobile, the judiciary paralyzed, and the police only partly effective. The issue is what can a weak political structure do when confronted by extremism, and more specifically how far can a democratically committed state go in repressing terrorism? While the European Court on Human Rights has criticized Italy for the slowness of its justice, a slowness which often leads to the release of criminals whose period of preventive detention has expired, the country's overall record on civil rights is not at all unfavorable, especially when compared to that of the Federal Republic of Germany, under a lesser threat. In spite of pressure from the right, Parliament passed no laws that curtailed the basic constitutional liberties of the citizens. Where Parliament, and especially the government, failed was in the early period of the terrorist attacks, when the center-left was showing its weaknesses and the preliminaries to the historic compromise were not yet fully clear. Tottering governments engaged in benevolent neglect and failed to provide police forces with the powers they needed to face the emergency. Only in response to crisis, and with the DC and the PCI both supportive of resolute action, would Parliament rather haphazardly provide the necessary resources in the form of the Reale Law in 1975, promptly challenged by the extreme left in a referendum. By 1980, rather than punitive legislation, the state would seek recuperative legislation designed to obtain information from the terrorists, to rehabilitate those willing to repent, and to make room in the jails for common criminals.

Such actions may be viewed as the product of weakness—and to the extent that they are reactive rather than anticipatory they may be—but they can also be deemed opportune and opportunistic: legislating terrorism out of business, if at all possible, is improbable without effective police and judiciary. Perhaps the State could accept its weakness and seek to muddle through the emergency, in the manner of the famous Italian gift for *arrangiarsi*, because the society on which it rested rejected terrorism and never took the Brigades too seriously. The State's decision-making was reactive and often ambiguous, and Italy today is still struggling with measures to reform the judiciary, while the police still needs to be unified, and the codes both seek to apply are sorely in need of revision. But in spite of all apparent contradictions, the State reacted, the government legislated, the police enforced, and together they thwarted terrorism.

II. THE TERRORIST EMERGENCY: THE LEGAL RESPONSE

To arrest and prosecute terrorists, the police and the courts of republican Italy were entirely dependent on the fascist codes of 1930. The nature of the codes was not an issue, but rather the fact that 40 years after their inception their provisions did not give the police sufficiently effective powers to respond to the new circumstances. Meanwhile the procedural code allowed justice to proceed at a pace incompatible with the load it had to confront. The issue would be how to deal with terrorism and how to deal with justice; the State would only address the first persuasively.

A second matter rendered the task of the judiciary more complex: the republican constitution guaranteed fundamental rights and explicitly invoked the need for judicial intervention before the police could seek to limit them, and then only in cases where an imperative need was demonstrated. The recently established Constitutional Court (1956) also made it clear that the maintenance of public order had to be fully compatible with the maintenance and preservation of fundamental rights.

Certain instruments of intervention were available to the State prior to 1975. The Italian Constitution in article 18 recognizes the right of association, with the exception of neo-fascist organizations (transitional provision No. 12), secret organizations, and those based on military struc-tures.[38]   The penal code in article 270 is specific: "Whoever in the territory of the State promotes, constitutes, organizes or directs associations intent upon violently establishing the dictatorship of one social class over another, or violently suppressing a social class, or otherwise violently subverting the economic and social order of the State is punished by imprisonment for five to twelve years." Articles 271 and 273 deal with "associations intent on destroying or undermining the national sentiment" and "unauthorized international associations" and complete the enumeration. Article 272 addresses the case of subversive propaganda aiming at "the establishment of the dictatorship of one class over the others," etc., punishable by a sentence of one to five years. The programs of terrorists of both left and right are clearly covered by these articles. Attacks against the Constitution and the form of government by means not recognized by the Constitution are subject to a minimum sentence of twelve years, while attacks and plots against the State and its constitutional bodies are also severely repressed. In the case of armed insurrection, even if the weapons are only stored and never used, article 284 calls for death, which the Republic changed to a life sentence for those who promote it and three to fifteen years for the participants. Death, now life, is also the sanction for "whoever attacks the security of the State, commits an action which leads to devastation, pillage or slaughter" (art. 285).

Articles 302 and 303 deal with the crime of instigation by individuals of an attack against the internal or international personality of the State, and article 304 deals with the same in the case of conspiracy by several individuals. In brief, incitement to the actions covered by articles 270-273 and 283-285 is sufficient cause for sanction, not to exceed one half of the sanction called for by the specific articles.

The programs, as well as the actions of terrorists whose aim it was to change by violent means the nature of the State, the relationship between the classes, and the economic order were severely sanctioned by the law, which called for terms of twelve years to life. What was lacking were better means to arrest, hold, and jail the terrorists. These would be granted to the police in 1975.

Under Aldo Moro's prime ministership, in response to Red Brigade kidnappings, to revelations about the role the secret services had played in rightist plots, to requests from police authorities and the judiciary, Parliament passed law 152, on May 22, 1975, the *legge Reale*. Within two years Parliament would complete or remove imperfections of the law, and the extreme left would seek its repeal, via popular referendum.

The law provided the police with the means to detain, stop, and search individuals, Italian or foreign, who associated with the extreme left, the extreme right, or the mafia. For crimes committed under articles 283-285, attempted murder, as well as for the creation of circumstances leading to civil war (art. 286), participation in armed bands (306), provoking railroad disasters (436), epidemics (438), poisoning of waters (439), violent robbery (628), extortion (629), kidnapping (605, 630), and any crime involving the use of military weapons or explosives, provisional liberty could not be granted. And in those cases where it might be possible, the judge was required to determine that the person released was not inclined to commit further crimes against the collectivity (art. 1). The length of preventive detention could be extended by the judge if its term were to be approaching, by a simple declaration of urgency of the trial (art. 2). The law provided in article 3 for a new reading of article 238 of the penal code: in case of suspicions, or of available circumstantial evidence of participation in attacks involving the use of military weapons or explosives, suspects could be detained by the police and isolated for a time sufficient to pursue proper inquiries, subject to immediately informing the public prosecutor, who was then required to question the suspect within 48 hours and either release or detain him. In exceptional circumstances in the course of police operations, police could search individuals and their vehicles, to ascertain if they were in possession of weapons. The police powers of search and detention had been considerably increased; crack-downs on terrorist hideouts would be numerous in the fall of 1975.

The law also established clearer parameters on what could be considered a dangerous organization and/or a reorganized fascist party, and it increased penalties for those who belonged (art. 7-13), while also forbidding the use of helmets in public manifestations (a disguise favored by fascist thugs).

To deter kidnapping and robbery article 15 called for sentences of two to eight years for those who harbored or attempted to recycle "dirty" money. Furthermore the judge could temporarily suspend the administration of personal property by the suspect if he considered his conduct, behavior or activity socially dangerous (art. 23-24). While applicable to suspected terrorists, these articles would serve as the basis for prosecution against the mafia. The final provisions offered further protection to the police. In the case of arrest in the course of commission of an act of violence against a policeman, judgment had to be rendered against the accused within 20 days. Simultaneously it was made even more difficult to prosecute policemen for their use of firearms or physical force while in service.

To summarize, judicial discretion was increased at the expense of individual's rights; and the criteria for arrest and continued detention became more flexible. The police obtained sweeping powers, which it used vigorously against those who threatened the State.

On August 8, 1977, the Reale Law was completed. The sentences of those who robbed armories and gun stores were raised to 15 to 20 years. Special provisions were made for the sale of the rockets and flares used on board ships. Buildings that were the seat of associations and in which arms and ammunition were discovered were subject to confiscation. Finally the law was amended to allow the wearing of protective helmets by athletes in sporting events!

To the extreme left, the law was abhorrent: defendants were less free, penal justice was in the hands of the police, lawyers were absent at critical junctures. "The law makes abundant use of 'police powers,' which in a state of law are usually recognized as untrustworthy and in contrast with clear constitutional principles. . . . These have been called preventive measures . . . [but they are informed] by a cynical scorn for the inviolable rights of man and ignore fundamental constitutional principles."[39] In 1977 the Radical Party quickly gathered the 500,000 signatures required to hold a referendum to repeal the law; it was held on June 11, 1978, a month after Moro's death. While a majority supported the maintenance of the law (76.5 percent voted against its abrogation), abstentions (24 percent) and the variations in abstentions (35 and 36 percent in the South and the Islands, 18 and 19 percent in the North and Center) indicated less than strong enthusiasm for its contents.

On March 16, 1978 the Red Brigades kidnapped Aldo Moro. Five policemen of his escort were killed. He was later shot, on May 9. On March 21, the Andreotti Government—installed on March 16 with the support of most parties in Parliament (the liberals opposed)—presented a decree law. On May 18, 1978 it would become law 191: "Penal and trial norms for the prevention and repression of serious crimes."

The reaction to the kidnapping was fast, and even hasty. The new law introduced distinctions that would complicate the task of the judiciary.[40] Kidnapping related to terrorism, *or* to the overthrow of the democratic order, (art. 289) required sentences of 25 to 30 years, and a life sentence in case of death. If a terrorist dissociated himself from the criminal enterprise and the kidnap victim returned to freedom, the sentence would be two to eight years. In cases of kidnapping for purposes of extortion (by terrorists or others, i.e. mafia), the penalties were identical. The laundering of money could bring four to ten years. Attacks on public buildings, research and computer centers—favorite terrorist objectives—produced article 419, with penalties of three to eight years.

The police were given increased powers to track terrorists: magistrates and/or the ministry of the interior could request information about trials and investigations in progress, if useful to other criminal investigations or to prevent the commission of a crime. Public prosecutors could grant the police verbal authorization to wire-tap telephones for periods of up to 30 days for investigative purposes, without any special demonstration of cause. And while information gathered in such ways could not be used for a trial related to the specific case under consideration, it could nevertheless be used in other trials if deemed relevant.

Police were also allowed to detain for up to 24 hours anybody who refused to reveal his/her identity or whose papers could be considered suspicious; and in case of emergency (art. 225) they were entitled to obtain summary information (not better defined) from suspects or from persons caught flagrante delicto, without a lawyer present.

Terrorist activity reached its zenith in 1979. Further, "Urgent measures to preserve democratic order and public safety" were drafted in December by the government (D.L.15.XII.79 no. 625) and became Law 15 on February 6, 1980. A new article 270 of the penal code was introduced to deal with "Associations the aim of which is terrorism *and* the overthrow of democratic order": "Whoever promotes, constitutes, organizes, directs associations that intend to commit acts of violence to overthrow the democratic order is punishable by seven to fifteen years of prison." In the same breath, the law declared that for all crimes of terrorism or subversion of the democratic order that were not punishable with life, sentences would be doubled. It also increased the penalties for unsuccessful attempts made on a person's life to 20 years, 18 in case of "serious lesions" (knee-capping), the penalties to be increased by one third if the crime was committed against a member of the government, parliament, the judiciary, or the police (art. 280).

For a period of one year, the police could arrest individuals suspected of terrorism and detain them for 48 hours. In executing an arrest warrant against anybody involved in suspected terrorist activity, upon authorization of the public prosecutor (even by phone), "officers of the judiciary police may proceed to search premises, including entire buildings, and blocs of buildings, where they have reason to believe that the person, or things that could be subject to seizure or indices that could be destroyed, may be located. In case of necessity or utmost urgency the officers of the judiciary police may also proceed without authorization of the competent magistrate, subject to informing the public prosecutor as soon as possible." (art. 224 p.c.)

To add to the arsenal of the judiciary, terms of preventive detention in cases of terrorism were increased by one third. Simultaneously the law considered favorable action for those who would dissociate themselves "from the others, would try to prevent criminal activity being carried to its full consequences, or would concretely help the police and the judicial authority to obtain decisive proof to identify and capture" terrorists. In such occurrences, life sentences could be reduced to 12 to 20 years, and other sentences would be diminished by half.

It was the most stringent of all laws passed against terrorism. It was also, in the views of many, the most generous, and generosity rather than severity would provide the more effective results. The law was clear-cut on kidnapping and other terrorist acts, and punishment was severe. Police powers were pushed to extremes, notably in the case of arrest and detention of suspects: those powers were also limited in time (one year) and required that the minister of the interior report to Parliament every two months on their implementation, but the law also considered the possibility of reduced sentencing for those terrorists willing to cooperate with the police. Very soon terrorists would begin to come forth and provide information to the public authorities. The movement would still fight back but the beginnings of its unraveling were close. Italian legislation on terrorism would enter its third phase, systematically searching for cooperation among repentant terrorists and seeking to limit the size of the prison population.

On May 29, 1982, Law 304, effective June 2, was published under the title "Measures in defense of the constitutional order." The title was a superb piece of legerdemain, and the law quickly became known as the law on the *pentiti*, which is exactly what it was. All but one of its provisions dealt with reducing sentences in cases of cooperation. The exception (art. 11), made it clear that the term "overthrow of the democratic order" corresponded in terms of juridical effect to "overthrow of the constitutional order."

For crimes committed prior to January 31, 1982, repentant terrorists, under specific circumstances, and for 120 days, could enjoy what would resemble a rampant amnesty. Members of terrorist organizations subject to prosecution under articles 270, 270 bis, 304, 305, and 306 p.c., would not be punished if their only crime was that of association, if they were willing to dissolve the terrorist group, or withdraw from it, or peacefully surrender and provide information. The non-punishment was to be confirmed by a judge. The terms of terrorism were no longer "Never Without a Rifle"[41] but rather "Lay down your gun and go home."

The law introduced an interesting distinction between dissociation from terrorism and collaboration with the authorities. For those terrorists who prior to final sentencing would confess all their crimes dissociating themselves from their companions, life sentences were reduced (15 to 21 years), and all other sentences decreased by a third, and not to exceed 15 years. For collaborators who helped the police and the judiciary obtain decisive proof to identify or capture terrorists with whom the collaborators had engaged in crimes they had confessed, or who would provide relevant instruments of proof to permit the reconstruction of the crime and the discovery of its authors, life sentences were reduced to ten to twelve years and other prison sentences by half, not to exceed ten years. In cases of exceptional information, those sentences could be further reduced by one third—in other words, a life term could become seven to nine years.

Additional bonuses were provided for consecutive sentences: to the longest sentence, one fifth of any other would be tacked on with a maximum of 16 years to be served in case of collaboration, or 22 otherwise. For verdicts of less than four and a half years, the sentence could be suspended. Provisional liberty now became possible for exceptional collaborators, subject to the judges' discretion and opinion that the ex-terrorist no longer represented a danger for the collectivity. In cases where one half of the sentence had been served, and the condemned gave evidence through his behavior that he/she had reformed, provisional liberty became mandatory.[42]

Two months later, on July 29 (Law 398), a further effort was made to decrease the prison population. New limits were set on the length of preventive detention, now called cautionary detention. The terms, if not met, assured the release of the person incriminated; they varied from five months for crimes calling for a sentence of less than three years, to six years in case of a sentence of twenty, or life. Furthermore, judges were required to question the defendant within 15 days of his arrest or release him. Minors under 18, pregnant women, or women who breast-feed, people who are sick or over 65—these could be kept under a state of arrest in their own home, if their crimes were not of a serious nature.

Law 398 of July 29 was a house-keeping law which attempted to address the issue of preventive detention, which had seen up to 30,000 Italians in jail awaiting trial. But Law 304 on the *pentiti* was truly exceptional in character. It literally depenalized serious crimes, going well beyond the normal effects of a guilty plea.[43] The legal requirements for dissociation and/or collaboration are not clear proof of re-socialization, which should be the bottom line for releasing a criminal. The granting of provisional liberty to terrorists who have served one half of their time, while not extending the same benefits to those who have committed "ordinary" crimes, is striking indeed.[44] The point is that the law had one exclusive purpose: to bring terrorists forward so terrorism could be defeated, to induce jailed terrorists to accept their defeat, admit their guilt, and inform on others to end the cycle of violence. A few *irreducibili* have refused to give in, but their numbers are becoming ever more exiguous.

In February 1987, the minister of justice presented a final law dealing with the terrorist emergency. He considered it "a message of pacification sent to those who, after having embraced the cause of terrorism, have separated themselves from it, both in words and deeds."[45] Law 34, of February 18, 1987, clearly states its purpose: "Measures in favor of those who dissociate themselves from terrorism." Its provisions applied for 30 days from the date of its publication on February 22. Terrorists were offered fewer advantages than in 1982, life sentences being commuted to 30 years while sentences for serious terrorist crimes were decreased by one quarter rather than a half. However, conditional liberty could be granted to those whose sentences did not exceed ten years. The law also applies only to crimes committed prior to December 31, 1983, but covers crimes for which final sentencing has taken place. The law seeks to define dissociation, which applies to those who have "definitively abandoned the organization, the terrorist or subversive movement to which they belonged and who in conjunction with this have also admitted to the activities in which they partook; objectively and unequivocally engaged in behavior that is incompatible with the maintenance of the association; repudiated violence as a method of political struggle." (art. 1)

By the end of May 1987, the law will have led to the release of 269 allegedly repentant terrorists. Three thousand and thirteen still under judgment may yet benefit from it. For example, Valerio Morucci and Adriana Faranda who headed the Roman column of the Red Brigades and helped organize the kidnapping of Aldo Moro will be free within a year. They spent Christmas 1986 at home, on furlough. The Italian State is confident it has defeated terrorism. But other organizations linked with terrorism threaten it, in ways perhaps far more insidious.

Both the mafia and Masonic Lodge P2 have sought to undermine the Italian democratic and constitutional order. In Italian legislation, they are consequently considered subversive and equivalent to terrorist organizations. We will however keep our discussion of these phenomena to a minimum, emphasizing only the terrorist links.

Licio Gelli entered the Justinian Masonic Lodge in Rome in 1970. A self-made millionaire and supporter of the neo-fascist MSI, he sought and bought influence in the world of politics, banking, the army, industry, and television, among others. The peddling of favors was at the heart of his network; it would also turn out to involve the cover-up of coups, such as the Miceli-Borghese coup in the early seventies, and subversive efforts to exploit the democratic order, or disorder. The rumor in Rome had it that the lodge was the real *stanza dei bottoni*—the command post. In the exploration of various scandals, not the least of which was the collapse of the Sindona bank in New York and the Banco Ambrosiano in Milan, the police came across the membership list of Gelli's *Propaganda 2*, a secret organization within the Justinian Masonic Lodge. Of 962 members, there were 4 ministers and 3 undersecretaries of state, 36 parliamentarians, and nearly 200 military officers, including the highest ranks of the international branch of the Secret Service. SISMI, it became clear, was engaged in smuggling arms, in cooperation with the mafia; it also had several sabotage attempts against the PCI to its record.

The government soon fell, and the reins of power escaped the DC to go first to a Republican (Spadolini) and then to a Socialist (Craxi). The parliamentary inquiry committee concluded that the lodge was in fact subversive, that it exploited its influence for illegitimate purposes, one of which may have been to prevent the left from acceding to power. On January 25, 1982, Law 17, article 5, disbanded the lodge and confiscated its assets.

The mafia is more complex. A conservative estimate of its income in its various Italian incarnations would probably start with $500 million yearly derived from business protection. In Sicily and Calabria 10 to 15 percent of cost is factored into all major transactions for such purposes. The drug trade, notably heroin, may add between $5 and $10 billion. Recycled money in legitimate business operations may provide $1 to $2 billion more. So much for economics. The mafia counts well in criminal matters. Among its recent victims are General Dalla Chiesa, the prefect of Palermo, who was a major factor in the battle on the Red Brigades; the Regional secretary of the Sicilian Communist Party; and the head of the Christian Democratic Party in Palermo. The mafia does not discriminate politically.

Many assert a connection between the mafia, terrorism, and politics. But because the mafia kills, most assertions are based on circumstantial evidence. A parliamentary commission in 1970 published a three-volume study which gives some indications of the linkage.[46] More recently, the final summary by the State, in the trial of 707 mafiosi held in Palermo, referred to the "contiguity of important business and political milieux with Cosa Nostra." It called General Dalla Chiesa's diary an "implacable indictment against an irresponsible ruling class." In it the general wrote on April 6, 1981: "I made it clear to Andreotti [the prime minister] I would use no gloves with that part of the electorate on which his people rely," and on April 30 following the assassination of Pio La Torre, regional secretary of the PCI,

Dalla Chiesa disparagingly referred to the DC, "which in Palermo cohabitates with the worst of mafioso activism and political power."[47] In 1980, Senator Benedetti (PCI) publicly asserted: "There are vast areas of encounters between terrorism, mafia and organized criminals, in their search of common goals."[48] In 1986, the president of the Police Union referred to "the links between black terrorism, mafia and P2 which are a concrete reality." The mafia is "engaged in plotting against the institutions. . . ."[49]

For many analysts the mafia danger is greater than the terrorist threat. Interestingly enough, it is legislation against terrorist activities that has been used as the first stepping-stone against the mafia. "An association is of the mafioso type when those who belong to it exploit its force of intimidation, subjugation and silence (omerta) to commit crimes, acquire directly or indirectly the gestion or control of economic activities, concessions, authorizations, contract and public services, with the aim of obtaining profits or unfair advantages for themselves or others." (Art. 416, penal code)

The law that opened the way to prosecute the mafia was the *Legge Reale* of 1975, a first step and a model for the 1982 law. Its Article 18 extended the State's reach to "those who were preparing acts that could subvert the constitutional order through the commission of crimes," though it did not "establish the presumption that particular individuals must be dangerous." In this way it became possible to prosecute mafiosi.[50] The law also put another block on the mafia's path, allowing for the temporary suspension of the administration of personal patrimony, which the law of 1982 picked up with a vengeance (art. 10-31). The finance police can now question any individual's standard of living, financial resources, patrimony, and their origins; they can suspend his right to administer his affairs, and seize and attach his property if any suspicion emerges with regard to the legitimacy of its acquisition. It is essentially a policy of "scorched earth"[51] that the state inaugurated once it felt secure it had defeated national terrorism.

III. ITALY AND INTERNATIONAL TERRORISM

The links between Italian terrorists and terrorists elsewhere have been amply documented. The *modus operandi* in the Bologna station explosion and the Oktoberfest bombing were quite similar, and there is also some evidence that the French *Action Directe* may have had a hand in delivering the explosives to Italy. Italian terrorist of the left have trained in Czechoslovakia, North Korea, Lebanon, and Libya which has led, it is rumored, to their infiltration by the Israeli Mossad. A special link should also be mentioned: France has not only granted political asylum to some of the most prominent figures of *Autonomia*, such as Toni Negri and Orante Scalzone, but also to 160 other terrorists.[52]

Italian terrorist writings always have had an international flavor and attacked the "imperialist state of multinational companies" dominated by American interests. They have opposed warmongering foreign policy and wanted Italy out of NATO. But the international commitment of the Italian terrorists has only become a reality in weakness rather than in strength. Their most visible operation, the kidnap of General Dozier in December 1981, also became their most clamorous failure, when he was freed, albeit after 42 days, by the Italian police. It also indicated a new direction of operations: the penetration of the Italian peace movement.

Since the State has become more effective in controlling terrorism and has proved less willing to let Italy serve as a safehaven for international terrorists, especially the PLO (apparently agreed to by Aldo Moro), the country has become a center for transnational terrorist activities. On February 15, 1984 General Leamont Hunt, an American who was director of the Multinational Force in the Sinai, was shot to death in Rome. In 1985 a plot to blow up the U.S. Embassy was foiled. On December 27, 1985, 16 people died at the Rome airport when a terrorist suicide squad opened fire on the TWA and El Al check-in counters. Countless episodes of violence involving Libyan, Jordanian, Syrian, and United Arab Emirates diplomats and citizens have taken place in Rome during the last five years.[53] The

State has engaged in a full-fledged operation against foreign terrorists since 1982.

The most dramatic international terrorist act against Italy was the seizure on the high seas of the Italian cruise ship *Achille Lauro* in October 1985 by a commando team under the orders of "Abu Abbas." An elderly, invalid, American passenger, Leon Klinghoffer, was shot to death. Italy quickly sought to negotiate the release of the ship and its several hundred passengers and both the PLO and Egypt were involved. The agreement called for the ship to dock in Alexandria, where the terrorists would surrender to the Egyptian authorities who would provide them with safe conduct. The operation involved total secrecy, until the Egyptian plane which carried the commando, Abu Abbas (supposedly representing the PLO and traveling on a Syrian diplomatic passport), 18 Egyptian diplomats, and 8 soldiers, was intercepted in international air space by United States fighter aircraft and forced to land at the NATO base at Sigonella, in Sicily. Italian *carabinieri* immediately surrounded the Egyptian aircraft; they in turn were surrounded by the American special Delta Force. A stand-off ensued, until agreement was reached between Rome and Washington that Italy should exercise jurisdiction over the passengers of the Egyptian plane. It would release Abu Abbas on the grounds of a lack of evidence that he had directed the commandoes (the Italian position would later be reversed) and would try the four members who had seized the ship and killed a hostage.

What was the Italian legal position on the takeover by terrorists of a ship flying the Italian flag and on the American actions in Sicily? With regards to the first issue,[54] as the ship was under Italian jurisdiction it was Italy's choice to select the most adequate tactic to deal with the situation, "the only limit admissible deriving from humanitarian considerations in the sense that the primary aim of intervention would be the safeguarding of human life over the punishment of the terrorists."[55] And Italy successfully negotiated the release of the passengers with the PLO, using Egypt as intermediary and guarantor. Italy considered the interception and forced landing of the Egyptian plane as a violation of international law, possibly a case of violent self-help. But a self-presumed right of the United States to consign the guilty parties to justice could not justify the operation.

As much as is known of agreements that exist between the United States and Italy, we may presume the base of Sigonella is under exclusive Italian control and responsibility. Authorization to land was solicited from the Italian commander both by the Egyptian plane which requested emergency landing procedures, being low on fuel, and by the U.S. fighter planes. Authorization to land was granted after a telephone conversation between Prime Minister Craxi and President Reagan. (The helicopters carrying Delta force troops landed in place of the Tomcats and hence without Italian consent.) The orders from Rome explicitly stated that local authorities should take charge of the four Palestinians. The jurisdiction of the flag state over crimes committed on its own ships had actually materialized, and whatever arrangements may have been reached between Egypt, Italy, and the PLO on the conditions of the release of the *Achille Lauro*, Italy would have to submit the commandoes to Italian criminal law where prosecution is mandatory. Furthermore the Italians could invoke the principle *male captum, bene judicatum*, to which Egypt had agreed.[56]

In the Italian perspective, it was absolutely clear the United States had no jurisdiction in the case, and Rome stood its ground. The terrorists were judged according to Italian law and received relatively mild sentences. Under no circumstances could the tragic events be considered under the existing Italian-American extradition treaties on Mutual Assistance in Criminal Matters (1973, 1982, and 1983),[57] because the latter two only came into force on November 13, 1985. Furthermore these treaties emphasize criminal matters, especially as they relate to narcotics. In fact the 1982 treaty on Mutual Assistance in Criminal Matters explicitly allows a party to deny assistance in the measure that a request relates to a purely military offense, or to a matter considered a political offense by the requested state. The 1983 extradition treaty also allows an exception for political crimes.

There is a natural tendency among States "to avoid dealing with terrorism outside their borders . . . [especially] out of a desire to evade the difficult political problems caused by a sustained terrorist campaign."[58] The European states, nevertheless, have sought to enter into legal agreements that deal with the issue of terrorism, and especially of extradition. The major seat of such activity has been the Council of Europe in Strasbourg. In May 1973, the Consultative Assembly[59] condemned "acts of international terrorism . . . whatever their cause," and invited member governments "to reach a common definition of 'political infraction' so that such a 'political' justification could not be invoked each time a terrorist act endangers innocent lives." On January 27, 1977, the European Convention for the Repression of Terrorism was signed; Italy, in November of 1985, would ratify it with reservations (as did most of the signatories).[60] The Convention clearly states in article one that certain breaches of law cannot be considered political, connected to, or inspired by political motives. These are skyjacking and acts against the safety of civil aviation; attacks against the life or physical integrity or freedom of individuals entitled to diplomatic protection; the kidnapping and seizure of hostages; violations involving the usage of bombs, grenades, rockets, fire-arms, etc. The Convention covers both the authors of the crimes and their accomplices.

The Convention has been a failure. The text itself, in its articles 5 and especially 13, allows a state, regardless of article 1, to introduce a reservation whereby it is the sole party allowed to define what it considers a political crime with regard to extradition. Furthermore, the Convention is not an extradition treaty and creates no obligation on the state with regard to extradition. France refused Italian requests for the extradition of Franco Piperno during the Moro kidnapping and would base its extradition of a suspect involved in the Bologna station bombing on the 1946 peace treaty signed with Italy, rather than refer to the Convention.[61]

Unfortunately, however much goodwill may be directed towards the repression of terrorism by European states and by Italy in particular, "what is necessary is not a continuous gush of vibrant resolutions condemning terrorism, but rather the adoption of concrete measures."[62] And of these, the sovereign states of Europe have taken very few. In September 1986, at the request of France, then the center of terrorist attacks, the twelve ministers of the interior of the European Community unanimously agreed not to negotiate with terrorist states and to collaborate against them. Italy, in the Trevi group of justice ministers, which she coordinates, proposed subjecting diplomatic pouches to metal detectors, while Britain and France sought to make access to the Community more difficult for citizens of third countries.[63] Subsequent hostage-taking in Lebanon and ensuing negotiations did not provide convincing evidence that the European states were standing by their resolutions.

International terrorism is the most elusive and difficult to control. It is also particularly difficult to deal with when it involves Arab states and the PLO, to which Italy has extended *de facto* recognition by receiving Yassir Arafat and treating with his envoys. Despite the fact that the PLO has supplied arms to the Red Brigades, Italy follows a pro-Arab policy. Italy may have, in the seventies, agreed to allow Middle East terrorists free transit through her territory in exchange for a truce.[64] But the eighties have seen too many terrorist attacks involving Middle Easterners in Rome to believe that any such agreement may still be in effect. The events of the *Achille Lauro* serve as partial confirmation of that sad truth.

* * * * * *

Immobile, weak, unstable, overloaded, and ineffective are epithets frequently applied to Italian governments. On the one hand, this wry litany is said to be the product of a multiparty system in which a single party, of relative majority, the Christian Democrats, is the inevitable and dominant partner in any governmental combination; it may as well bespeak a lack of alternation between the parties due to the existence of an almost equally strong Italian Communist Party, sometimes considered anti-system, because the PCI's accession to power, at least in its present form, would be unwelcome by Italy's American and European allies. On the other hand, this peculiar system has kept the DC in uninterrupted power since 1945. It has brought the Italian economy to fifth place in the world and the Italian standard of living is about to exceed the British, a story of amazing success.

Italy's battle against terrorism is one of only relative success. Unfortunately slow in perceiving the danger, the system reacted vigorously once the emergency was declared. Until 1973, the Christian Democrats sought to exploit the *strategia della tensione* for limited electoral gains. They offered no coherent policy towards the Brigades (or the right). While the terrorist organizations were infiltrated by the police, the judiciary was thwarted by the secret services—the responsibility of the political world remains to be determined. For this slow and fragmented reaction, Italy would pay a heavy price in deaths and violence; an efficient police and judiciary supported by loyal secret services could have truncated the Red Brigades well before the end of the decade.

Jolted, the system responded. One branch of the police, the *carabinieri*, the least political of all three, was given priority to break the terrorist threat. Legislation was written to support the effort. The first and fundamental law, the Reale law, took a rather scattered approach, revising articles of the penal code and extending police powers. It was the first in a series of laws that escalated police powers as terrorist actions became more numerous and violent. It was capped by Law 15 of February 6, 1980. That same law started the process of decriminalizing terrorist acts and offering rewards for dissociation from terrorist groups, offers repeated in 1982 and 1987 as the intensity of the threat declined. The vigor of the State response increased as terrorism advanced, heightening police powers and punishment, while offering incentives as the emergency diminished.

At the same time, fundamental civil liberties were maintained. While police powers were considerably expanded, especially with regard to arrest and detention, time limits were set and careful monitoring was enforced by Parliament in general, and by the Radical party in particular. No *Berufsverbot* was considered by Italy. Episodes of police brutality do not appear to have been numerous, and while the use of firearms by the police increased considerably (with some untimely deaths), the situation did not become distressing.

Thus the Italian legal response to terrorism was by and large successful. Several troublesome questions nevertheless remain unsolved: the police are needlessly divided, and the state over-reliant on the *carabinieri*; it is unclear how reliable the secret services may be; it is uncertain when the judicial system will abandon its partisan political commitments. Can the State address these problems effectively? The answer suggested by the Italian case may be uncertain. However, the Italian case provides interesting perspectives on how even a weak democratic system can handle a serious terrorist threat.

In conclusion it is extremely difficult for an overloaded and weak political system quickly to perceive the intensity and the seriousness of a terrorist threat. Consequently considerable time lags may occur before an organized and effective response answers the threat. Such a delay imposes heavy costs on the system in terms of loss of life and destruction.

One fact is clear: it is imperative that all (or most) parties be loyal and supportive of the democratic and constitutional order if a state is to organize an effective answer against terrorism. If a weak democratic political system can defeat a serious terrorist threat, then the long-term commitment of the population to democracy will be increased and the political system will be strengthened. In Italy, the slow but persistent legal response to terrorism gave the State the means to defeat terrorism. But the real base for an effective response lies in the country's anti-authoritarian political culture.

ENDNOTES

1.   Foreign Broadcast Information Service, 25 February 1987, p. VII, L2.

2.   *The Economist*, 23-30 July 1983.

3.   Gianfranco Sanguinetti, *Del terrorismo e dello stato*, 1979.

4.   Giorgio Galli, *Storia del partito armato*, 1986, notably pp. 207, 231-233, 253.

5.   Paul Furlong, "Political Terrorism in Italy: Response, Reactions and Immobilism," in *Terrorism: A Challenge to the State*, Juliet Lodge, ed., 1981, pp. 79-80.

6. *Id.*

7. W. Lacqueur in Alberto Ronchey, "Guns and Grey Matter: Terrorism in Italy," *Foreign Affairs*, 1979, p. 926.

8. Furlong, *op. cit.*, p. 60.

9. Martha Crenshaw, "The Causes of Terrorism," *Comparative Politics*, 1981, p. 396.

10. Vincenzo Manzini, *Trattato di diritto penale italiano*, vol. 4, 1985, p. 568.

11. See pp. 111-113.

12. Lorenzo Bedeschi, *Malefatte della rossa Emilia*, 1953.

13. U.S. Senate Committee on the Judiciary, Security and Subcommittee on Terrorism, *Terrorism in Italy, An Update Report 1983-1985*, 1985, p. 12.

14. Frederic Spotts & Theodor Weiser, *Italy: A Difficult Democracy*, 1986, pp. 185-93.

15. Sabino Acquaviva, *Guerriglia e querra rivoluzionaria in Italia*, 1979.

16. Giorgio Bocca, *Il terrorismo italiano 1970-1978*, 1978, pp. 7-8.

17. Ronchey, *op cit.*, p. 928.

18. Furlong, *op. cit.*, p. 63.

19. Bruce Hoffman, *Right Wing Terrorism in Europe*, 1982, p. 18.

20. *Id.*

21. Luigi Cavalli, "La violenza politica," *Citta e regione*, 1977, p. 23.

22. See Acquaviva, *op. cit.*, chapters 5 & 6.

23. Antonio Negri, *Dominio e sabotaggio*, 1979, pp. 17 & 59.

24. Spotts, *op. cit.*, p. 182.

25. *Ibid.*, p. 180.

26. Furlong, *op. cit.*, pp. 78-79.

27. Richard Collin, *The DiLorenzo Gambit*, 1976.

28. Thomas Sheehan, "Italy: Terror on the Right," *New York Review of Books*, January 22, 1981.

29. *Id.*

30. Spotts, *op. cit.*, p. 178.

31. Galli, *op. cit.*, p. 220.

32. *Ibid.*, pp. 223-224 and 140-142.

33. Guido Corso, "La difesa dell' ordine pubblico," in *Manuale di diritto pubblico*, Giuliano Amato, ed., 1984, pp. 959-976.

34. M. Cherif Bassiouni, "Terrorism, Law Enforcement and the Mass Media," *Journal of Criminal Law and Criminology*, 1981, p. 31.

35. Ronchey, *op. cit.*, p. 935.

36. Spotts, *op. cit.*, p. 156.

37. *Id.*

38. We follow Manzini, *op. cit.*, in the section.

39. Giorgio Gregori, "Variazioni penalistiche sul tema delle leggi Reale," *La questione criminale*, 1978, p. 323.

40. See p. 91, *supra*.

41. Alessandro Silj, *Never Again Without a Rifle*, 1979.

42. Maurizio Laudi, *Terroristi pentiti e liberazione condizionale*, 1984.

43. E. Resta, *L'ambiguo diritto*, 1984, p. 125.

44. Laudi, *op. cit.*, p. 13.

45. *Corriere della Sera*, 11 February 1987.

46. Alfonso Madeo, ed., *Testo integrale della relazione della commissione parlamentare d'inchiesta sul fenomeno della mafia*, 1973.

47. Corrado Stajano, ed., *Mafia, Atto di accusa dei giudici di Palermo*, p. 230.

48. P. L. Vigna, *La finalita di terrorismo ed eversione*, 1981, p. 130.

49. *La Repubblica*, 21 February 1986.

50. Oliviero Drigani, "Misure di prevenzione," *Nuovissimo Digesto Italiano*, 1980, p. 1183.

51. *Ibid.*, p. 1192.

52. *Resto del Carlino*, 16 February 1987.

53. U.S. Congress, *op. cit.*, pp. 28-32.

54. Natalino Ronzitti, *L'uso della forza control azioni terroristiche in alto mare*, 1986.

55. *Ibid.*, p. 7.

56. Laura Picchio, *The Status of US Bases in Italy and its Impact on the Egyptian Plane Affair*, 1986.

57. Paolo Mengozzi, "A view from Italy on Judicial Cooperation Between Italy and the United States," *Journal of International Law and Politics*, Spring 1986.

58. R. M. Govea, "The European Response to Terrorism" in *The Harmonization of European Public Policy*, Leon Hurwitz, ed., 1983, p. 97.

59. Conseil de l'Europe, *Rapport explicatif sur la Convention europeenne pour la repression du terrorisme*, 1973.

60. Maria Riccarda Marchetti, *Instituzioni europee e lotta al terrorismo*, 1986, p. 155.

61. Paolo Mengozzi, "Diritto internazionale, ordinamento italiano e violazioni gravi dei diritti dell' uomo di tipo terroristico" *Rivista trimestrale di diritto e procedura penale*, 1982, p. 120.

62. Marchetti, *op. cit.*, p. 115.

63. *Il Sole/24 Ore*, 25 November 1986.

64. *La Repubblica*, 28 November 1986.

BIBLIOGRAPHY

Acquaviva, Sabino, *Guerriglia e querra rivoluzionaria in Italia*, Milan, Rizzoli, 1979

Bassiouni, M. Cherif, "Terrorism, Law Enforcement, and the Mass Media: Perspectives, Problems, Proposals," *Journal of Criminal Law and Criminology*, vol. 72, n. 1, 1981

Bedeschi, Lorenzo, *Malefatte della rossa Emilia*, Bologna, ABES 1953

Bocca, Giorgio, *Il terrorismo Italiano 1970-1978*, Rizzoli Milan, 1978

Bonsanti, Sandra, "*L'Europa unita contro il terrore*," *La Repubblica*, Rome, 28-Ix-1986

Calabro, M. Antonietta, "Dissociati dal terrorismo," *Corriere della Sera*, Milan 11-II-1987

Camera dei Deputati, *Estradizione e Reati Politici*, Quaderni di Documentazione n. 2, Roma 1981

Cavalli, Luigi, "La violenza politica," *Citta e Regione*, 1977

Chelazzi, Giorgio, *La dissociazione dal terrorismo*, Giuffre, Milano 1981

Collin, Richard, *The DiLorenzo Gambit: The Italian Coup Manque of 1964*, Sage Publications, Beverly Hill, 1976

Corso, Guido, "La difesa dell'ordine pubblico" in *Manuale di diritto pubblico*, Giuliano Amato and Augusto Barbera, ed., Il Mulino, Bologna, 1984

Counseil of Europe, *Rapport explicatif sur la Convention europeenne pour la repression du terrorisme*, Strasbourg, 1978

Crenshaw, Martha, "The Causes of Terrorism," *Comparative Politics*, vol. 13, July 1983

Drigani, Oliviero, "Misure di Prevenzione," *Nuovissimo Digesto Italiano*, 1980

"Eppur si muove," *The Economist*, London, vol. 288, 23-30 July 1983

Foreign Broadcast Information Service, Western Europe, 25 February 1987

Furlong, Paul, "Political Terrorism in Italy: Responses, Reactions and Immobilism" in *Terrorism: A Challenge to the State*, Juliet Lodge, ed., St. Martin's Press, New York, 1981.

Galli, Giorgio, *Storia del partito armato*, Rizzoli, Milan 1986

Govea, Rodger M., "The European Response to Terrorism, in *The Harmonization of European Public Policy*, Leon Hurwitz, ed., Greenwood Press, Westport, 1983

Gregori, Giorgio, "Variazioni penalistiche sul tema delle leggi 'Reale'," *La Questione Criminale*, vol. 4, n. 2, 1978

Hoffman, Bruce, *Right Wing Terrorism in Europe*, Rand Corporation N. 1856 AF, Santa Monica, 1982

Labriola, Silvano, "La gestione costituzionale del caso dell' Achille Lauro," *Rivista di diritto internazionale privato e processuale*, vol. 22, n. 2, 1986

Lumley, Bob and Schlesinger, Philip, "The Press, the State and its Enemies: The Italian Case," *Sociological Review*, 1982

Maddalena, M., *Le circostanze attenuanti per terroristi pentiti*, Giuffre, Milano, 1984

Madeo, Alfonso, ed., *Testo integrale della relazione della commissione parlamentare d'inchiesta sul fenomeno della mafia*, vol. 1, 2, 3, Cooperativa Scrittori, Rome, 1973

Manzini, Vincenzo, *Trattato di Diritto Penale Italiano*, Vol. 4, 5th edition, UTET Milano, 1985

Marchetti, Maria Riccarda, *Instituzioni europee e lotta al terrorismo*, Cedam Padova, 1986

Mengozzi, Paolo, "Diritto internazionale, ordinamento italiano e violazioni gravi dei diritti dell'uomo di tipo terroristico, *Rivista Trimestrale di Diritto e Procedura Civile*, v. 36, n. 1, 1982

Mimmi, Vittorio, "Allarme del Siulp," *La Repubblica*, Roma 21-SI-1986

Moran, Sue Ellen, *Court Depositions of Three Red Brigades*, Rand Corporation N. 2391 RC, Santa Monica, February 1986

Negri, Antonio, *Dominio e sabotaggio*, Feltrinelli, Milan, 1979

Picchio, Laura Forlati, "The Status of U.S. Bases in Italy and its Impact in the Egyptian Plane Affair," I.A.F.E., Castelgandolfo, 19-20 May 1980, Typescript

Resta, E. "Il Diritto penale premiale," *L'Ambiguo diritto*, Angeli, Milano 1984

Resto del Carlino, Bologna, 16-II-1987

Ronchey, Alberto, "Guns and Gray Matter: Terrorism in Italy," vol. 57, n. 4, *Foreign Affairs*, 1979

Ronzitti, Natalino, "Il caso dell 'Achille Lauro. Aspetti giuridici della crisi," I.A.F.E., Castelgandolfo, 19-20 May 1986, Typescript

Sanguinetti, Gianfranco, *Del terrorismo e dello stato*, Milan, 1979

Sheehan, Thomas, "Italy, Terror on the Right," *New York Review of Books*, January 22, 1981

Silj, Alessandro, *Never Again Without a Rifle: The Origins of Italian Terrorism*, New York, Karz, 1979

Silvestri, Stefano, "Una risposta europea al terrorismo," *Sole/24 Ore*, Milan 25-IX-1986

Spotts, Frederick, & Weiser, Theodor, *Italy, A Difficult Democracy*, Cambridge, Cambridge University Press, 1986

Stajano, Corrado, ed., *Mafia, Atto di accusa dei giudici di Palermo*, Rome, Editori Riuniti, 1986

Sterling, Claire, *The Terror Network*, Holt, Rinehart & Winston, New York, 1981

U.S. Senate, *Terrorism in Italy: An Update Report 1983-1985*, Subcommittee on Security and Terrorism, 99th Congress, 1st session

Vigna, Pierluigi, *La finalita di terrorismo ed eversione*, Giuffre, Milano 1981

CHAPTER FOUR

Politics of Emergency Powers:
The Case of Korea

YOUNG C. KIM

Introduction

The objective of this paper is twofold: first, to examine legal provisions concerning the use of presidential emergency powers under the Fourth and Fifth Republics, and second, to review briefly actual cases in which emergency powers were invoked.

Part One will begin with an examination of the existing legal provisions on emergency powers under the Fifth Republic (1981 to the present). Then, a brief note on the legal provisions under preceding regimes (1948-1971) will be followed by a discussion of comparable provisions under the Fourth Republic (1971-1981).

Part Two notes the circumstances and the purposes for which emergency powers were invoked as well as the consequences of their use. The eight cases to be examined are as follows:

1. The student revolution of April 19, 1960

2. The military coup of May 16, 1961

3. The Korea-Japan Talks of 1964

4. The state of national emergency of 1971

5. The revitalization reforms of 1972

6. The emergency measures of 1974-1979

7. Political disturbances and the assassination of President Park in October 1979

8. Political disturbances and the Kwangju incident of May 1980

PART ONE: LEGAL PROVISIONS[1]

I. Requirements For the Invocation of Emergency Powers

A. Objectives and Circumstances

The president can invoke Article 51 to take emergency measures to defend the state when speedy measures are deemed necessary in the face of natural calamity or a grave financial or economic crisis, or in a state of belligerency or similar state of emergency threatening the security of the state. The powers of emergency are to be invoked as a reactive measure to overcome a major crisis and to restore or maintain the security of the state, but not to positively promote an objective such as public interest.

There is some disagreement among scholars as to whether emergency powers can be legally invoked only as ex post facto measures or for preventive purposes in anticipation of major crises. Some scholars argue that the president can take emergency measures *before* crises occur as the Constitution empowers the president to invoke emergency powers "in case of *a similar* grave state of emergency," in addition to natural calamity, a grave financial or economic crisis, or a state of war threatening the security of the state.

B. Determining the Need for Invocation and its Procedure

Whether or not a state of emergency exists is to be determined primarily by the president. Article 65, paragraph 5 of the Constitution specifies that the question of presidential emergency measures shall be referred to the State Council for deliberation. Another relevant provision is Article 67, paragraph 1, which specifies that the national Security Council shall advise the president on matters related to national security prior to their deliberation by the State Council. Furthermore, as with other acts by the president, the presidential decision on the use of emergency

powers must be provided in a written document, counter-
signed by the prime minister and relevant members of the
State Council (Article 58). These procedural requirements,
however, do not operate as significant constraints on
presidential prerogative in a presidential system of
government such as the Fifth Republic.

Another procedural requirement for invocation of the
president's emergency powers is a constitutional stipulation
that the president shall notify the National Assembly
without delay and obtain its approval (Article 51, paragraph
3). If the proclamation of emergency measures occurs while
the National Assembly is in recess or is out of session, the
president must request a convocation of a special session.
The emergency measures lose legal validity when National
Assembly approval is not obtained.

A difference of interpretation exists among legal
scholars as to whether the president can take emergency
measures during the period between the dissolution of the
National Assembly and the convoking of a new National
Assembly. One view holds that the president cannot, while
another view asserts that approval may be sought when a
new National Assembly convenes. This procedural
requirement for National Assembly approval is—at least
potentially—a meaningful constraint on the president's misuse
of emergency powers, depending in part on the political
composition of the Assembly.

C. Contents and Effects of Emergency Measures

According to Article 51, paragraph 1, when the
circumstances specified above are present, the president
shall have power to take the necessary emergency measures
within the entire range of state affairs, including internal
affairs, foreign affairs, national defense, economic or
financial affairs, and judicial affairs. Furthermore, when
the president deems it necessary, he shall have the power to
temporarily suspend the freedom and rights of the people as
defined in the Constitution and to take emergency measures
with regard to the rights and powers of the Executive and
the Judiciary (Article 51, paragraph 2).

The president is deemed unable to amend the
Constitution itself through emergency measures, although he
can suspend parts of the Constitution temporarily.
Moreover, the standard interpretation has it that the

National Assembly cannot be dissolved nor its powers revoked through emergency measures. Even though there is no explicit constitutional provision to that effect, such an interpretation is said to be tenable in view of the fact that Article 51 obligates the president to notify and obtain approval from the National Assembly and that the Constitution contains separate stipulations for the dissolution of the National Assembly. Furthermore, the National Assembly is deemed to retain legislative powers with regard to matters not regulated by emergency measures. Emergency measures cannot be applied to the powers of the Constitutional Committee since specific reference of Article 51, paragraph 2 govern only the Executive and the Judiciary.

The question of whether military government rule can be effected through emergency measures has conflicting interpretations. The majority view appears to be negative, on the grounds that the Constitution contains separate stipulations concerning the proclamation of martial law.

D. The Period of Emergency Measures and Controls after Invocation

The Constitution stipulates that emergency measures are to remain operative for the shortest period necessary for the realization of their objectives. The president is obligated to lift emergency measures as soon as the cause for their invocation has been removed. The intent of this provision is to rectify the past precedent of long-term emergency measures. Should the president fail to lift the measures even after their objective is deemed to have been attained, or when the president is deemed to have resorted to emergency measures improperly, the National Assembly can demand that the emergency measures be lifted. When a majority in the National Assembly so demands, the president must lift emergency measures (Article 5, paragraph 5). Should the president refuse to comply with this request, the president may be subject to impeachment. The dissolution of emergency measures requires deliberation of the State Council (Article 65, paragraph 5). The validity of emergency measures ends from the time the measures are lifted. Furthermore, the National Assembly can presumably exercise some restraint over presidential use of emergency powers in other ways as well. The National Assembly can

not only exercise its legislative powers with respect to
matters not regulated by the emergency measures but can
also exercise its investigate powers: it has the right to
summon the prime minister and other ministers for
questioning, and the right to pass a resolution of dismissal.

Presidential use of emergency measures is presumably
subject to a degree of judicial control. The Constitution of
the Fourth Republic (1972-1979) had a provision which
explicitly excluded the president's emergency powers from
judicial review. Since the present Constitution of the Fifth
Republic has no such stipulation, some scholars are of the
opinion that emergency measures could be the object of
judicial review. Since the present Constitution of the Fifth
Republic has no such stipulation, some scholars are of the
opinion that emergency measures could be the object of
judicial review. Other scholars are skeptical even in theory.
At any rate, all legal scholars appear to believe that in all
probability, judicial review will be avoided on the grounds
that the acts involved are political and are acts of
governing.

In this connection a question arises as to whether the
Judiciary may exercise some control by way of determining
if the invocation of emergency measures has conformed to
formal procedural requirements. Judicial control in this
respect might be possible. There is, however, a legal
precedent in Korea in which the Judiciary refused to render
judgment as to whether a law was passed appropriately by
the National Assembly out of respect for the independence
of the National Assembly. It is then highly likely that the
Judiciary will refuse to take up a case involving the
president's use of emergency measures.

The emergency powers of the state encompass the
proclamation of martial law as well as the enforcement of
emergency measures. Martial law refers to a system where
the president can take special measures in accordance with
the law in time of war or similar national emergency when
the maintenance of public safety and order dictates the
employment of armed forces. In such an event, the martial
law commander exercises jurisdiction over part or all of the
administrative and judicial functions within his purview,
even at the infringement of the constitutionally-guaranteed
basic rights of the people.

II. Requirements For the Proclamation of Martial Law

A. *Conditions*

First, the state of martial law may be proclaimed in accordance with the law only in time of war, *sabyon* (disturbances), or similar national emergencies. *Sabyon* refers to acts of violence by armed rebellious groups with the objective of either seizing territory or disturbing the constitutional order. "Similar national emergencies" refers to social disorder caused by natural calamity or by armed or unarmed groups or masses without the aim of seizing territory or disturbing the constitutional order (Article 51, paragraph 1).

Such emergencies must have actually occurred before martial law may be proclaimed. The proclamation presumably is not to be made in a situation merely characterized by the anticipation of such an emergency. It is understood that disturbances to social order must be of such a magnitude to threaten the survival of the state or its constitutional order.

Second, a state of martial law may be proclaimed only under circumstances where there is a military necessity or when it is required to maintain public safety and order through the use of armed forces. "Military necessity" refers to the operational necessity for the safety of armed forces. "Public safety and order" refers to the maintenance of order under police law such as the security and tranquility of the society; but even under such circumstances, the proclamation of martial law is justified only when the use of police is inadequate in achieving the objective, thereby requiring the use of armed forces.

B. *Who May Proclaim*

The Constitution empowers the president to proclaim martial law. The Martial Law of 1981, currently in force, specifies that the minister of defense or the minister of internal affairs may through the prime minister propose the proclamation of martial law to the president when the appropriate conditions have developed.

C. *Procedure*

Upon the proclamation and before the termination of martial law, these matters must be referred to the State Council for deliberation. Article 3 of the Martial Law requires that at the time of proclamation the president must specify the reason, kinds of martial law, the effective date, the affected area, and the martial law commander. Furthermore, the president must notify the National Assembly without delay (Constitution, Article 52), and if the Assembly is in recess, the president must request without delay a special session of the Assembly.

D. *Kinds of Martial Law*

There are two kinds of martial law: security (precautionary) martial law and extraordinary martial law (Martial Law, Article 2, paragraphs 2 and 3). Security martial law is proclaimed to maintain public safety and order in the district where, at the time of war, disturbances, or similar national emergency, social order is so disturbed that it is not possible to safeguard public security by normal administrative organs alone. Extraordinary martial law is proclaimed either because of military necessity or for the maintenance of public safety and order in the district where at the time of war, disturbances, or similar national emergency, hostile actions of enemies are underway and social order is so extremely disturbed as to make the execution of administrative and judicial functions very difficult.

E. *Changes in Martial Law*

Following deliberations by the State Council, the president may make changes with respect to the areas to be placed under martial law, to the kinds of martial law, and regarding the martial law commander (Martial Law, Article 2, paragraphs 4 and 5).

F. *Effects of Martial Law*

Article 52 of the Constitution states that under the extraordinary state of martial law special measures may be taken, as provided by law, with regard to the warrant system, freedom of speech, press, assembly, and association, or with regard to the rights and powers of the Executive or the Judiciary. According to Martial Law, Article 7, upon the proclamation of *extraordinary* martial law, the martial law commander shall have jurisdiction over *all* administrative and judicial affairs within the district under martial law. In the district under extraordinary martial law, the martial law commander may in the case of military necessity take special measures with regard to apprehension, detention, seizure, search, residence, mobility, speech, publication, assembly, association, or group activities. Prior to such measures, the said commander shall make an announcement as to the nature of the measure (Article 9).

Within the district under extraordinary martial law, the martial law commander has the authority to make material and human requisitions in accordance with the relevant law and to check and register articles intended for military use and to issue injunction orders concerning such articles. Furthermore, the commander may, when unavoidable, destroy or burn property of the people for operational purposes (Article 9, paragraph 3). In such a case, proper compensatory damages will be paid for the loss in accordance with the procedure to be specified by presidential decree (Article 9, paragraph 4).

Any person within the district under extraordinary martial law who has not complied with specified instructions and measures of the martial law commander (e.g., violations of the provisions of paragraphs 1 and 2 of Article 9), or who has committed any of the enumerated crimes, shall be tried by court martial. However, the martial law commander may request a civilian court to conduct such a trial. The list of crimes includes those relating to civil war or rebellion, foreign aggression, arson, and homicide. If there is no court in a district under extraordinary martial law, or if communications with the competent court are interrupted, all criminal cases shall be tried by court martial.

Upon proclamation of martial law (whether security or extraordinary) all administrative and judicial organs in the district must be placed under the direction and supervision of the martial law commander without delay (Article 8). Upon the proclamation of *security* martial law, the martial law commander will have jurisdiction over administrative and judicial functions for *military* affairs (Article 7, paragraph 2).

It is also noteworthy that during the enforcement of martial law, apprehension or detention of a National Assembly member is specifically forbidden, except in cases of flagrant law violation.

G. *Termination of Martial Law*

The president must proclaim the termination of martial law without delay when the conditions mentioned in paragraphs 2 and 3 of Article 2 of the Martial Law—having necessitated the proclamation of martial law—have returned to normal, or the National Assembly has made a request for termination. Here again, deliberations by the State Council are to precede the presidential decision to terminate martial law (Article 11).

Upon termination of martial law, all administrative and judicial functions will return to normal. All cases pending trial by court martial under Article 10 will be transferred to the jurisdiction of an ordinary court. However, whenever the president deems it necessary, the judicial functions of the court martial will be extended for a period not to exceed one month (Article 12).

H. *Constraints on the Proclamation of Martial Law*

As already mentioned, the minister of defense or the minister of internal affairs may *propose* to the president the termination of martial law. Since the ministers are appointed by the president, the provision may not be meaningful. The National Assembly may, with the consent of a majority of the membership, request that martial law be terminated. Since the president is obliged to comply with this request, this constitutional provision constitutes a restraint on the president's martial law power. Moreover, the National Assembly may, to a certain extent, exercise restraint on this presidential power by using several powers it holds, such as the right to investigate national affairs, the right to institute impeachment proceedings, the right to demand the presence of the prime minister and other ministers, and the right to pass a resolution of their dismissal. Of course, the degree of restraint the National Assembly may be able to exercise will depend in part on its political composition. It is interesting to note here that Korea has had both precedents, one in which the National Assembly request was complied with and another in which the president refused. Even under the Fourth Republic of President Park, there was an explicit constitutional provision specifying the president's obligation to comply with the National Assembly request for termination of martial law. In addition, the old version of the Martial Law then in force had an explicit stipulation limiting the presidents martial law power in this way (Article 21 of the Martial Law of 1949).

The question arises whether judicial review is possible with regard to martial law. Some legal scholars contend that individual acts of martial law authorities may be subject to judicial review. On the other hand, the act of a martial law proclamation by the president itself may, in theory, be subject to judicial review. But the Supreme Court, in practice, has tended to disagree with these views on the grounds that such an act constitutes a political act of governance.

So far, we have examined the emergency powers of the president under the Fifth Republic. These legal provisions currently in force represent a substantial curtailment of the president's power as compared with similar provisions under the Fourth Republic (1972-1979). With regard to the requirements for invoking emergency powers, and the constraints imposed on their invocation by the president, the relevant provisions of the Fourth Republic were far less stringent even in comparison with Article 16 of the Constitution of the French Fifth Republic or with Article 48 of the Weimar Constitution.

The next section will address the constitutional and other relevant legal provisions concerning the emergency powers of the president under the Fourth Republic. First, however, a brief survey of the history of the constitutional provisions concerning the use of emergency powers is in order.

III. Constitutional Provisions Concerning the Use of Emergency Powers (1948-1971)

The Constitution of 1948 provides for the president's power to proclaim martial law in accordance with the law

(Article 64). It also provides for the presidential power to issue legally valid orders and to make financial dispositions, when emergency measures are needed to maintain public safety and order in times of trouble (at home and abroad), natural calamity, or grave financial or economic crisis. These orders and dispositions must be reported without delay to the National Assembly for the latter's approval. When Assembly approval cannot be obtained, these decrees and dispositions immediately lose their validity and the president must so proclaim to the public.

The power of emergency orders was deleted from the Constitution of 1960, while the powers of emergency financial dispositions and of emergency financial orders were recognized (Article 57). With regard to the proclamation of martial law, the president's veto power over a State Council decision was recognized. Also, detailed regulations were enacted concerning special measures that may be taken during a state of martial law (Article 64).

The Constitution of 1962 provides not only for the president's powers regarding emergency financial and economic dispositions and emergency financial and economic orders, and the proclamation of martial law, but also for the power of emergency orders. The requirements for invoking the emergency powers are specified in detail and the invocation of the power must be reported to the National Assembly for approval. While the country was still under the Constitution of 1962, President Park took an extra-constitutional step of proclaiming the state of national emergency on December 6, 1971, rammed through the National Assembly the Special Measures Law on National Defense on December 27, 1971, and went on to take extra-constitutional emergency measures on October 17, 1972.

It is useful to identify the major provisions of the Special Measures Law on National Defense. The stated objective of the law is to ensure the safety of Korea and solidify national defense by effectively and promptly taking necessary domestic, diplomatic, and defense measures related to national security under the state of emergency. Under this law the president may proclaim a state of national emergency—through the advice of the National Security Council and the deliberation of the State Council—when it is necessary to counter promptly and effectively a grave threat to national security or to safeguard the nation by the maintenance of social peace and order.

The president is given a wide range of powers under the state of emergency. The president may impose restrictions on the economy, i.e., he may issue orders restricting commodity prices, wages, and rents for a specified period following the deliberation of the State Council. The president must notify the National Assembly without delay when he issues such orders.

Also, following State Council deliberation, the president may issue a national mobilization order for effective mobilization, control, or management of human and material resources throughout the country, or in specified areas of the country, when it is necessary for national defense. The president must promptly notify the National Assembly when a national mobilization order is issued. The president may also take necessary measures on migration into or out of specified areas when a military necessity arises, or for the protection of the lives and property of the people. The removal of certain installations from designated areas is permitted.

Also under a state of emergency, the president may take special measures to restrict or prohibit outdoor assembly and demonstrations when it is necessary for the maintenance of public peace and order. Concerning the press and publication, the president may also take special measures to regulate such matters as those on national security, and those liable to split national opinion or to contribute to confusion of the social order. The president is also empowered to impose restrictions on the right to collective bargaining and collective actions of workers and to take special measures to regulate collective actions of the employees of certain organizations, such as government agencies and public services, and those enterprises having an important influence on the national economy.

The president may take special measures with regard to the budget and accounting. If military necessity dictates, the president may, under the state of emergency, alter the government budget within authorized expenditures. The president must promptly notify the National Assembly if such action is taken. Under this provision, the chief of any central government agency may alter the items or nomenclature of the budget of his agency for national security purposes. In this case, the director of the Office of Audit and the minister of finance must be promptly notified by the chief of the agency.

The law specifies that the president shall remove the state of emergency without delay when the grave threat to national security for which the emergency was invoked has been eliminated. The National Assembly may recommend the removal of the state of emergency to the president, and in that case the president must remove the state of emergency unless he can put forward a particular reason against it.

Also noteworthy about this law is that the state of national emergency declared December 6, 1971 was specified as having been declared under Article 2 of the Special Measures Law of *December 27, 1971.*

IV. Emergency Powers Under the Fourth Republic (1972-1979)

A. *Circumstances*

Paragraph 1 of Article 53 of the Fourth Republic Constitution states that "when in time of natural calamity or a grave financial or economic crisis, and in case national security or public safety and order is seriously threatened, or it is anticipated to be threatened, making it necessary to take speedy measures, the president shall have power to take necessary emergency measures in the whole range of state affairs, including internal affairs, foreign affairs, national defense, economic, financial, and judicial affairs."

What is most striking about this constitutional provision is that unlike the comparable provisions of the Third Republic or of the Fifth Republic, emergency powers may be invoked even when a threat is *anticipated*, not just when an actual emergency has already occurred. In other words, emergency powers may be used for preventive purposes in anticipation of a crisis as well as for ex-post facto corrective purposes. This feature, along with the absence of any legal constraints on its use by the president, represents an exceptionally powerful instrument at his disposal.

Aside from the preventive character for which the powers may also be invoked, the scope of the permissible circumstances is similar to that enumerated in the Fifth Republic Constitution. It refers to natural calamity or a grave financial or economic crisis, and serious threat to national security or public safety and order. While the wording of the Fifth Republic Constitution refers in part to the state of war (armed conflict) threatening national security or a similar grave state of emergency, the Fourth Republic Constitution uses the expression "serious threat to national security or public safety and order." It should be emphasized that the Fifth Republic Constitution does not provide for emergency measures of the Fourth Republic type.

B. Determination of the Existence of the State of Emergency

Without consultation with other branches of government, the president is empowered to determine whether or not a state of emergency necessitating the use of emergency powers exists.

C. The Procedure

In exercising emergency powers, the president is subject to the following procedural requirements. The Constitution specifies that matters such as emergency measures and the state of martial law must be referred to the State Council for deliberations (Article 66). On matters related to national security, the president is to be advised by the National Security Council before deliberation by the State Council (Article 67). The president's acts must be done in the form of documents and the co-signatures of the prime minister and other ministers concerned are required.

Given the presidential system of government, it is evident that these provisions pertain to procedure only, and impose no constraint on the president's use of emergency powers.

The president is to issue a special statement explaining to the people the necessity for emergency measures and, upon the proclamation of emergency measures, the National Assembly must be notified without delay.

D. The Contents of Emergency Powers

When the above-mentioned requirements for invoking emergency powers are met, the president is empowered to take emergency measures with regard to the entire range of state affairs, such as internal affairs, foreign affairs, national defense, economic, financial, and judicial affairs (Article 53, paragraph 1). The president is also empowered to take emergency measures while temporarily suspending the freedom and rights of the people as defined in the Constitution and to enforce emergency measures with regard to the rights and powers of the Executive and the Judiciary (Article 53, paragraph 2). There is some question whether these provisions are to be taken as enumerative or restrictive in nature.

With regard to the emergency powers of a preventive nature, the Special Measures Law concerning National Security is illuminating. According to the law, under the state of emergency the following matters may become the object of presidential emergency powers: the economy, national mobilization orders, restrictions on residential mobility into certain designated areas, mass rallies and demonstrations, speech and publication, collective bargaining and collective activities, and changes of national budget.

While emergency measures may be taken with regard to matters normally subject to legislation by the National Assembly, during the specified period it would be impermissible to deprive the National Assembly of its powers, or to dissolve the National Assembly by emergency measures. This interpretation is based on the fact that Article 53, paragraph 2 makes no reference to the rights and the powers of the National Assembly under emergency powers, whereas those of the Executive and the Judiciary are mentioned explicitly as being within the domain of presidential emergency powers.

The interpretation that the National Assembly cannot be dissolved is supported by a constitutional provision that the president shall notify the National Assembly without delay of emergency measures which the president may take under paragraphs 1 and 2 (Article 53, paragraph 3). Another provision stipulates that the National Assembly may recommend to the president the lifting of emergency measures (Article 53, paragraph 6). All this implies that the National Assembly may not be dissolved by emergency measures. Besides, the Fourth Republic Constitution explicitly grants the president the power to dissolve the National Assembly under Article 59. A related interpretation has it that the use of armed forces in connection with, or at the time of taking emergency measures is not permissible since there is no specific constitutional provision—as provided for in Article 48 of the Weimar Constitution—and also because there are separate constitutional provisions concerning the proclamation of martial law.

Similarly, special measures cannot be directed towards the powers of the National Conference for Unification or the Constitutional Committee as Article 52, paragraph 2 contains no explicit provision in this regard.

There is the question of whether the Constitution can be amended by emergency measures. Though such a interpretation has been advanced, a prevalent interpretation appears to be that emergency measures may be taken to suspend temporarily the validity of constitutional provisions, but cannot be used to permanently amend them.

E. Termination of and Constraints over Emergency Measures

When the causes behind the proclamation of emergency measures cease, the president must terminate these measures without delay (Article 53, paragraph 5). Whether the reason for cessation exists is a matter for the president to decide. However, the National Assembly may recommend to the president the lifting of emergency measures with the approval of more than one half of the members duly elected and seated, and the president must comply with this unless there are special circumstances and reasons. In essence, then, the president alone, in actuality, determines when to terminate emergency measures. This contrasts with the provisions of the Fifth Republic Constitution. It will be recalled that there are two explicit provisions in the Fifth Republic Constitution that the National Assembly must be notified without delay when emergency measures have been taken, and unless approved by the National Assembly, the measures will lose this validity and that when requested by the National Assembly—with the approval of a majority of the membership—the president must terminate emergency measures without delay unless there are special reasons.

It is, however, unrealistic to expect such an Assembly recommendation to emerge, given the political balance in the Assembly and a constitutional stipulation enabling the members elected by the National Conference for Unification (read, selected by the president) to occupy a substantial proportion—one third—of the membership of the Assembly.

In theory, however, the Assembly has the power to recommend termination, and such an Assembly resolution, if it occurs, has some political significance, even though it is not legally binding.

Particularly noteworthy about the questions of restraints on emergency measures is an explicit constitutional provision stipulating that the emergency measures set forth in Article 53, paragraphs 1 and 2, "shall *not* be subject to judicial deliberations thereon." Neither the courts nor the Constitutional Committee may rule on the constitutionality of emergency measures. Even on the question of whether the courts can rule on *procedural* aspects concerning the invocation of emergency measures, the dominant interpretation appears to be negative.

So far as the proclamation of martial law is concerned, the constitutional provisions of the Fourth Republic are virtually the same as those under the Fifth Republic. The contents of the Martial Law in force during the Fourth Republic (Law #69, November 24, 1949) are substantially similar to those of the Martial Law adopted on April 17, 1981 (Law #3462), of the Fifth Republic, though under the former a wider range of matters was subject to the jurisdiction of court martial. Also, somewhat less stringent or precise specification is given for both the circumstances necessitating the proclamation of the state of martial law, and for the types of martial law.

PART TWO: CASE STUDIES[2]

I. The So-called Student Revolution of April 19, 1960 and Martial Law

Security martial law was proclaimed in Seoul effective at 1:00 p.m., April 19, 1960. The immediate cause of martial law was massive anti-government demonstrations staged by several tens of thousands of citizens in Seoul. The demonstrations were in protest of the irregularities accompanying the elections of March 15. The demonstrators declared the elections to be null and void, and called for new elections, the resignation of President Rhee, and the restoration of democracy. Several thousand demonstrators converged on the Presidential Palace and began to destroy barbed wire erected near the entrance to the Palace. A volley of police fire resulted in the death of a few scores of demonstrators. Demonstrations of varying sizes—ranging from a few hundred to a few thousand—took place in other major cities. Security martial law was extended to Pusan, Taeju, Taejon, Kwangju, and Masan at 4:40 p.m., and these cities as well as Seoul were placed under extraordinary martial law at 5:00 p.m. the same day. On that day alone (April 19, 1960), the number of deaths nationwide reached 186, with 6,026 persons sustaining injuries. Under martial law, curfew hours were extended, mass media were subject to censorship, and schools and universities were closed.

This massive demonstration occurred in the context of major political instability over the March 15 elections for the president and vice president of the Republic. The opposition party had indeed declared, on the afternoon of March 15, that the elections were null and void, charging the ruling Liberal Party with various election irregularities and fraud. This outrage was translated into a concrete demonstration on April 6, attended by about 4,000 persons.

Concomitant with the increasing stirrings within political circles, the level of student political activism grew as well. Two incidents in particular fueled student activism. The incident of March 15 in Masan, where police mercilessly fired upon street demonstrators, resulted in 8 deaths and 172 injuries. The so-called Second Masan Incident, the demonstration of April 11, followed the discovery of a body of a student missing since the demonstration of March 15. This was followed by the April 18 Korea University demonstrations and subsequently by the so-called April 19 Student Revolution.

To return to the state of martial law, martial law troops moved into Seoul on the 19th to restore order. Following the introduction of a National Assembly resolution calling for the termination of martial law, the state of extraordinary martial law was changed to security martial law on April 25. However, martial law troops were not to fire upon demonstrators. On the 25th, demonstrations were staged by a group of professors calling for the release of arrested students and the resignation of President Rhee. The students and citizens joined the demonstrations and they continued all night. Extraordinary martial law was reinstated as of 5:00 a.m. on the 26th. Despite the state of martial law, on the morning of the 26th, the demonstrators— about half a million people—took to the streets again. The residence of Vice President Elect Lee Kipoong was destroyed, President Rhee's statue was torn away from a park and dragged around the city, and his official residence was surrounded by the demonstrators. The martial law commander advised President Rhee that it was difficult to control the situation. On the same morning, President Rhee announced his willingness to resign his post if the people so desired. The National Assembly unanimously passed a resolution calling for Rhee's resignation at 3:25 p.m., and Rhee's announcement of his resignation came at 6:00 p.m.

The collapse of the Rhee government brought in the interim government headed by Hu Jung. With the improvement in public order, the government changed the state of extraordinary martial law to that of security martial law on May 28. The termination of security martial law came on July 16.

II.   The Military Coup of May 16, 1961 and Martial Law

On May 16, the "Revolutionary Government" proclaimed the state of emergency martial law throughout the country as of 9:00 a.m. The proclamation came in the form of Order #1 of the Military Revolutionary Committee and was announced in the name of the chairman of the Committee, Major General Chang Do-young. This was done without the explicit approval of General Chang. When the military coup led by General Park Chung-hee began in the early morning hours of the 16th, General Chang was the chairman of the Joint Chiefs of Staff.

On the morning of the 16th, Major General Park tried to persuade Lieutenant General Chang to support the military coup but General Chang wanted more time to think about it. When General Park sought General Chang's consent regarding the proclamation of the state of martial law, General Chang responded by suggesting that the proclamation be issued in accordance with legal procedures, following consultation with President Yun. General Park reportedly answered that there was no use in talking about legal procedure when the on-going revolution itself constituted an unlawful act.

Having concluded that it would be impossible to obtain General Chang's agreement on the state of martial law, General Park ordered its proclamation. The proclamation was broadcast in the name of General Chang, however. It was not until after 4:30 p.m. on the 16th that General Chang indicated his willingness to participate actively in the revolution, and accepted the chairmanship of the Military Revolutionary Committee.

At 5:00 p.m., the Military Revolutionary Committee issued a proclamation which stated in part: (1) the Committee would inherit in full the powers of the current government of Chang Myun by 8:00 p.m.; (2) the National Assembly was abolished; (3) political activities by all political parties and social groups were forbidden; (4) cabinet and other state ministers were under arrest; and (5) all the functions of the state machinery would be performed by the Military Revolutionary Committee.

At 1:00 p.m. on the 18th, two days after the military coup, the then-Premier Chang Myun conferred with other ministers and decided on the following steps: (1) to recognize and so recommend to the president, in accordance with Article 72 of the Constitution, the validity of the state of martial law proclaimed by the chairman of the Joint Chiefs of Staff on May 16; and (2) to resign en masse, assuming political and moral responsibility for the military revolution.

At 3:30 p.m., President Yun proclaimed the state of martial law throughout the country. This was done in accordance with Article 64 of the Constitution by way of acknowledging the validity of the measure already taken by the Military Revolutionary Committee on May 16. On the 19th (at 8:30 p.m.), President Yun issued a statement indicating his resignation from the presidency, but the following day (the 20th), he announced in the presence of General Chang Do-young and General Park Chung-hee that he would remain in the post (which he did until March 22, 1962).

In the meantime, the Supreme Council of National Reconstruction was established on May 19, 1961 to replace the Military Revolutionary Committee. The Council was to serve as the supreme state organ. The Emergency Measures Law on National Reconstruction was proclaimed (effective June 6, 1961 and partially amended on July 3, 1961), which in effect replaced the Constitution of the time. It made it clear that even the basic rights of the people specified in the Constitution were not guaranteed if they contravened the revolutionary tasks. In case any constitutional provisions contravened the Emergency Measures Laws, the latter would prevail.

The Supreme Council pledged, on August 12, 1961, that the transfer of political power to a civilian government would occur in the summer of 1963. The Supreme Council accepted the resignation of President Yun on March 24, 1962, and resolved to have the chairman of the Council, Park Chung-hee, serve as acting president by amending the Emergency Measures Law of National Reconstruction—until a new government was set up.

On November 5, 1962, a constitutional amendment was announced under Article 9 of the Extraordinary Measures Law, and after the approval by the Supreme Council on December 6, it was put to a national referendum on December 17. On December 5, at midnight (beginning on December 6), the government terminated the state of security martial law, which had been in force since May 27, 1962. The state of extraordinary martial law proclaimed on May 16, 1961 had been changed to security martial law on May 27, 1962. Shortly after the termination of martial law, a national referendum was held on December 17 which resulted in a 78.8 percent approval of the Constitution of the Third Republic.

Presidential elections occurred on October 15, and new National Assembly elections on November 26. Park defeated Yun Bo-sun by a narrow margin (about 50,000 votes).

On December 17, 1963, the Third Republic was born, with President Park sworn in as its president.

III. Korea-Japan Talks of 1964 and Martial Law

On June 3, 1964, martial law was proclaimed in Seoul. President Park's statement issued on the eve of the proclamation contains the following points: (1) this decision was taken most reluctantly as the situation had become unbearable and that this was the measure he was compelled to take for the democratic development of the country; (2) for some students, the Constitution does not exist, nor does the National Assembly, nor the government. The government had been trying to deal with the students with patience, but the prolongation of patience would have led to the further deterioration of the situation, and this step was inescapable since an effective measure to prevent a catastrophe was urgently needed rather than ineffective ex post facto measures; (3) the government would try to restore stability within the shortest possible period, strengthening administration power that has been rendered chaotic by demonstrations and redirecting all its efforts to the proper tasks of government and would promptly terminate the state of martial law.

Martial Law Decree #1, issued in the name of the Martial Law Commander Min, had the following provisions:

1. Both indoor and outdoor assembly and demonstrations were forbidden with the exception of ceremonies for coming of age, marriage, funeral, ancestral worship, and the presentation of movies;

2. Speech, press, and publications were to be subject to censorship;

3. All acts of reprisal were forbidden;

4. No one was allowed to desert one's job;

5. Fabrication and distribution of rumors was forbidden;

6. Until further notice all the elementary and secondary schools, and colleges and universities in Seoul would be closed;

7. A curfew would be imposed from 9:00 p.m. to 4:00 a.m. and these hours were to be strictly observed;

8. Violators of these provisions would be subject to seizure, search, arrest, and detention without warrant.

The proclamation of martial law was a culmination of three months of political and social unrest characterized by a series of demonstrations staged by members of opposition parties, other social, religious and cultural organizations, as well as students, all of whom were opposed to the Korea-Japan talks then underway.

Following the military revolution of 1961, talks on the normalization of relations between Korean and Japan had been resumed and had been going on intermittently. By November 1962, the major problem of reparations was resolved in principle, leaving the problem of fisheries as the most difficult issue impeding the conclusion of the normalization treaty. As of February 1964, all indications pointed to the government's readiness and determination to seek an early resolution of the fisheries issued by early March, followed by a cabinet level political meeting with a view toward the conclusion of the treaty sometime in May. President Park's speech on March 1 spoke of normalization in the near future and by March 23 both sides agreed to complete the draft treaty in late April and to sign it in early May.

In the meantime, the opposition forces were proceeding with their plans for blocking the version of the treaty being promoted by the government. On March 6, the Pan National Struggle Committee Against Low Posture Diplomacy toward Japan was organized with the participation of all the opposition parties.

A few days later, these opposition parties, together with the representatives of social, religious and cultural groups and other prominent personages, formed the Pan National Struggle Committee Against Humiliating Diplomacy toward Japan. This Committee played a major role in leading the movement to oppose the Korea-Japan talks. The Committee took to a series of speaking tours in Pusan (March 15) and Seoul (March 21), demanding an immediate end to the Korea-Japan talks and urging the preservation of the so-called Peace Line.

It is in this context that the massive student demonstration of March 24 occurred. About four to five thousand students from Korea University and Yonsei University staged demonstrations at the National Assembly building following meetings denouncing the talks at their respective campuses. About 250 persons were injured. Of 283 students arrested, all were released with the exception of 40. On their part, the students of the College of Liberal Arts and Sciences of Seoul National University issued a series of resolutions calling for the cessation of the Korea-Japan talks, termed inimical to national interest, the expulsion of the vanguard of Japanese monopoly capital from Korea, and the elimination of comprador capitalists, the lackeys of Japan.

Their beliefs were expressed in the form of a declaration that the national independence of Korea was again on the verge of being swallowed by the imperialistic monopoly capital of Japan. On the following day, these demonstrations spread to numerous universities and high schools involving several tens of thousands of students in Seoul and other localities. By March 26, students of other universities and high schools participated in a series of demonstrations on a virtually nationwide scale. On that day, President Park issued a special statement urging students to return to their studies. In the statement, he expressed his understanding of the patriotism of the students and indicated that he would send instructions to the Korean delegates in Tokyo asking them to bear in mind the spirit and stance of the students, and to do their utmost to realize the objectives of the Korean side. He pledged that within 24 hours of the conclusion of the treaty he would make public all the secret documents concerning the Korea-Japan talks so as to seek the people's judgment.

The student demonstrations subsided for a while, only to be revived in mid-April (the 17th to the 21st). A government spokesman stated on April 22 that the demonstrations had lost moral justification and that they constituted a fundamental threat to the lives of the citizenry and jeopardized the basic order of the state; he warned that the government was compelled to take stern measures urging school authorities to take appropriate action against students violating the law.

The beginning of another wave of student demonstrations occurred on May 20. On that day, students from nine universities assembled at the College of Liberal Arts and Sciences at Seoul National University to hold a funeral for "national democracy." During their demonstrations, near the entrance to the college of Law, students clashed with police. A denunciation meeting, attended by about two thousand students and a thousand citizens, demanded an end to the humiliating negotiations with Japan which they charged would lead to subservience to Japan, and the punishment of wicked comprador capital-financial cliques.

The confrontation with the police lasted five hours and resulted in injuries to 21 students, 28 citizens, and 16 policemen. Altogether, 94 students and 91 citizens were arrested. The judge issued a warrant for the arrest of three persons out of the 27 requested by the prosecutor. The prosecutor instructed the police to detain 82 citizens and 20 students who either injured persons or destroyed property by throwing rocks.

On May 21, the district court issued a warrant for the arrest of 33 persons out of the 135 the prosecutors requested. The student rallies and demonstrations continued at various universities, and on May 30 the students of the

College of Liberal Arts and Sciences started a hunger strike. The number of students on the hunger strike grew to 130 by June 2, and by then 13 of them had fainted. The demonstrations of June 2 which occurred at various universities were particularly fierce, and at the Korean University campus the slogans included a demand for "the resignation of the government and the end of dictatorship." On June 2 alone, 622 students and 7 citizens were arrested. The presidents of student organizations of various colleges of Seoul National University decided to resort to force instead of hunger strikes. June 3 saw the students of about a dozen universities staging demonstrations, some of whom appeared before the National Assembly Hall, the Central Government Building, and the Presidential Palace.

The student demonstrators clashed with the police at various points in the city. Some of them took over police vehicles and four police substations were damaged by rocks. These scenes reportedly resembled the student uprisings of April 19, 1960. It will be recalled that martial law was proclaimed on June 3 of that year.

On June 15, 1964, the major opposition party (Minjung Party) unsuccessfully attempted to place on the agenda the issue of terminating martial law. The government's position was summarized in a special speech which President Park made on the 26th at the National Assembly. It stated that while he wanted to terminate martial law promptly, it must be preceded by a firm guarantee that the unfortunate situation would not recur, expressing his hope that talks between government and the opposition parties be resumed.

On July 6, an extraordinary session of the National Assembly was convened, giving impetus to discussions aimed at the reconciliation of the opposition demand for the termination of martial law and the government's demand that laws be enacted on regulating the activities of the press and the universities with regard to acts of violence. These talks finally led to the passage on July 28 of a resolution calling for the termination of martial law, jointly submitted by the government and opposition parties. On the same day, President Park proclaimed the termination of martial law and urged a prompt enactment of the necessary legislative measures.

As of June 17, about two weeks following the proclamation of martial law, the number of arrests had reached 348 persons. (Of 168 students arrested, 53 had been turned over for prosecution.) On June 23, the first public session of court martial was held for several student activists (including Kim Jung-tai, Hyun Seung-il, Kim Do-hyun, all of the College of Liberal Arts and Sciences of Seoul National University) on charges that they led a series of unlawful assemblies and demonstrations since the March 24 demonstration. Likewise, on June 29, the first public trial by court martial was held for 13 students on charges of insurrection and disturbances.

On July 18, the interior minister issued a report on the causes that led to the student demonstrations. The demonstrations, of nationwide scale, were manipulated by the Society of Flame, a Marxist-Leninist group which had as its ultimate objective the establishment of a communist society. The Society of Flame was organized six years earlier by Kim Jung-kang and Kim Jung-nam, both of whom were students at Seoul National University.

At a public trial on July 20 for 20 civilians who were arrested on June 3 for having seized trucks and participated in demonstrations, 13 were given a sentence of a year and a half, with the remainder found not guilty. With the termination of martial law, student activities such as Kim Jung-tai were turned over to a civilian court. Following appeals to the justice minister by the presidents of major universities in early August, the government began releasing the detained students and on August 22, 31 of 137 students who had been arrested were released.

On September 1, a resolution was adopted by the plenary session of the National Assembly calling for the release of the detained students and the repeal of penalties imposed on them. The disposition of the cases against the major leaders of student demonstrations shows the attitude of the government authorities at that time. The charges for Kim Jung-tu, Hyun Sung-il, and Kim Do-Hyun were changed from rebellion to violations of the law of assembly and demonstration. The prosecutors demanded five years of imprisonment for the first two and four years for the third but at the subsequent trial of October 28, the three defendants were given two years of suspended sentence. The court decision stated that the May 16 meeting—the so-called "funeral services for national democracy"—had not followed a specified legal procedure for assembly. In any event, the proclamation of martial law led to the indefinite postponement of the Korea-Japan talks.

IV. The National Emergency of 1971

On December 4, 1971, President Park proclaimed a state of national emergency. This was preceded by the invocation of the Garrison Law in mid-October. At the request of the mayor of Seoul, army troops moved onto university campuses on October 15. As a result, student leaders were arrested and a number of colleges suspended classes. Over a hundred students were expelled from their colleges. The garrison decree was terminated on October 30. Throughout that year, student demonstrations had been occurring intermittently, protesting compulsory on-campus military training, government corruption, press censorship, and the illegal intrusion of army troops onto the Korea University campus.

According to the declaration of national emergency, South Korea faced a grave situation from a national security point of view due to rapid developments internationally, such as China's admittance to the United Nations and all out efforts by North Korea to invade South Korea.

The declaration urged citizens to acquire a new system of values while giving priority to national security, and to be prepared in the worst case to sacrifice some of their freedoms. The mass media was told to refrain from irresponsible debates on national security issues. The government on its part reiterated its position that national security was the top priority of government policy programs, and that it would not tolerate any sources of social instability. The opposition forces denounced the measure, declaring that they would not tolerate the restrictions on fundamental rights under the political pretext of national security.

In order to provide a legal basis for the state of national emergency, the ruling party submitted to the National Assembly a draft Law on Special Measures for National Protection and Defense. (The Special Measures Law and its provisions are summarized above.)

Following the obstructionist tactics employed by the opposition forces, the ruling party assemblymen alone convened a plenary session of the National Assembly and passed the law on the 27th. The opposition party protested, declaring the law invalid on the grounds that it violated the

Constitution and National Assembly Law.   The law was promulgated on the same day.

V. Emergency Martial Law and the Revitalization Reforms Constitutions of 1972

Emergency martial law was proclaimed again on October 17, 1972. The action was justified as a measure to overcome historical trials facing the nation, to prevent anticipated disturbances to and confusion in social order, and to protect the lives and property of the people. The social disturbances were said to accompany the projected reforms of the political system designed to bring about peaceful unification.

Under Proclamation #1 of the emergency martial law, a number of measures were put in effect, some of which were:

1.   All indoor and outdoor assembly and demonstrations for the purpose of political activities were banned. Other types of non-political assembly required prior approval with the exception of marriages, funerals, and religious worship.

2.   Press, publications, and broadcasts were subject to prior censorship.

3.   Universities were closed temporarily.

4.   Fabrication and dissemination of rumors were banned.

The special statement of President Park announcing the emergency measures contains, inter alia, the following points by way of justification:

1.   Disorder and inefficiency were rampant and politicians were deeply engrossed in factional and partisan strife. Such a representative organ that had been victimized by irresponsible political parties and partisan strife could not be expected to carry out the task of peaceful unification.

2.   It was imperative to establish a system which would provide a solid support for North-South dialogue, and that could positively respond to the volatile changes in the international situation. The current Constitution

and laws were enacted during the Cold War era, and Korea needed to carry out great revitalization reforms to establish a system that could cope with the new situation.

3. Since these reforms could not be achieved by normal methods, the president, being faithful to the task given to him, decided to carry out the reforms suitable for the circumstances so as to vigorously promote North-South dialogue and to better cope with rapid changes in the international situation.

The four emergency measures specified were as follows:

1. The validity of certain provisions of the Constitution were to be suspended, i.e., the National Assembly would be dissolved and party activities banned.

2. The functions specified in the suspended constitutional articles were to be taken over by the Emergency State Council.

3. The Emergency State Council would proclaim, by October 27, 1972, a draft of the revised Constitution aimed at peaceful unification of the fatherland and have it ratified by national referendum within a month following its proclamation.

4. The normal constitutional order would be restored by the end of the year in accordance with the new revised Constitution.

On October 27, 1972, a draft Constitution was approved by the Emergency State Council and was promulgated. The official rationale and characterization of this new proposed Constitution is noteworthy. The following characteristics of the proposed Constitution were alleged:

1. It aimed at the realization of peaceful reunification of the fatherland.

2. It aimed at indigenization (Koreanization) of democracy.

3. It represented reforms of the ruling structure and other related systems designed to better organize national strength and to maximize efficiency.

4.   It would enhance political, economic, cultural, and social stability and consolidate the foundation for national prosperity.

5.   It guaranteed the basic rights of the people to the maximum extent possible consistent with the situation.

The proposed Constitution was approved in a national referendum of November 21, 1972. It provided the president with a vast array of power, reducing the powers of the legislative and judiciary branches. Civil and political liberties were restricted. The president was to be elected for a term of six years indirectly by the members of the National Conference for Unification and he was to appoint one-third of the National Assembly.

Schools were allowed to reopen on November 28, and the North-South Coordinating Committee was inaugurated on November 30. The termination of emergency martial law came on December 13, 1972.

V.   President Park and Emergency Measures

What follows is a brief examination of several emergency measures that were issued under President Park. It will be recalled that under the Fourth Republic the president enjoyed the power to take emergency measures.

Emergency Decrees #1 and #2 were issued on January 8, 1974. The government was confronted with enormous pressure to relax political control and there was a report that an anti-government group gathered about a million signatures in support of a petition to revise the Yushin Constitution. Emergency Decree #1 prohibited any challenges to the government or the Constitution.

The text of decree #1 specifies acts which were prohibited. It was prohibited for:

1.   any person to deny, oppose, misrepresent, or defame the Constitution;

2.   any person to assert, introduce, propose, or petition for revision or repeal of the Constitution;

3.   any person to fabricate or disseminate false rumors;

4. any person to advocate, instigate, or propagate any act or acts which are prohibited in the above provisions or communicate such act or acts to others through broadcasting, reporting, publishing, or by any other measures; and

5. any person who violated the provisions of the emergency measure and any person who defamed the measure would be subject to arrest, detention, search or seizure, without warrant thereof, and would be punished by imprisonment for not more than 15 years;

6. any person who violated any provision of the emergency measure would be tried and sentenced in the Emergency Courts-Martial.

Emergency Decree #2 established an Emergency General Courts-Martial system to try persons convicted under the emergency measures.

We have already examined the legal provisions concerning the use of emergency measures. What interests us here is the official rationale given for their use. President Park issued a special statement when proclaiming emergency measures in January 1974. The opening paragraph states that these measures are proclaimed "in order to consolidate the foundation of constitutional government and ensure national security." The statement cites the rapidly changing international situation, particularly the fluctuations of the international economy and various acts of provocations by North Korea as constituting an extremely harsh situation for the fatherland. The statement goes on to say that it is imperative to maintain political and social stability and to organize and foster national strength, and that the only way to achieve this national task is to firmly maintain and develop the Yushin system. The statement points out that the Yushin Constitution was given all-out support by the people in the national referendum of November 21, 1972.

The statement refers to "some impure elements obsessed with delusion" who had begun to engage themselves in activities purporting to deny and overthrow the Yushin structure, the legitimate constitutional order of the nation. They were accused of attempting to create social unrest and confusion by agitating the general public and spreading malicious and false rumors. These activities were labeled a direct challenge to the legitimacy of a popular mandate and a serious threat to the basic order and security of the nation. The statement goes on to say that despite the stern warnings issued by the prime minister and the president, "anti-Yushin utterances and activities" would not stop and yet, if these activities were left unchecked, national security, as well as public safety and order would be seriously impaired. Hence, the president said he was compelled to proclaim emergency measures through the deliberation of the State Council under Article 53 and 66 of the Constitution.

Emergency Decree #3 was imposed on January 14, 1974. The objective was to overcome a national economic crisis caused by shocks from the world economy. It provided for economic stabilization, especially for people in the lower income brackets, restraints on consumption of luxury goods, conservation of raw materials, development of domestically produced raw materials, improvement of the nation's international balance of payments position, and special budgetary measures. For example, for the benefit of people in low-income brackets, the government would reduce rates on income and residence taxes, raising the exemption base for property tax. The prices on daily necessities and public utility taxes would be lowered. Large funds would be set aside to ensure a higher level of employment for needy people and special low interest loans could be provided to small and medium industries. A number of measures would be taken to improve working conditions. Emergency Decree #3 was lifted on December 31, 1974.

Emergency Decree #4 was imposed on April 3, 1974, outlawing the National Federation of Democratic Youth and Students. It banned student protest and empowered the ministry of education to expel students. Emergency Decree #5, declared on August 23, 1974, lifted Emergency Decrees #1 and #4. Emergency Decree #6 was declared to lift Emergency Decree #3. Emergency Decree #7, imposed on August 8, 1975 closed down Korea University, banned demonstrations and assemblies there, and authorized the stationing of troops on that campus. Emergency Debate #8, declared on May 13, 1975, was to lift Emergency Decree #7.

Perhaps the most well-known and infamous emergency decree was #9, which was promulgated on May 13, 1975. This decree remained in force until December 1979.

The Emergency Measures for Safeguarding National Security and Public Order (Emergency Decree #9), were promulgated on May 13, 1975, to borrow an official expression, "in order to consolidate national unity, to coalesce national opinion and to enable all people to prepare themselves thoroughly for an impregnable posture of national security."

The logic of the government's justification was that the communist victory in Indochina was a source of great encouragement to the North Koreans, and there was a heightened threat of aggression from North Korea. To the South Korean government—and perhaps to many informed South Koreans—a series of events such as the fall of Saigon, President Kim Il Sung's trip to Beijing, President Kim's militant speech, and the substance of the Sino-North Korean Joint Communique were deeply disturbing. Deep division in public opinion and persistent political instability in Cambodia and Vietnam were cited as the major causes of communist victory. The most important lesson drawn from the turbulent situation in Indochina was that the biggest obstacles to defeating communism were wasting national strength, splitting national opinion, and acting counter to national unity.

From the perspective of the government, certain politicians were causing political confusion in the blind pursuit of power, while reckless students were indulging in demonstrations and rallies for no justifiable reasons, undermining national unity. All acts of this sort which were detrimental to national solidarity had to be rooted out.

The official justification also speaks of the Constitution as being the foundation of the state, and therefore, the security of the state means the security of the Constitution. Any dispute over the Yushin Constitution was tantamount to a dispute over national security, and thus detrimental to the coalescence of national opinion. The official explanation went on to state that some journalists supported and publicized reckless demands for constitutional amendments, thereby attacking the Yushin Constitution and misleading the public by fanning futile controversies over constitutional amendments—hence, the emergency decree's bans on the press. Whatever the justification of Emergency Decree #9, its restrictions on basic freedoms were sweeping. These measures were condemned as arbitrary and repressive measures by church groups, intellectuals, students, and journalists, although the critics were severely limited in their means to articulate and disseminate their views.

VII. Assassination of President Park and Martial Law

President Park Chung-hee was assassinated on the night of October 27, 1979. The following morning, effective 4:00 a.m., October 27, emergency martial law was proclaimed throughout South Korea, except for the Cheju islands.

A government spokesman announced that an extraordinary meeting of the State Council was called at 11:00 p.m. following the "accident" involving President Park, during which it was decided 1) to proclaim emergency martial law; 2) that Premier Choi Kyu-ha would serve as acting president in accordance with Article 48 of the Constitution; and 3) that the chief of the army staff, General Chung Seung-wha would be the martial law commander.   Proclamation #1 issued by the commander specified, inter alia, that 1) curfew hours be extended to run from 10:00 p.m. to 4:00 a.m.; 2) all universities would be closed; 3) unauthorized assembly would be forbidden; and 4) press and publications would be subject to censorship.

As will be shown later, the martial law decree of October 27, 1979 remained in force until May 18, 1980 when martial law was extended to the entire country, i.e., including the Cheju Islands. It was not until January 25, 1981 that martial law was terminated.

The universities were allowed to open within a few weeks; technical colleges and graduate schools opened on November 12 and regular colleges and universities on November 19.   The extended curfew hours were lifted throughout the country by November 26. By the end of the year, criteria for censorship of the press were gradually relaxed with the coverage of non-political matters exempted from prior censorship.   The statistics published by the martial law commander throw light on the activities of the court martial during the period of October 27 to December 28. Out of 439 cases received, 180 were given sentences, 107 were dropped (non-prosecution), 18 were referred to the ordinary courts, 25 were under trial, and 109 were under investigation.

During the same period, the martial law commander also dealt with numerous other cases: of a total of 25,518 people arrested, 15,691 were booked without detention, 4,426 were detained in custody, 4,896 were referred to summary hearings, with 505 freed after given a warning.

One of the celebrated cases involving the violation of martial law was the so-called YWCA unlawful assembly case. According to the announcement of the martial law commander of November 27, 1979, about 400 people assembled without approval at the YWCA auditorium under the pretext of a wedding ceremony. The assembly was in fact a "National Conference" to block the election of a president by the delegates of the "National Conference for Unification," and a statement calling for the formation of a pan-national cabinet was issued. Some of those assembled staged a street demonstration. In connection with this incident, 14 prominent citizens were turned over to court martial for trial, and 4 others, including former President Yun Bo-sun, were booked with detention. On January 25, 1980, the court martial sentenced 17 defendants to imprisonment ranging from 1 to 4 years and of those, Mr. Yun Bo-sun and Hahn Suk-hun were given suspended sentences a few days later.

On December 6, 1979, Acting President Choi was formally elected president of the Republic by the National Conference for Unification in accordance with the Yushin Constitution. On December 7, 1979, following the deliberation of the State Council, President Choi proclaimed the termination of Emergency Decree #9 effective December 8, 1979, a move the president characterized as one intended to promote national harmony. He stated that since the death of President Park, the government and the people had been exerting common efforts for social order and for overcoming the difficult situation, and a national consensus had been formed to press forward with national development in an orderly manner. He added that the termination of Emergency Decree #9 was a part of a larger political development he was envisaging.

Accordingly, on December 8, 1979, all 68 persons who had been detained on charges of violating Emergency Decree #9 were released. Prior to this measure, the government had already released 193 persons on suspended sentences who were in custody for violating Emergency Decree #9, and the government had dropped charges against the 224 persons who had been either under investigation or trial without detention. By the termination of Decree #9, Kim Dae-jung, who had been released by suspended sentence earlier, won complete exemption from the remaining term of one year and four months and the protective observation measure, i.e., house arrest, was removed for him as well. Kim Young-sam, who also had been under trial, was acquitted on December 15, and amnesty was granted to 33 persons who had been convicted of violating Emergency Decree #1 and #9, and the sentences for 31 persons who were convicted of Emergency Decree #4 violations were commuted on December 27. The Supreme Court acquitted 10 persons charged with violating Emergency Decree #9.

By December 20, 1979, the court martial concluded its trials of 8 persons implicated in the case of assassination of late President Park. Seven persons, including Kim Jai-kyu, were sentenced to death, with one person sentenced to three years of imprisonment.

In the meantime, on December 12, 1979, General Chung Seung-wha, Army chief of staff and the martial law commander, was arrested by forces loyal to General Chun Du-huan, commander of the Army Security Command, who was serving as the chief of Joint Investigation Headquarters of the Martial Law Command. The arrest, as justified by the minister of defense later, was for his alleged complicity in the assassination of President Park, his potential misuse of power as martial law commander, and the danger of disturbances that might be caused by the forces loyal to General Chung.

It should be added that the act of assassination followed the disturbance that occurred in the cities of Pusan and Masan. Mass protest demonstrations against the government took place in early October 1979, and the government responded by declaring emergency martial law in Pusan on October 18 and by imposing a garrison decree in Masan, Kimhae, and Changwon on October 20.

VIII.   The Kwangju Incident and Martial Law

Effective May 18, 1980, extraordinary martial law was extended to include the entire country. Martial law had been in force in all of Korea except on the Cheju Island since the assassination of President Park. The move was followed by what some analysts call a virtual coup d'etat. A number of major political leaders and intellectuals were arrested and all political activities were banned. This state of martial law was to remain in force until January 25, 1981.

A brief sketch of the developments that led to the imposition of martial law in all of South Korea is now in order. The death of President Park in October 1979 unleashed powerful currents of yearnings and expectations for democratization of the political system. The successor, Choi Kyu-Ha, in his inaugural presidential address on December 21, 1979, spoke of a revision of the Yushin Constitution to be followed by a presidential election. Thus began "the era of the Three Kim's." "The Three Kims" refers to opposition leader, Kim Dae-jung, who had his political rights restored, another, Kim Young-sam, president of the major opposition party, and the third, Kim Jong-pil, president of the then-ruling party. All three aspirants began preparing for what they thought would be the forthcoming presidential elections of 1981.

The students returned to their campuses in March and began staging various demonstrations throughout the country. The appointment of General Chun Du-huan to the post of acting director of the Korean Central Intelligence Agency on April 14 heightened concern over the emergence of the military, especially of the hardline faction led by General Chun who simultaneously held the position of commander of the Defense Security Command. It will be recalled that General Chun had emerged as the leading military figure following the "coup" of December 12, 1979.

Beginning on May 1, student demonstrations in the streets of Seoul were gathering momentum. Those which occurred from May 14 to 15 are said to have involved 50,000 to 100,000 students. The demands of the students were succinctly expressed in the resolution adopted by the delegates to the National Conference of Student Representatives of Public and Private Universities on May 17. The resolution labeled Prime Minister Shin Huon-ho and General Chun as enemies of the people and demanded their withdrawal from public office by the 22nd. It also demanded the immediate termination of martial law, and the release of all political prisoners and detained students. Unless the government made its intentions clear, the resolution warned, the students would launch nationwide demonstrations beginning on the 23rd.

The decision to impose extraordinary martial law in all of South Korea—technically speaking, to expand the scope of existing martial law to the entire country—was made at an extraordinary meeting of the State Council on the evening of April 17. The move transferred the power of command and supervision of martial law from the minister of defense to the president. With the consent of the president, which is not difficult to obtain, the military then could impose de facto military rule.

The decision regarding the expansion of martial law and simultaneous moves against major political leaders, intellectuals, and student leaders appear to have been based on several considerations. First, the scale and intensity of student demonstrations strengthened those in the military favoring hardline countermeasures. Second, two opposition party leaders (Kim Dae-jung and Kim Young-sam) reportedly had endorsed on the 16th the student demand that Prime Minister Shin and General Chun resign from public office. Third, the opposition party (the New Democratic Party) was planning to submit a resolution calling for the termination of martial law to the extraordinary session of the National Assembly scheduled to be convened on the 28th, and that there were some indications that the ruling party (the Democratic Republican Party) was sympathetically inclined to the idea. It will be recalled that under the Fourth Republic Constitution, a National Assembly resolution demanding the termination of martial law was legally binding on the president unless he could cite special reasons for non-compliance. Aside from the legality of presidential action, non-compliance in the face of a National Assembly resolution would have grave political ramifications.

Despite the imposition of martial law in all of Korea and school closings, student demonstrations in Kwangju continued on to May 18. About 200 students of Chonnam University took to the streets—by 2:00 p.m. the number grew to about 1,000—throwing rocks at the police and burning police jeeps. Army paratroops were eventually brought in at 4:40 p.m. The violent clashes between the two sides escalated, and on the 19th, a local broadcasting station was burned down. By the 21st a virtual state of insurrection was evident, with some demonstrators seizing armored vehicles and weapons, and firing M16 automatic rifles at martial law troops. Major public offices such as provincial government buildings and city halls were occupied by demonstrating students and citizens. Martial law troops were withdrawn from the city temporarily but they returned on the 27th, spearheaded by tanks to crush the "armed uprising." The statement issued by the martial law command characterized the situation created by the armed rioters in Kwangju as "anarchical". The statement said the actions of the demonstrators exceeded the bounds of expression of opinion. It also described intensifying violence and disorder, including the acts of killing, destruction, arson, and looting by armed mobs of rioters. According to the martial law commander, altogether 189 persons were killed: 162 civilians, 23 soldiers, and 4 policemen. Altogether, 175 persons were tried in connection with the Kwangju incident. Subsequently, at the court martial of North Cholla and South Cholla provinces of October 25, 1980, five student ringleaders were sentenced to death and seven others to life imprisonment. Two of these death sentences were commuted to life imprisonment; one by the superior court martial on December 29, and the other by the martial law commander.

A comprehensive treatment of the political developments subsequent to the Kwangju incident is not within the scope of this paper. However, a brief review of major political developments up to the termination of martial law in January 1981 is necessary, for such a review, however cursory, throws light on the objectives which emergency powers may potentially pursue.

On May 31, a few days after the "Kwangju uprising" was crushed, the government established the Committee on National Defense Emergency Countermeasures. The Committee consisted of ten civilian cabinet officials and 14 military leaders and was to be headed by the president. The Committee was declared to be an advisory organ with the objective of enabling the president to command and supervise the affairs of martial law and to deepen the cooperative relationship between the cabinet and martial law authorities. According to a government spokesman, the establishment of the Committee was based on Articles 9, 11, and 12 of the Law on Martial Law, Article 7 of the Implementation Decree of the Law on Martial Law, and Article 5 of the Government Organization Law.

In order to "examine and coordinate" the matters delegated by the Committee, a Standing Committee was established with General Chun appointed by President Choi to serve as chairman. This 30-man Standing Committee was to coordinate and control the process of examining national policies. These committees were reconstituted as the

National Security Legislative Council (81 men) on October 22, 1980. The council served as an interim legislature until April 1981, when the new National Assembly came into being. During this period, a purification campaign was launched with about 8,000 government officials, and about 840 politicians, purged and barred from political activities for a period of eight years.

President Choi's resignation on August 16 prepared the way for the inauguration of a new president, General Chun. Mr. Chun was elected on August 30 by the National Conference for Unification as specified in the Fourth Republic Constitution. In accordance with a pledge he made in his inaugural address, a new constitution was then drafted by a government-appointed committee. It won popular approval at the national referendum on October 22, 1980. President Chun was re-elected on February 25, 1981, under the terms of the new constitution and the general election for a new National Assembly was held on March 15, 1981. It will be recalled that martial law was terminated on January 25, 1981, i.e., just a month before the presidential elections. It is worth noting that the major changes that were brought about in Korea since the Kwangju incident, such as the transfer of political power, and the popular plebiscite on a new constitution, took place while Korea was under martial law.

IX. Summary and Conclusions

Case #1, the so-called Student Revolution of April 19, 1960, shows the "unsuccessful" implementation of emergency powers resulting in a transfer of political power. Confronted with massive popular protests against election irregularities—a clear challenge to the very legitimacy of the government—the state of martial law was proclaimed. However, the leadership, political and military, chose not to employ the level of force necessary for the suppression of the protest movement. President Rhee's resignation resulted in the establishment of an interim government, and subsequently a new political system. Case #1, then, illustrates a transfer of power and a major, fundamental change in the constitutional order.

Case #2, the military coup of May 16, 1961, represents a case which involved the imposition of martial law by the leaders of a military coup d'etat, i.e., a transfer of political power preceded its proclamation. This case also resulted in a major and fundamental change in the constitutional order. This may be said to be a case of "effective" implementation by the coup leaders, but from the perspective of the defenders of the then-existing constitutional order, it was a case of the failure of the leadership of the legitimate government to even invoke emergency powers.

Case #3 represents an effective utilization—effective from the government's viewpoint—of the instrument of martial law to deal with a serious social disturbance caused by a major opposition challenge to a specific governmental policy regarding Japan. An ineffective implementation of martial law might have resulted in a major change in the controversial policy or even in the composition of the governing elite.

Case #4, involving the declaration of the state of emergency in 1971—justified legally ex post facto by the enactment of the Special Measures Law of National Security—represents a case without apparently compelling causes for taking emergency measures, constitutional or extra-constitutional. It may have been an intended pretext for, and a prelude to, the adoption of more authoritarian and restrictive political practices. The subsequent enactment of the Special Measures Law and other developments that followed sustain such an interpretation.

Case #5 constitutes the use of martial law to effect a fundamental change in the constitutional order in accordance with the conception of requirements as entertained by the ruling political leadership. The Revitalization Reforms of 1972, resulting in the establishment of the new regime of the Fourth Republic, were carried out under the state of martial law. It may be said that a fundamental change in political arrangements occurred, although no transfer of political power from one group to another took place.

Case #6 represents the use of emergency powers— through a series of emergency measures—to cope with and counter growing criticism by the opposition, and challenges to the legitimacy of the constitutional order and President Park's rule. As we have seen, the government's rationale was to consolidate national unity in the face of grave threats to social order and the security of the nation. It is debatable whether the threat posed to social order and national security was of such a magnitude as to justify the imposition of such restrictions on basic freedoms. In any event, case #6—with the obvious exceptions of Emergency Measures designed to terminate previous measures—represents the exercise of emergency powers in defense of the existing constitutional order.

Case #7 constituted a response of the government to an emergency caused by the assassination of President Park, though a series of disturbances in southern cities had already led the government to impose extraordinary martial law in Pusan and a garrison order in other cities. This response had the obvious objective of defending against any threats to the then-existing constitutional order, social order, and national security. However, the process of political succession, occasioned by the sudden death of a strong leader, occurring in the context of martial law, facilitated a factional power struggle with the armed forces, and the increasing involvement of the military in the political process. The transfer of political power was effected with a new civilian president succeeding under the terms of the then-existing Constitution.

Case #8 represents the invocation of emergency powers—via the extension of martial law to the entire country—to cope with a serious threat to social order and national security. These threats were caused by widespread demonstrations which called for the rapid democratization and civilianization of politics and the prompt removal of emerging military leaders from public office.

Martial law facilitated the assault of the military leadership on civilian political leadership and on the normal constitutional political process. The Kwangju incident further accelerated military domination of politics, or what some analysts call the usurpation of political power by the military. It was under martial law that a series of changes were effected, culminating in the establishment of a new constitutional system—the Fifth Republic—with its new ruling elite. Whether these changes represented a departure from the system and practices of the Fourth Republic is a separate question.

ENDNOTES

1. For the preparation of Part I, the following works were consulted:

Books:
Yun, Se-chang, *Sin Honbob*, 1983, pp. 223-27.
Kwon, Yong-song, *Honbobhak Wonron*, 1981, pp. 63-73, and 651-79.
Kang, Mun-yong, *Honbob*, 1961, pp. 224-28, and 377.
Han, Tae-yon, *Honbobhak*, 1973, pp. 453-66.
Kim, Chol-su, *Hyundai Honbobron*, 1979, pp. 650-59.
_____, *Honbobhak Gairon*, 1982, pp. 611-25.
_____, *Honbobhak Sinron*, 1984, pp. 449-58.
Kim, Ki-bom, *Hanguk Honbob*, 1973, pp. 378-90.
Ku, Pyong-sak, *Hanguk Honbobron*, 1985, pp. 541-66.
Han, Sang-bom, *Hanguk Honbob*, 1973, pp. 263-70.
Mun, Hong-ju, 1963, pp. 453-57, and 563-67.
Albert Blaustein and Gisbert Flanz, eds., *Constitutions of the Countries of the World: Korea*, Oceana Publications, 1974.

Articles:
Chungang, February 1980, pp. 218-28.
Ibbob Josa Yongu, February 1974, pp. 5-9.
Buk Han, September 1972, pp. 32-45.
Bobhak, December 1964, pp. 38-76.
Yonsenoncho, May 1969, pp. 291-313.
_____, February 1968, pp. 457-77.
Kosige, November 1963, pp. 94-101.
_____, December 1963, pp. 130-137.
_____, September 1967, pp. 65-72.
Honbob Yongu, May 1972, pp. 69-96.
_____, May 1972, pp. 45-65.
_____, May 1972, pp. 3-44.
Bobjo, April 1968, pp. 1-10.
_____, August 1974, pp. 1-7.
Bobjung, July 1964, pp. 31-35.

Sindonga, March 1984, pp. 154-79.
_____, January 1980, pp. 186-93.
_____, September 1964, pp. 44-53.
Jong Kyong Yongu, January 1972, pp. 138-45.
_____, February 1974, pp. 159-69.
_____, February 1974, pp. 61-68.
_____, February 1974, pp. 150-58.
_____, February 1972, pp. 147-59.
_____, January 1972, pp. 10-13.
Ibbob Josa Wolbo, February 1974, pp. 5-9.
Emergency Measures No. 9, May 15, 1985.
Emergency Measures Proclaimed by the President of the Republic of Korea, January 8, 1974.

2.   The following works were consulted for the preparation of Part II:

Books:

Haebang Samsibnyonsa, Vol. 2-4, 1976.
Young W. Kihl, *Politics and Policies in Divided Korea*, 1984.

Annuals:

Hanguk Nyonkam, 1980.
Hapdong Hyonkam, 1961, 1965, 1972, 1973, 1980.
Asahi Nenkan, 1965, 1972-82.
Kokusai Nempo, 1960-62.

Newspapers:

Dong-A Ilbo.

Asahi Shimbun.

*The author wishes to thank Drs. S. S. Cho and K. P. Yang for their valuable advice and for all the courtesies they accorded to me during my research at the Library of Congress. I wish also to thank Ms. S. A. Ahn for her able research assistance.

CHAPTER FIVE

Laws on Emergency Powers in Taiwan

TAO-TAI HSIA,
WITH WENDY ZELDIN

When martial law (*chieh yen*) was first declared by the Republic of China (ROC) on Taiwan, there was a real and pressing need to protect the island enclave from the threat of armed takeover by the Communist forces of the People's Republic of China (PRC). With time, over the last 38 years, Taiwan has emerged as an economically strong, socially stable polity whose authoritarian cast has been tempered by the ruling party's steady, if grudging, attempts to edge closer to a system of full-fledged constitutional democracy. Critics at home and abroad have questioned ever more vociferously the government's adherence to martial law, but until recently the ruling Kuomintang (KMT) party resisted calls for its abolition.

In March of 1986, however, President Chiang Ching-kuo appointed a 12-man group comprised of the KMT's Central Standing Committee[1] to examine proposals for lifting the emergency decrees that activated martial law and for enacting legislation that would allow the formation of new political parties in Taiwan.[2] The committee studied six sensitive issues: lifting martial law, removing the ban on political parties, allowing self-administration by local governments, rejuvenating legislative bodies through elections, and improving the KMT's administrative efficiency. Their recommendations were submitted to the President on October 2, 1986,[3] and on October 15 President Chiang publicly announced that martial law was to be lifted and opposition parties would be allowed to participate in the political process.[4] Premier Yu Kuo-hua then instructed the three government ministries concerned, the Ministries of Justice, the Interior, and National Defense, to draw up a draft National Security Law. The joint body formed by the three ministries was also to draft amendments to the existing laws on civic organizations and on election and recall of public functionaries.[5]

On April 9, 1987, the KMT Central Policy Coordination Committee passed a resolution to revise some articles in the draft national security law based on the suggestions of lawmakers, scholars, and officials. The revised draft was presented on April 15 to the KMT Central Standing Committee (which sets party policy) for deliberation.[6]   It was approved by the Legislative Yuan's committees on the interior, national defense, and judicial affairs as the final draft of the National Security Law on June 15, 1987.[7] After being submitted to the floor of the Legislative Yuan for final approval, it was enacted into law on June 23.[8] Martial law was lifted only after the National Security Law was in place.   Even though the emergency decrees that had activated martial law were rescinded, the new National Security Law replaces some of their provisions.   The law's proponents maintain that "political reality dictates that some form of modified martial law remain";[9] those opposed to it, especially members of the opposition (*tangwai*), contend that other laws and regulations still on the books could adequately provide for security needs.[10]

Against this background, let us consider in turn the legislative history of emergency powers legislation in the Republic of China (ROC), the lifting of the decree on martial law in Taiwan and the arguments for and against it, and the features of the new National Security Law.

I.   THE LEGISLATIVE HISTORY OF MARTIAL LAW IN ROC, TAIWAN

A.   Emergency Power Orders (*jinji mingling*)

The dynastic laws of China never contained any provisions on emergency powers; only towards the end of the Ch'ing dynasty did certain laws of a constitutional nature, imported from Western Europe, come to embody such provisions.[11]   Thus, China did not have any emergency power laws until the beginning of the twentieth century, when, impressed by Japan's victories first over Ch'ing forces and then over the Russians, Chinese leaders came to believe that Japan's strength lay in her constitutional form of government. As a result, there was a movement in China to emulate Japan. In 1908, a draft constitution in outline form, entitled "Outline of the Constitution" (*Hsien fa ta kang*) in 23 articles, was prepared.[12] It borrowed heavily from Japan's Meiji Constitution, and had provisions on *chieh yen* as well as on the issuance of independent orders. For example, one provision stipulated that when the parliament was not in session, in the case of an emergency an imperial order might be issued in place of a law, and such an order also might be issued for the purpose of raising necessary funds. However, such matters were to be submitted to the forthcoming parliament for consideration.[13] The first half of this provision was taken from Article 8, on emergency orders, and the second half from Article 70, on emergency fiscal measures, of the Meiji Constitution. This was the first time that an emergency powers provision appeared in a Chinese legal document. Nevertheless, the "Outline of the Constitution" was only prepared as a guide for drafting a Constitution and did not have the force of law.[14]

The first valid constitutional document to incorporate emergency power provisions was the "Nineteen Articles of the Constitution" (*Hsien fa shih chiu hsin t'iao*) promulgated on September 13, 1911. Although it was implemented as a temporary Constitution, it nevertheless had the force of a permanent one. Article 11 stated: "An order (*mingling*) cannot be issued in place of a law but only to implement the law, and only if authorized by a certain law. Emergency orders are an exception, however." Despite this reference to emergency orders, the document did not prescribe any procedures for issuing them.[15]

After the founding of the Republic of China in 1912, the first constitutional document to be formulated was the "Outline of the Organization of the Provisional Government" (*Lin shih cheng fu tsu chih ta kang*). Both in form and in spirit this document was an attempt to emulate the Constitution of the United States, and so it did not contain provisions on emergency powers. As it was being revised, Sun Yat-sen, provisional president of China, also submitted a "Draft of the Organic Law of the Provisional Government of the Republic of China" (*Chung-hua min kuo lin shih cheng fu tsu chih fa ts'ao an*) to the legislature for consideration.

Article 25 of Sun's draft law was on emergency power orders: "When the provisional president deems it necessary because of an extraordinary emergency, he may issue orders that carry the force of law.   However, such orders shall then be submitted to the legislature for ratification."[16] This draft document never became law, however, and the provisional Constitution that was subsequently enacted had no provision on emergency powers.[17]

When Yuan Shih-k'ai became president in 1913, he found the Provisional Constitution too restrictive and sought to have provisions on emergency dictatorial powers and emergency fiscal powers incorporated in it. Yuan's proposal was rejected by parliament, however; since a Constitution was just in the process of being drafted, that body saw no need to amend the provisional document.   The draft Constitution, known as the "Temple of Heaven Draft" (*T'ien tan hsien fa ts'ao an*) was completed shortly thereafter, at the end of October 1913.   It contained provisions on emergency orders (Art. 65), on *chieh yen* (Art. 71), and on emergency fiscal measures (Art. 104).[18]   Yuan Shih-k'ai was still dissatisfied, however, because these provisions on emergency powers had many restrictions which he argued would defeat the purpose of maintaining the security of the country during times of crisis.   Due to his objections, the "Temple of Heaven Draft" was abandoned and on May 1, 1914, a new Constitution, the Constitutional Compact (*Chung-hua min kuo yueh fa*), which became known as the Yuan Shih-k'ai Constitution (*Yuan shih yueh fa*), was promulgated.[19]   It was based on the presidential system in form, but concentrated so much power in the hands of the president that it actually institutionalized a system of dictatorship.   Article 20 of the Yuan Shih-k'ai Constitution, on emergency orders, and Article 55, on emergency fiscal measures, were drawn from like provisions in the Ch'ing "Outline of the Constitution" mentioned above, which emulated the Meiji Constitution.[20]

The first Constitution of the Republic of China, known as the Ts'ao K'un Constitution after the president in power at the time, was promulgated on October 10, 1923.   It did not have any provisions on emergency orders, but its Article 118 did provide for emergency fiscal measures.   After Ts'ao K'un was forced to abandon the presidency a little over a year later, the Constitution promulgated under him was abrogated (along with the Provisional Constitution of 1912, which had been restored by government decree in 1917).[21] The next major constitutional document, the Provisional Constitution for the Period of Political Tutelage (*Hsun cheng shih ch'i yueh fa*), promulgated on June 1, 1931, and various versions of the Organic Law of the National Government (*Kuo min cheng fu tsu chih fa*), did not provide for emergency powers of any kind. It was only when the present Constitution of the Republic of China was adopted in 1946 that a provision on emergency orders, Article 43, was finally incorporated.[22]

Thus, the constitutional basis of emergency orders in Taiwan lies in Article 23 of the ROC Constitution, which states:

> In case of a natural calamity, an epidemic, or a national financial or economic crisis that calls for emergency measures, the President, during the recess of the Legislative Yuan, may, by resolution of the Executive Yuan Council and in accordance with the Law on Emergency Orders, issue emergency orders, proclaiming such measures as may be necessary to cope with the situation. Such orders shall, within one month after issuance, be presented to the Legislative Yuan for confirmation; in case the Legislative Yuan withholds confirmation, the said orders shall forthwith cease to be valid.[23]

Article 43 has never actually been applied, however, because the "Law on Emergency Orders" to which it refers has never been enacted. Instead, the *de facto* legal basis for emergency powers lies in the "Temporary Provisions Effective During the Period of Communist Rebellion" (*Tung yuan k'an luan shih ch'i lin shih t'iao k'uan*), which were adopted by the National Assembly on April 18, 1948, as an amendment to the Constitution.[24] The advantage of the Temporary Provisions lies in the fact that they virtually free the president from the procedural restrictions of prior Legislative Yuan approval or ratification contained in Articles 39 and 43, respectively. According to item 1 of the Temporary Provisions,

> The President during the Period of Communist Rebellion may, by resolution of the Executive

Council, take emergency measures to avert an imminent danger to the security of the State or of the people, or to cope with any serious financial or economic crisis, without being subject to the procedural restrictions prescribed in Article 39 or Article 43 of the Constitution.[25]

Although item 2 of the Temporary Provisions states that "the emergency measures mentioned in the preceding paragraph may be modified or abrogated by the Legislative Yuan in accordance with paragraph 2 of Article 57 of the Constitution,"[26] the president still retains veto power over any such resolution made by the Legislative Yuan and the Legislative Yuan must have a two-thirds majority vote in order to override it.[27] Item 3 of the Provisions does away with the two-term restriction on the offices of the presidency and vice-presidency imposed by Article 47 of the Constitution. Item 6 provides for election of new members to the three national elective bodies (the National Assembly, the Legislative Yuan, and the Control Yuan) by removing the restriction imposed on election to those bodies by Articles 26, 64, and 91 of the Constitution, respectively.

It was on the basis of the Temporary Provisions that the Martial Law (*Chieh yen fa*) was promulgated on May 19, 1948.[28] The Law contains 13 articles and 2 appendices (the first appendix is the order declaring martial law for all of China; the second is the order for Taiwan Province specifically). One set of emergency powers legislation has been enacted on the basis of the *Chieh yen* Law; another set has been enacted on the basis of the National General Mobilization Law (*Kuo chia tsung tung yuan fa*), which was formulated in 1942 for the purpose of carrying on the war against the Japanese.[29]

Presidents of the ROC have invoked emergency powers on five occasions.[30] The first time was in order to cope with serious inflation. With the country on the verge of financial and economic collapse, the president issued an order calling for implementation of four types of emergency measures in order to improve the desperate situation. These measures (*banfa*) included: 1) measures governing the issuance of gold dollar certificates (in 17 articles); 2) measures governing the disposition of gold, silver, and foreign currencies owned by the people (in 15 articles); 3) measures governing the registration and control of foreign exchange deposits in foreign countries owned by Chinese (in 15 articles); 4) measures governing the adjustment of finances and the strengthening of control over the economy (in 33 articles). At the time, the Executive Yuan, empowered by the president, enacted a number of auxiliary rules and regulations to implement the above measures. The second occasion on which emergency powers were invoked was December 10, 1948, in accordance with item 1 of the Temporary Provisions, when martial law was declared throughout China. The third occasion was on January 19, 1949, when the president called for the issuance of short-term bonds for gold. On the fourth occasion, August 7, 1958, the president issued an order for disaster relief work to be carried out in central and southern Taiwan in the wake of major flooding there. The last occasion was on December 16, 1978, when the armed forces were placed on full alert due to the pending derecognition of the Republic of China on January 1, 1979, which meant the abrogation of the U.S.-ROC mutual defense treaty one year later.

Although the legality of the Temporary Provisions and the need for their continued existence have been challenged, various arguments have been advanced in support of keeping them in place. Premier Yu Kuo-hua, for example, has maintained that the foundation of the ROC government rests on the Constitution, the Temporary Provisions, and the three elective bodies whose members were originally elected in accordance with the Temporary Provisions.[31] Many defend the legality of the Provisions by stressing the fact that they were enacted in accordance with Article 174, paragraph 1 (on amendments), of the Constitution, and that, being in the form of an amendment to the Constitution, they are legal as such. To the argument that the Constitution should have been altered to incorporate them in the first place, the counterargument has been made that since the Constitution itself was newly promulgated at the time, revising it so soon afterwards might have undermined its continuation in force.[32] Furthermore, it is pointed out, the Temporary Provisions were enacted to cope with an extraordinary situation that had not been anticipated when the Constitution was adopted in 1948. Some contend that the "temporary" status of the Provisions is actually a boon, because it means that they can only freeze certain parts of the Constitution and will be easier to remove when no longer needed.[33] Others maintain that the Provisions need to be kept in place as long as the communist threat still exists, because the president may have to invoke emergency measures to deal with that threat.

B. Martial Law (*chieh yen*)

The term martial law as applied to Taiwan is something of a misnomer. As Professor Hungdah Chiu has stated, "The state of 'martial law' in the ROC is, in fact, similar to a 'state of siege' in the civil law countries and is different from the concept of martial law in common law countries."[34] The Republic of China's "martial law" (*chieh yen*, "emergency") originates by way of Japan from the French legal system's "state of siege" (*état de siège*). The Japanese used the Chinese characters *chieh* (*kai*, "warning, be alert to") and *yen* (*gen*, "danger, crisis") when they borrowed the French legal notion, and China simply appropriated the Japanese term.   Unfortunately, in Japanese-English legal dictionaries the term "*kaigen rei*" is translated as "martial law" rather than "state of siege," and that practice has been carried over to the translation of the Chinese term *chieh yen* as well.   *Chieh yen* refers to the state's temporary restriction or suspension of people's freedoms and rights during times of war or quasi-war (i.e., civil disorder), in order to meet the need of placing the executive power and judicial power of a given area under that area's military organ.

The difference between martial law and state of siege has been explained as being rooted in the common and civil law systems'

> divergent attitudes . . . toward the origin of this emergency measure. The "martial law" emphasizes the suspension of certain normal rules of law, whereas "state of siege" emphasizes the emergency as an effective threat against public safety and order. . . . under [the civil law state of siege,] the civilian courts may still function and only those crimes against national security, the constitution, and the public safety and order are under the jurisdiction of military courts. The civil and military powers within the government work side by side. . . . Another major difference should not be overlooked. The executive and/or

the legislature in civil law countries has the final word as to whether an emergency situation has arisen; the courts assume this function under the common law.[35]

The legislative history of martial law in the Republic of China begins with the Provisional Constitution of the ROC, which was promulgated on March 11, 1911. Its Article 36 provided that the provisional president could declare *chieh yen* in accordance with the law. On December 15 of the same year, the Martial Law (*Chieh yen fa*) was promulgated. This law was similar in content to the Japanese edict on *chieh yen*.[36] According to its Articles 2 and 3, when a war or other extraordinary situation took place and necessitated the use of a garrison force, the president could either declare *chieh yen* in accordance with this law, or empower others to make such a declaration. The areas under *chieh yen* were divided into two types: 1) security areas and 2) combat areas. During a war or extraordinary situation, the military commanders of various areas could declare temporary *chieh yen* (Arts. 4 and 5). However, they were to report such action to the president and to the senior military officers under him (Art. 7).[37]

On July 29, 1926, the Nationalist government in Canton promulgated a *Chieh yen* Law in 11 articles, which was more concise than the previous *Chieh yen* Law. In October 1930, the military committee of the Legislative Yuan prepared a new draft *Chieh yen* Law, which, according to a report submitted by the committee, was prepared on the basis of both the 1911 *Chieh yen* Law and the 1926 *chieh yen* regulations, as well as Japan's edict on *chieh yen*. The final version of the law was adopted and promulgated on November 29, 1934, ten months after the founding of the Nationalist government on January 29, 1934.[38]

The 1934 *Chieh yen* Law was later amended twice, first on May 19, 1948, then on January 14, 1949. Like the 1911 law, it divided the areas where *chieh yen* would apply into two types, security areas and combat areas. However, this *Chieh yen* Law was much more detailed than that of 1911 and contained many more restrictions. For example, it stated that *chieh yen* could only be declared when war or rebellion broke out (Art. 1) and did not include, as did the 1911 law, extraordinary situations. Shortly after the *Chieh yen* Law was amended for the first time, in May 1948, the present Constitution of the Republic of China was promulgated, on December 25, 1948.[39]   Its Article 39 provides for the declaration of *chieh yen*:

> The President may, in accordance with law, declare martial law with the approval of, or subject to confirmation by, the Legislative Yuan. When the Legislative Yuan deems it necessary, it may [by] resolution request the President to terminate martial law.[40]

Chiang Kai-shek, in accordance with the "Temporary Provisions Effective During the Period of Communist Rebellion," issued the decree for implementation of the *Chieh yen* Law for the mainland in 1949, but this decree did not cover Taiwan province.   With the removal of the Republic of China government to Taiwan, the enforcement of an emergency law in the province was proclaimed by the Taiwan Provincial Garrison Headquarters on May 19, 1949, and the law went into effect the following day, May 20, 1949, [41] in accordance with Article 3 of the *Chien yen* Law. On November 2 of the same year, at its 94th meeting, the Council of the Executive Yuan declared that the whole country, including Hainan Island and Taiwan, was to be treated as a war zone where the *Chieh yen* Law would be in effect.   On November 22, the Executive Yuan requested the Legislative Yuan to approve the *Chieh yen* Law retroactively for these areas, which it did on March 14, 1950, in accordance with Article 2 of the *Chieh yen* Law.[42]   Two days later, the Legislative Yuan sent its notification of approval to the president as well as to the Executive Yuan. On March 28, the Executive Yuan sent an order to the Ministry of National Defense regarding the implementation of the *Chieh yen* Law in the Taiwan region.   In this way, the implementation of "martial law" in Taiwan became part of the *chieh yen* decree that had been applied to the whole of China.   Since autumn 1958, however, when the Communists launched an unsuccessful attack against Quemoy, the Taiwan Straits have been relatively peaceful, especially since January 1, 1979, when the Chinese Communists announced the cancellation of their policy of bombarding Quemoy on alternative days.[43]

The *Chieh yen* Law contains 13 articles and two appendices.   The first appendix is the order declaring martial law for all of China; the second is the order for Taiwan Province specifically.

The *Chieh yen* Law, as well as the National General Mobilization Law, which was formulated in 1942 for the purpose of conducting war against the Japanese, each spawned different sets of additional emergency power measures. The lifting of martial law entailed not only the lifting of the decree that put the *Chieh yen* Law in force but also the abolition of various measures (*banfa*) that were enacted on the basis of the law.[44] The National General Mobilization Law and the measures associated with it, however, are to remain in effect. Some of the 16 measures abolished in conjunction with the lifting of martial law include: 1) Measures Governing the Control of Entry into and Exit from the Taiwan Region During the Period of Suppression of Rebellion. These measures affect freedom of residence as provided for in Article 10 of the ROC Constitution. The criteria for approval or rejection of an application are vague, as is the law in general, and when a request for entry or exit is rejected, there is no effective recourse. 2) Measures Governing the Examination of Passengers Entering or Leaving Taiwan Harbor and Airport Inspection of Passengers Entering or Leaving Taiwan During the Period of Suppression of Rebellion. These measures, too, contravene Article 10 of the Constitution. 3) Measures for Dividing What Kinds of Cases Are To Be Tried by Military Organs and What Kinds Are To Be Turned Over to the Civil Court for Trial During the Period of Martial Law in the Taiwan Area. These measures contravene Article 9 of the Constitution, which states that only those in active military service are to be tried by a military court. 4) According to provisions of the Military Trial Law, which is followed by the military courts, a final appeal cannot be lodged in the Supreme Court. This goes against Article 77 of the Constitution, which says that the Judicial Yuan is the supreme judicial organ in charge of trying criminal matters. 5) Measures Governing the Control of Publications During the Period of Suppression of Rebellion in the Taiwan Area contravene Article 11 of the Constitution on freedom of speech, teaching, writing, and publication, since they are administered by military officers, lack any procedure for remedy, and also lack any objective standard by which to judge controversial publications. 6) Measures Governing Implementation of the Provisions for Preventing Illegal

Assembly, Association, Demonstration, Petition, or Strike. These measures restrict the constitutional right of assembly and association provided for in Article 14 of the ROC Constitution, and can be used to ban the formation of new parties.

It should be noted that over the years the scope of military trial jurisdiction in Taiwan has gradually been reduced, first in 1952 and then in 1954 and 1967. Initially, there were 104 charges that could be lodged against an individual who was to be tried before a military court.[45] Military courts' jurisdiction over nonmilitary personnel was also whittled down to cover four categories of crimes: sedition and espionage, theft or unauthorized sale or purchase of military equipment and supplies, or theft or damage of public communications equipment or facilities.[46] While their jurisdiction expanded in 1976 to cover nine serious crimes, referral to a military court was not automatic,[47] and application of martial law still decreased overall. The number of people charged, the number of detentions, and the number of prosecutions also declined significantly over the years.

II. PROS AND CONS OF MARTIAL LAW

In May 1982, the Subcommittee on Asian and Pacific Affairs of the Committee on Foreign Affairs, U.S. House of Representatives, held hearings on martial law in Taiwan and its implications for human rights and American foreign policy. In the course of these hearings, various arguments were raised in favor of or against the lifting of martial law on Taiwan. At the time, the Taiwanese government had not yet instituted on its own initiative any review of its martial law policy.

The most conservative view presented at the hearings mirrored the KMT government's position that a very real threat from Communist China still existed, that martial law was still needed for internal security, that it was necessary for continued economic, social, and political progress, and that it interfered very little with the daily lives of the people or with the development of democracy. One spokesman stated, "Martial law is self-defense, and it is the state's sole power to decide whether or not circumstances require the implementation of self-defense."[48] It was also mentioned that a stable Taiwan figured in the larger picture of the triangular equilibrium among the three superpowers, the U.S., the Soviet Union, and the PRC.

A more moderate view represented was that martial law is an "understandable if regrettable necessity." The external threat from the mainland was put into quantitative terms to show that the PRC's military capacity exceeded that of Taiwan. It was also argued that the mainland did not even really have to launch an invasion, that a trade blockade could be equally effective in incapacitating Taiwan. Another argument made against the lifting of martial law was that it might make it easier for terrorists to destabilize the government and thereby provide the PRC with a pretext to step in to restore order on Taiwan to "protect" its people. The fear of an increased internal threat from the implementation of a united front strategy by the Communists was also expressed. Others argued that the existing martial law might be more palatable in the end than new legislation that the government might enact to ensure its *de facto* continuation. Yet another argument advanced by those who reluctantly advocated keeping martial law was that problems endemic to Asia as a whole—instability due to the strains of economic development, real military threats, thorny ethnic issues—made martial law in the region a commonplace necessity.

The most radical view in favor of lifting martial law posited that no military threat existed from mainland China and that "martial law has increasingly affected freedom of speech, freedom of assembly, and freedom to strike," creating a pattern of more oppression, not less.[49] Adherents of this view charged that the situation of political prisoners had actually worsened and that "while economic conditions have improved, the mechanisms of invisible repression have also improved."[50] Another argument adduced in favor of lifting martial law was that it would put an end to the KMT's alleged state terrorism, carried out by means of "arbitrary authority, secret proceedings and vigilante groups," and would mean the dissolution of the "network of Taiwan spies at home and abroad, which affects Taiwan students in particular." It was also pointed out that Taiwan had had martial rule longer than any other country, and that even the Philippines and South Korea had lifted martial law.

Others acknowledged the presence of a threat from the PRC, but argued that martial law did not make Taiwan any better protected, and that lifting martial law would not mean that the military or the police would be done away with. One commentator remarked that if necessary martial law could easily be reinstituted:

> The point about martial law supposedly is that it is to facilitate emergency orders in times of invasion or in times of open warfare. That is definitely not going on now . . . and in no way would getting rid of martial law weaken Taiwan's ability to resist or react.[51]

There were those at the hearings who claimed that even though the public at large might not feel oppressed by martial law, the unpredictability of the imposition of certain restraints did have a "chilling effect" on people.[52] This effect of martial law was described as "submerged authoritarianism," not necessarily obvious but at the back of people's minds because of three changes that were made in martial law in 1954. 1) The Statute of Denunciation was added, stipulating that failure to report if someone were a Communist or engaged in subversive activity or sedition would be punished; 2) the notion of collective responsibility was institutionalized by martial law; 3) Chiang Ching-kuo remarked in 1954 (and thereafter) that democracy could never be fully implemented as long as Communism existed.

The views of the opposition party on the subject of *chieh yen* might be represented by the five-point position set forth by Mr. K'ang Ning-hsiang, a member of the Democratic Progressive Party (DPP) caucus in the Legislative Yuan, in March 1987. 1) The Legislative Yuan should pass a resolution to lift the *chieh yen* edict and request the president to make a declaration to that effect. 2) As of the day *chieh yen* is lifted, all executive orders that were issued on the basis of *chieh yen*, except for those governing exit into and exit from the country and the law on coastal defenses, should become void. 3) Within six months of the lifting of *chieh yen*, new laws should be enacted to fill the vacuum resulting from the abolition of those executive orders if the regular laws currently in place are not sufficient to cope with Taiwan's security situation. 4) All of the present executive orders should be screened and speedily revised or abolished if they are in conflict with the Constitution or the law. 5) The president should declare termination of the period of national mobilization for suppression of rebellion and also abolish the Temporary Provisions for the Period of National Mobilization for the Suppression of Rebellion.[53]

The Chinese Communist view of *chieh yen* in Taiwan is also of interest. As might be expected, the Chinese Communists by and large supported the *tangwai's* call for elimination of *chieh yen*. A radio broadcast by the Central People's Broadcasting Station on April 20, 1983, stated that

> at present none of the legitimate demands of the people of Taiwan for restoration of political and democratic rights can be satisfied because the Taiwan authorities, under the pretext of averting a Chinese Communist takeover and of preventing Taiwan independence elements from betraying the country, refuse to abolish their *chieh yen* law. The myth of the spread of Chinese Communism, which is their excuse for not abolishing *chieh yen*, will only disappear after reunification with the mainland, because only then would both of their pretexts cease to exist. The KMT authorities would therefore have no reason to maintain the *chieh yen* law.

A similar broadcast made on May 23, 1983, stated that "after reunification Taiwan will become a Special Administrative Region of our country. At that time there will no longer be any pretext for having a *chieh yen* law, since there will no longer be any threat from Chinese Communism."

Professor Hungdah Chiu has interpreted the Communist Chinese position as follows. Even though most of those who oppose the *chieh yen* law are pro-Taiwan independence, which is against the Communists' interests, the Communists still support them because they put the KMT government on the defensive. If the Taiwan authorities suppress Taiwan independence activities in order to enforce martial law, the KMT government's international image would be tarnished, especially in the eyes of the United States. Furthermore, if activists in favor of Taiwan independence were to foment trouble or even overthrow the KMT government as a result of the lifting of *chieh yen*, the Chinese Communists could use the situation as a pretext for stepping into the breach. Their action might even be applauded by their own people and by overseas Chinese as an act of nationalism.[54]

III. THE LEGISLATIVE HISTORY OF TAIWAN'S NATIONAL SECURITY LAW

The legislative history of the National Security Law can be divided into five stages.[55]   The first stage occurred in December 1986. Before the Executive Yuan prepared a draft of the law, the Central Policy Committee of the KMT invited members of the three committees of the Legislative Yuan concerned (committees on the interior, national defense, and judicial affairs) to two meetings, held for the purpose of discussing the essential points of the forthcoming law and giving the committee members the opportunity to make comments.   KMT Secretary-General Ma Shu-li and Deputy Secretary-General Ma Ying-chiu also invited scholars of law and political science to participate in discussions of the bill. The Central Policy Committee of the KMT held six meetings with the leaders of the two minor legally recognized political parties in Taiwan, the Youth Party and the People's Socialist Party, as well as with *tangwai* members of the Legislative Yuan, to solicit their views. The Executive Yuan, taking into consideration the opinions expressed at these various meetings as well as the relevant laws of other countries, prepared a draft national security law. In the process, it regularly consulted with the Central Policy Committee of the KMT.   The bill went through several revisions, and the 14 articles of the original version were gradually whittled down to 10.   The draft law was adopted at the January 8, 1987 session of the Executive Yuan Council and passed on to the Legislative Yuan for deliberation.   Initially, it appeared that Legislative Yuan approval would occur in March 1987 and that martial law would be lifted at that time as well, but the legislative process was delayed because of certain controversial provisions in the draft law. The government wanted more time to work with the opposition in ironing out problems; it sought to avoid any hint of confrontation that might tarnish its image abroad.

The second stage in the process of formulating a National Security Law began in March 1987. The Legislative Yuan's committees on the interior, national defense, and judicial affairs examined the bill submitted by the Executive Yuan and held hearings on it. In the meantime, the Central Policy Committee of the KMT not only held numerous consultations with KMT members of the Legislative Yuan but also gathered together the views expressed by legal and political scholars at the hearings. The three committees held six joint review sessions, including one in which political and legal scholars gave testimony. During this period the KMT determined the direction that revisions would take.

The third stage occurred between March and April. The Central Policy Committee of the KMT held two policy coordination meetings to which all KMT members of the Legislative Yuan and the Ministers of the Interior, National Defense, and Justice were invited. Subsequently, representatives from the Executive Yuan and the Legislative Yuan formed a task force to synthesize the views expressed by KMT members of the Legislative Yuan. The synthesis of views was to be used as the basis for revising the draft law.

The fourth stage is marked by June 3, when the Standing Committee of the Central Committee of the KMT adopted the resolution made by the policy coordination committee. The Central Policy Committee of the KMT then held consultations with members of the Legislative Yuan who are members of the two non-KMT parties or the *tangwai* to solicit their views on the revised draft. At the same time, the three committees of the Legislative Yuan held nine review sessions, which, combined with the six meetings held earlier, meant that 15 such sessions were held in all. A record 338 statements were made on the bill by members of the Legislative Yuan. KMT spokesman stressed that seven of the ten articles of the draft law were revised to incorporate the views of the *tangwai*.

The fifth stage of the process occurred on June 19, when the bill was enacted by the Legislative Yuan after having gone through a second and third reading. Between the fourth and fifth stages, KMT Secretary-General Ma held four coordination meetings with key officials of the Executive Yuan and the Legislative Yuan. Deputy Secretary-General Liang Su-jung of the Central Policy

Committee of the KMT and key KMT members of the Legislative Yuan held six coordination meetings with all the KMT members of the three committees. Members of the Democratic Progressive Party, which has yet to be legally recognized, boycotted the meetings. Finally, on June 23, 1987, the National Security Law was passed at the 79th session of the Legislative Yuan.[56]

On July 2, 1987,[57] detailed regulations on the implementation of the National Security Law were enacted by the Executive Yuan in accordance with article 10 of the Law, which states that "The enforcement regulations of the present law and the date of its coming into force shall be made and determined respectively by the Executive Yuan." The enforcement regulations consist of 50 articles in seven chapters. The chapters are: 1) General Principles; 2) Permits for Entry Into and Exit From the Taiwan Region; 3) Security Examinations for Entry Into and Exit From the Taiwan Region; 4) Permits for Entry Into and Exit From Restricted Zones; 5) Prohibition or Restriction of Construction in the Restricted Zones; 6) Transfer of Cases From Military Courts to Civilian Judicial Organs; 7) Appendices. Articles 2 and 3 of the regulations provide a definition of the terms "entry into and exit from" and "persons in active military service." Article 4 to 10 prescribe the application procedures administered by the Entry and Exit Service Bureau of the National Police Administration, Ministry of the Interior.

Articles 12 and 13 of the enforcement regulations are the most controversial. They state that the Entry and Exit Service Bureau may deny permission to enter or exit the Taiwan region (as the case may be) to people who lived in the "lost areas" (i.e., Communist-occupied areas) and have not lived continuously in the free area for five years; to those who have lived in the free area for five years but have not obtained the right of residency or who have lineal blood relatives in the Taiwan region; to those who have been to Communist-occupied areas. Some are of the view that these stipulations exceed what is set forth in Article 3 of the National Security Law. The Secretary-General of the Executive Yuan, Wang Chang-ch'ing, however, contends that they are necessary because of the danger of Communist infiltration and the need to protect national security. It should be noted that the articles state that the Bureau "may," not "shall," deny entry and exit permission.

Furthermore, means of recourse is provided in the last paragraph of Article 3 of the National Security Law, which states: "The Ministry of the Interior shall organize a review committee composed of, *inter alia*, generally recognized impartial personages to review cases of denial decided pursuant to subparagraph (2), paragraph 2 of the present Article."

Finally, on July 7, the Legislative Yuan voted unanimously to cancel the emergency decree. According to Article 72 of the Constitution, the president is to promulgate a bill passed by the Legislative Yuan within 10 days of receiving it.[58] While the proposal to lift the emergency decree did not necessarily have to be governed by this decree, since it was not a statutory bill, the president nevertheless repealed the decree less than 10 days later by issuing a presidential order on July 14 to the effect that the decree would be repealed as of July 15, 1987. Once this proclamation was made, the Executive Yuan announced that the National Security Law and its implementation regulations would take effect on July 15.

IV. PROS AND CONS OF THE NEW LAW

The government insists that a National Security Law is needed because threats and infiltrations from the Chinese Communists still exist. Opponents of the law have a different view of the magnitude of the Chinese Communist threat. They contend that the National Security Law is simply "old wine in a new bottle" and that existing laws and regulations are sufficient to provide for Taiwan's security.[59] In particular, they point out that a group of special criminal regulations, including the Regulations for Punishing Sedition, the Regulations for Wiping Out Spies, and the Regulations for Punishing Robbers, among others, provide for much more severe penalties than those found in the criminal code, and that these special criminal laws, along with Articles 100, 101, and 103 to 115 of the criminal code, are sufficient to maintain state security.

Some legal experts are of the opinion that it would be better to enact specific new laws governing entry into and exit from the country, procedures for lifting martial law, assembly and association, and control of areas with military installations, instead of a National Security Law.[60]

Democratic Progressive Party members of the Legislative Yuan called for a return to the Constitution, without enactment of a National Security Law.[61] Supporters of the law have pointed out, however, that a return to the Constitution means a return not only to the Constitution proper but also to the Temporary Provisions that were adopted as a constitutional amendment on the basis of Article 174. Hence, they argue, enactment of the National Security Law is not in conflict with a return to the Constitution.[62]

V. PROVISIONS OF THE NATIONAL SECURITY LAW DURING THE PERIOD OF MOBILIZATION FOR SUPPRESSION OF REBELLION
(*Tung yuan k'an luan shih ch'i kuo chia an ch'uan fa*)[63]

The sources of legitimation of the National Security Law is Article 23 of the Constitution, which states that freedoms and rights shall not be restricted by law except by such as may be necessary to prevent infringement upon the freedoms of other persons, to avert an imminent crisis, to maintain social order, or to advance public welfare. Article 1, paragraph 1, of the law reflects this relationship to Article 23 in stating that the purpose of the law is to "safeguard national security and maintain social stability." Any question as to the legality of the law would have to be determined by the Council of Grand Justices, whose right it is to interpret the Constitution and to review laws for their constitutionality.

Seven of the 10 articles in the draft National Security Law presented by the Executive Yuan to the Legislative Yuan were altered by the latter, but the major differences between the draft version and the final version are found in articles 2 and 9.

Article 2 of the draft National Security Law, concerning assembly and association, has created the most controversy. It was criticized for being too vague, for not being couched in legal language, for being mainly a declaratory provision. The draft version of article 2 stated:

> No person may violate the Constitution or the national policy of anti-Communism [*fan kung kuo*

ts'e] or advocate separatism [*fen li i shih*] in the exercise of the people's freedoms of assembly and association.

The assembly and association of people mentioned above is to be governed by laws to be enacted separately.

DPP members of the Legislative Yuan objected to this version of Article 2, and specifically to the use of the term "separatism" (*fen li i shih*, literally, separation ideology, considered a code word for Taiwan independence), claiming that the government had improperly equated the DPP's call for "self-determination" for Taiwan with "separatism." The article as it stood could therefore have threatened the DPP's potential right to existence as a political party, since the KMT government has outlawed advocacy of Taiwan independence.[64] As a result of the strong opposition to the draft article, it was revised to read as follows in the final version:

> No person may violate the Constitution or advocate Communism [*kung ch'an chu i*] or the division of national territory [*fen lieh kuo t'u*] in the exercise of the people's freedoms of assembly and association.

Under the new law, and after the enactment of bills governing formation of civil groups and election and recall of public functionaries, the DPP and other political groups will be able to gain legal recognition. The KMT is at a critical juncture; while it remains strongly opposed to an independent Taiwan—the declaration of which might invite the mainland to use force to recover the island as part of one China—it must woo the majority of the populace, whose families have lived in Taiwan for generations, the *tai chi*, those whose place of affiliation is Taiwan. Without the support of *tai chi*, who represent 85 percent of the population, a candidate has little chance of getting elected, and so in recent years the KMT has tended to select more native Taiwanese as candidates. The children of the mainland Chinese who went to Taiwan after 1949 are not viewed as being "Taiwanese." Among native Taiwanese, moreover, there is less sense of nationalism for one China. In order to ensure its party's future commitment to one

China, therefore, especially since the old guard from the mainland is gradually expiring, the KMT must attract to its cause indigenous Taiwanese who appeal to the populace at large.

Articles 3, 4, and 5 of the National Security Law deal with travel restrictions, either across the country's borders or in certain designated security areas inside the country. Article 3 is on controls over entry into or exit from Taiwan. It describes the application procedure for entry or exit permits as well as the grounds of denial of such permits. Whereas the draft version, first paragraph, said that "A person who enters the Taiwan region without permission is subject to immediate deportation," the corresponding sentence in the law reads: "A person without permission may not enter into or depart from the Taiwan region." In its paragraph 2, the article lists three conditions under which exit or entry may be denied. The order of the second and third items is reversed in the final version, and the wording of the second item (item three in the draft version) is slightly altered. Thus, item two states that an application may be denied if the applicants "have been strongly suspected (versus simply "considered" in the draft version), on the basis of factual evidence, to be grave security risks to national security or social stability." The revision would seem to place a somewhat greater burden of proof on the authorities. Paragraph 3 of the draft stated that those denied permission "shall be notified in writing"; in the law the phrase "with reasons for denial" has been added. Last but not least, the law contains a fourth paragraph, which was not in the draft version, that provides for establishment of a review committee for cases of denial on suspicion of existence of a security risk (paragraph 2, item 2, cited above).

Article 4 provides for inspections by police authorities of passengers, crew, aircraft, or other vessels entering or leaving the country. "Security authorities" in the draft Article 4 was changed to "police authorities." Security authorities were to include the Taiwan Garrison Command, the National Police Administration under the Ministry of the Interior, the Military Police Headquarters, and the Bureau of Investigation under the Ministry of Justice.[65] The inclusion of the Taiwan Garrison Command in this list created a storm of controversy, however, and it was subsequently dropped. Thus, the Garrison Command will not handle matters related to the National Security Law, even though it will continue to exist.

Article 5 deals with the designation of restricted zones in order "to safeguard coastal defenses, military installations, and mountain areas." The draft version stated that "the Ministry of Defense may designate and declare" such zones; in Article 5 of the law this became the Ministry of Defense, "in consultation with the Ministry of the Interior. . . ." Zones deemed restrictable by the Ministry of Defense might prove inconvenient to the people, hence the importance of participation by the Ministry of the Interior in the decisions. Moreover, it is the practice in Taiwan for the Ministry of the Interior to be headed by a Taiwanese, which also might make the decision-making process in regard to restricted zones less arbitrary. Paragraph 3 of the article in its final form has also been changed slightly. The scope of construction allowed in the special zones "shall be determined jointly by the Ministry of National Defense, the Ministry of the Interior, and other related agencies." The draft version did not include the last phrase in regard to related agencies. The expansion of authority here, too, may make the decision-making process more equitable. A fourth paragraph, having to do with reduction of taxes and other levies on land where construction is restricted or prohibited, is a new addition to the article that is absent from the draft version. This modification would also seem to have been added with the interest of the people in mind.

Articles 6 and 7 set forth penalties of imprisonment or fines to be incurred for violation of the restrictions imposed in Articles 3, 4, and 5. The maximum penalty, for entering or exiting the country without permission, which violates Article 3, paragraph 1, is imprisonment for three years and/or a fine of 30,000 *yuan.* The penalties compare favorably with those imposed by other countries; indeed, penalties imposed under U.S. law are much more severe. Paragraph 2 of Article 6 has to do with violations of Article 4: "A person who without justifiable reason refuses or evades searches or inspections conducted pursuant to Article 4 shall be punished with imprisonment for not more than six months, detention, and/or a fine of not more than 5,000 *yuan.*" The draft version did not have the phrase "without justifiable reason," and the punishment was for not more than one year or a fine of not more than 10,000 *yuan.* Thus, the changes make it more difficult to punish people

and also lessen the punishments inflicted.   Similar changes
are found in Article 7.   Its paragraph 1 states:

> A   person   who   *without   reason*   violates
> paragraph 2 of Article 5 by entering into or
> departing   from   the   restricted   zones   without
> applying for permission *and refuses to leave after
> having been notified to do so* shall be punished
> with imprisonment for not more than six months,
> detention, and/or a fine of not more than 5,000
> *yuan.*

The italicized phrases above, which provide more procedural
protection, were not in the Executive Yuan draft version of
the article.   The term of punishment and fine set forth in
paragraph two of Article 7 were lessened along the same
lines as those in paragraph 2 of Article 6, and a procedural
modification was added as well (italicized phrases are new,
except for "*yuan*"):

> A person who violates paragraph 3 of Article 5
> concerning   prohibited   or   restricted   construction
> *and refuses to comply with instructions to cease
> construction* shall be punished with imprisonment
> for not more than *six months*, detention, and/or a
> fine of not more than *5,000 yuan.*

The modification will make it more difficult to carry out
summary   punishment.   When   some   members   of   the
Legislative Yuan voiced concern that punishments prescribed
in the draft versions of Articles 6 and 7 might be too light,
Minister of Justice Shih Ch'i-yang stated that they were
purposely made less severe in order to show the sincerity of
the government's intention in lifting martial law.[66]
     Articles 8 and 9 spell out the jurisdiction of civil and
military courts.   Article 8 is the provision which does away
with military trials of civilians, stating in paragraph 1 that
"Except for military personnel in active military service, no
person shall be subjected to military trial."   For criminal
matters, if the defendant is a civilian, the case will be tried
by a civil court, but if the defendant is a military
serviceman, the case will be under the jurisdiction of a
military court.[67]   Paragraph 2 of Article 8 provides for trial
by court martial of military personnel charged with crimes.

A proviso that was not in the draft version of the article was added at the end of the final version: " . . . unless the criminal offense committed is not provided for under the Criminal Code of the Armed Forces or other special enactments thereof but is provided for under Article 61 of the Criminal Code." This, too, makes it more difficult to carry out arbitrary punishment.

Article 9 covers court jurisdiction in transitional situations, for cases of civilians currently being tried under martial law or those tried prior to the law's enactment. This article aroused a great deal of debate, but was incorporated into the law unaltered from the draft version. The cases of civilians who are presently being prosecuted for commission of martial law crimes are to be turned over to a public prosecutor or to a civil court, depending upon the stage of litigation (para. 1). It is paragraph 2 of Article 9, on final judgments, that is especially controversial:

> Where criminal sentences have been finalized, appeal or interlocutory appeal to a competent court will not be allowed. But applications for retrial or extraordinary appeal may be lodged pursuant to law, if there are grounds for retrial or extraordinary appeal.

Under Article 10 of the *Chieh yen* Law, if a civilian is tried by a military court and his sentence has been finalized, he can still appeal to a civilian court: "Appeal against a judgment rendered in accordance with Articles 8 and 9 of this law may be instituted in accordance with law as from the day following the date on which martial law is repealed." It is likely that when the *Chieh yen* Law was enacted, the authorities did not expect that it would be enforced for almost four decades; it was an emergency decree, meant to be briefly enforced, which is why it provided for greater flexibility of appeal. Furthermore, if the authorities allowed all the cases in which final judgment had been rendered by a military court to be appealed to civilian courts, those courts might be flooded. Therefore some scholars are of the view that since criminal judgments rendered by a military court would probably not be as fair as those rendered by a civilian court, remedial measures should be taken to restore at least the political rights of those deprived of such rights as a result of those judgments. Eight thousand civilians were sentenced under the *Chieh yen* Law over the past 38 years, and 200 were still in prison when the proposal to lift the decree was approved by the Legislative Yuan on July 7.[68] According to paragraph 3 of the article, if a sentence has not yet been served or is just in the process of being served, the case shall be transferred to a public prosecutor for disposition. Objections to Article 9 have been raised by those who hold the view that 1) military personnel who violate the regular criminal code should also not be tried by a military court and 2) Article 9 contradicts Article 10 of the Martial Law, which does allow appeal.

Article 10 of the National Security Law stipulates that the Executive Yuan is to determine the issuance of enforcement regulations and the effective date of the new law.

VI. CONCLUSION

With the replacement of martial law by a new national security law have come the lifting of travel restrictions to Hong Kong and Macao,[69] the commutation of sentences for 237 non-military prisoners convicted under the emergency decree and restoration of their civil rights,[70] and the lifting of most foreign exchange controls.[71] In addition, a draft Civic Body Organization Law has been completed and the Assembly and Street March Law has been passed. The United States and other countries have applauded the lifting of the decree and have encouraged Taiwan to take other steps towards full-fledged democracy.

Nevertheless, opposition politicians consider it only a first step, at best. In particular, they point out the need for reform of the Taiwan National Assembly. Only one-fifth of the members are elected; most seats are held by Nationalists elected in 1947 for life, even though about 85 percent of the populace are indigenous Taiwanese.[72] Many of the members of the National Assembly and the Legislative Yuan are in their eighties. The government does not directly appoint replacements for these men when they pass away, but the procedure for choosing a new member is rather unique. According to law, a record has been kept of the candidate from each mainland legislator's province who received the next highest number of votes in the 1947 election. When a member who was elected on the mainland dies, the former runner-up, if still alive and in Taiwan, is to be considered as next in line for the position after being screened by the Ministry of the Interior. Given these various requirements, it is not a certainty that the vacancy will be filled by the former candidate. There are members of the Legislative Yuan who are directly appointed by the government, however—those who represent overseas Chinese for a certain term. The question has been raised by the Democratic Progressive Party as to whether some of these member-representatives might not in fact have U.S. citizenship as well as Taiwanese. Under the laws of the Republic of China, dual nationality is permissible, but those with foreign nationality are prohibited from serving as public functionaries. Since the president of Taiwan is indirectly elected by the Assembly, moreover, some of the opposition may now begin to call for direct elections. The suggestion has also been made that the KMT "should divest itself of its many business interests, which, they argue, give it an unfair financial advantage over any alternative parties."[73]

From a legal point of view, there is validity in the argument that a national security law is not really necessary in Taiwan, that the Constitution and laws currently on the books are sufficient for coping with emergencies that might arise. From a political standpoint, however, there is a need for such a law. It serves to pacify more conservative elements in Taiwan who are opposed altogether to the lifting of martial law by acting as a stopgap measure during the transition to normalcy. Moreover, absence of a security law would imply that Taiwan is in a state of normalcy, which most would agree is not the case. Taiwan still faces both internal and external threats, and so some form of emergency powers law is still a necessity.

Second, the language of the draft version of the National Security Law was criticized by many for being vague and ambiguous. While the language was made more precise and concrete, it is important to remember that no matter how well a law may be written, there is still the need to have in place a judicial organ capable of interpreting it; without the mechanism of judicial review, the most aptly phrased law might still prove inadequate. In Taiwan, the Grand Council of Justices serves this purpose.

Third, the National Security Law has an educative role. This is reflected especially in Articles 1 and 2. Article 1, which states that the aim of the law is to safeguard national security and maintain social stability, is declaratory in nature and carries no sanction. Because of its educative intent, the article does serve a certain purpose and is not superfluous, as critics have contended. Article 2 is basically a restatement of Chiang Ching-kuo's policy and the principles of the KMT government and is similarly educative and nonenforceable.

There are several reasons behind President Chiang's unexpected decision to lift martial law on Taiwan. His stated reason for terminating the emergency decrees was to foster constitutional democracy in his country.[74] But there are other very important reasons as well. First, pressure from the U.S. Congress to improve Taiwan's human rights record is a factor. Taiwan is still quite dependent on the U.S. and is aware of the need to improve its image. Second, there was Chiang's own desire to leave a legacy, to be remembered in China and the world as a leader with vision. Third, the influence of the *ch'ing nien ts'ai chun*, the relatively young talented elite, cannot be overlooked. Through various channels, they recommended to President Chiang that the order enforcing martial law be lifted. Many of this group are American-educated scholars who hold important KMT and government positions or who teach at universities in the U.S. Impressed by the American democratic political system, they want to help Taiwan emulate the American model. They are also sensitive to criticism of Taiwan's failure in the eyes of the world to make greater strides towards democratic rule, and so they urged Chiang Ching-kuo to take such steps. Chiang Ching-kuo, for his part, was quite responsive to the suggestions of this young elite as well as to the wishes of the populace in general. Fourth, at present many KMT members of the Legislative Yuan elected on the mainland are elderly and do not even attend some of the meetings. The government may have realized that the time is now ripe to enact a security law, because it will only become more difficult later as the old guard passes away and a younger generation with different views gains power.

Whatever the reasons behind the decision to lift martial law and to initiate political change, the challenge for Taiwan lies in creating a successful balance between maintaining stability and introducing more democratic reforms. During this transitional stage, it would seem advisable not to rush the Taiwan authorities into making more drastic changes, but to encourage their continued efforts to develop a more open society.

ENDNOTES

1. Joint Publications Research Service, *China Report: Political, Sociological, and Military Affairs*, Jan. 14, 1987, at 118 (hereafter cited as JPRS).

2. "Taiwan: The Winds of Change," *Newsweek*, Oct. 20, 1986. The KMT also initiated ground-breaking talks with members of the opposition (*tangwai*) shortly afterwards, in April 1986. Aside from the KMT, there are two other legal political parties in Taiwan, but they rarely present candidates to run against the KMT. Instead, before 1986, opposition candidates would run for office as independents without any party affiliation. In September of 1986, however, in defiance of the ban on formation of new parties, about 150 *tangwai* members formed their own Democratic Progressive Party.

3. *China Post* (Taipei, in English), Oct. 4, 1986, at 12, as reported in Foreign Broadcast Information Service, *China Report* (hereafter cited as FBIS), Oct. 9, 1986, at V2.

4. Julia Leung, "Taiwan's Democratic Opening Threatened," *The Wall Street Journal*, Nov. 28, 1986, at 14.

5. Central News Agency (CNA) (Taipei, in English), Oct. 24, 1986, as cited from FBIS, Oct. 28, 1986, at V1-V2. The Interior Ministry completed a draft revision of the Civic Organization Law, in 11 chapters and 66 articles, in September 1987. CNA, Sept. 19, 1987, as cited in FBIS, Sept. 22, 1987, at 24. The revised draft was

approved by the Legislative Yuan's Committees on the Interior and on Judicial Affairs in mid-December and awaits ratification. CNA, Dec. 12, 1987, as cited in FBIS, Dec. 15, 1987, at 43. In addition, on January 11, 1988, the Legislative Yuan approved the Assembly and Street March Law. This law was promulgated on January 20, 1988, and went into effect the same day. CNA, Jan. 20, 1988, as cited in FBIS, Jan. 21, 1988, at 40.

6.   CNA, Apr. 10, 1987, as cited in FBIS, Apr. 10, 1987, at V2.

7.   CNA, June 16, 1987, as cited in FBIS, June 16, 1987, at V2.

8.   *The Free China Journal*, June 29, 1987, at 1.

9.   Leung, *supra* note 4.

10. *See for example* Lin Shan-tien, "It Seems Unnecessary To Enact a National Security Law," *Tzu li wan pao*, Oct. 7, 1986, at 3, as translated in JPRS, Jan. 14, 1987, at 118-120.

11. *See* T'an Su-ch'eng, *Chin chi ming ling chih yen chiu* (Study on Emergency Orders) (Taipei, National Taiwan University, Graduate Institute of Political Science, Masters Thesis, 1966). The information that follows is based on the section "The Historical Evolution of Emergency Orders." *See also in general* William L. Tung, *The Political Institutions of Modern China* (The Hague, Martinus Nijhoff, 1964).

12. For a translation of the Principles of Constitution, *see* Tung, at 318-319 (Appendix A).

13. T'an, at 208.

14. *Id.*

15. *Id.*

16. *Ibid.*, at 209.

17. For a translation of the document that was enacted, the Provisional Constitution of the Republic of China (*Chung-hua min kuo lin shih yueh fa*), see *ibid.*, at 322-325 (Appendix C).

18. T'an, at 211-212.

19. *Ibid.*, at 213. For a translation of the Yuan Shih-k'ai Constitution, *see* Tung, at 326-331 (Appendix D).

20. T'an, at 214.

21. Tung, at 79. The restoration of the 1912 Provisional Constitution is mentioned on page 65.

22. *See* the chapter on "State Emergency Powers and Rights of Freedom" in Luo Chih-yuan, *Hsien fa lun ts'ung* (Collected Essays on the Constitution) (Taipei, Commercial Press, 1969). The Constitution of the Republic of China (*Chung-hua min kuo hsien fa*) was promulgated on January 1, 1947, and went into effect on December 25, 1947. For a translation of the Provisional Constitution for the Period of Political Tutelage, *see* Tung, at 344-349 (Appendix F).

23. "Constitution of the Republic of China," *in* A. Blaustein & G. Flanz, eds., *Constitutions of the Countries of the World* (Dobbs Ferry, N.Y., Oceana Publications, Inc., 1981).

24. The Temporary Provisions were promulgated on May 10, 1948, and subsequently amended in 1960, 1966 (twice), and 1972. An alternative translation also used for this emergency decree is "Provisional Amendments for the Period of Mobilization and Suppression of the Communist Rebellion." *See* Blaustein & Flanz, at 45-47.

25. Blaustein & Flanz, at 45.

26. *Id.*

27. *See* Art. 57, para. 2, of the ROC Constitution, in Blaustein & Flanz, at 8.

28. This law was originally promulgated and enforced on November 29, 1934, when the Nationalist government prepared for war against the Japanese. On January 14, 1949, the text of Article 8, concerning criminal offenses to be tried by military courts, was amended. *See Martial Law on Taiwan and United States Foreign Policy Interests*, Hearing Before the Subcomm. on Asian and Pacific Affairs, House Comm. on Foreign Affairs, 97th Cong., 2d Sess., May 20, 1982, 175, 177 (Washington, U.S. Govt. Print. Off., 1982) [hereafter cited as Hearing]. For the text of the *Chien yen fa* [Emergency Law] and the *Chieh yen ling* [Emergency Decree] *see* Tuan Shao-yen, comp., *Liu fa pan chieh hui pien* [Collection of Precedents and Interpretations on the Six Codes] 1785-1790 (Taipei, San-min Books, 1962).

29. For the Chinese text, *see Tsui hsin liu fa ch'uan shu* 981-984 (T'ao Pai-ch'uan, comp. Taipei, San-min Books, 1986). The Law was adopted on March 29, 1942, and went into effect on May 5 of that year. It contains 32 articles. According to Minister of Justice Shih Ch'i-yang, the National Mobilization Law consists of administrative control measures for specific matters, such as manpower and materiel, so that the grounds for abolishing it differ from those for lifting *chieh yen*. He stated that the government deems it undesirable at present to terminate or suspend the law. Reported in *Chung yang jih pao* [Central Daily News], International Edition, Apr. 1, 1987.

30. T'an, at 246-247.

31. Reported in *Chung yang jih pao*, International Edition, Mar. 25, 1987.

32. "Scholars All Agree That the Legality of the Temporary Provisions Cannot Be Questioned and That There Is a Need to Keep These Provisions To Cope With Changing Circumstances," *id.*

33. *Id.*

34. Hungdah Chiu & Jyh-pin Fa, "The Legal System of the Republic of China in Taiwan," 2 *Modern Legal Systems Cyclopedia* 645 (Charlottesville, VA., University of Virginia Press, 1984).

35. *Id.*

36. *See* Hsieh Chen-min, *Chung-hua min-kuo li fa shih* [History of Legislation of the Republic of China] (Chang Chih-pen, rev. Shanghai, Chen-cheng Press, 1948, orig. ed. 1937).

37. *See* Hungdah Chiu, "An Analytical Study of the Question of *Chieh yen* in Our Country," a paper prepared for the Human Rights Association of China, November 26, 1983.

38. Hsieh, at 633-636.

39. Chiu, *supra* note 37.

40. Blaustein & Flanz, *supra* note 23.

41. *Chung yang jih pao*, International Edition, July 3, 1987, at 1.

42. According to 1 *Li fa chuan k'an* [Special Gazette on Legislation] 244, *cited in* Chiu, *supra* note 37.

43. *Id.*

44. *Mei chou hua ch'iao jih pao* [China Daily News], Mar. 14, 1987, at 6.

45. *See* the testimony of Prof. A. James Gregor, in Hearing, at 127.

46. Chiu & Fa, at 318. Article 2 of the "Measures Governing the Classification of Cases To Be Tried by the Military Judicial Organs Themselves and Those Which Are To Be Turned Over to the Courts in the Region of Taiwan During the Period of Martial Law" provides for these restrictions.

47. *Id.* at 319.

48. Hearing, at 87.

49. *Ibid.*, at 131.

50. *Ibid.*, at 90.

51. *Ibid.*, at 116.

52. *Ibid.* at 129.

53. *Shih chieh jih pao* [World Daily News], Mar. 19, 1987, at 5.

54. Chiu, *supra* note 37.

55. *Chung yang jih pao*, International Edition, June 24, 1987, at 1.

56. *The Free China Journal* (Taipei, in English), June 29, 1987, at 2. The full text of the law in English translation is provided.

57. *Chung yang jih pao*, International Edition, July 5, 1987, at 1.

58. CNA, July 14, 1987, as cited in FBIS, July 15, 1987, at V1.

59. *See* editorial in *The Free China Journal*, Mar. 16, 1987, at 2.

60. *Kuo chi jih pao* [International Daily News], Mar. 19, 1987, at 7.

61. *Lien ho pao* [United Daily News], Mar. 12, 1987, at 1. Reporter Hu Yuan-hui is of the view that present circumstances do not permit a return to normalcy, but that the government should not overemphasize national security considerations at the expense of democratic reforms.

62. Wen Hsi, "The Juridical Basis of the National Security Law," *Chung yang jih pao*, International Edition, Mar. 14, 1987, at 1. Wen is a professor of law at a university in Taiwan.

63. For a book-length study of the National Security Law, *see* Ts'ao Ching-hui, *Tung yuan k'an luan shih ch'i kuo chia an ch'uan fa shih lun* [An Interpretive Discussion of the National Security Law During the Period of Mobilization for Suppression of Rebellion], Chang-ming Series on Legal Science No. 19 (Taipei, San-min Books, 1987).

64. Hsin-hsin Yang, Hong Kong AFP, in English, Mar. 18, 1987, as cited in FBIS, Mar. 20, 1987, at V3.

65. *China Post* (English), Mar. 10, 1987, at 12, as cited in FBIS, Mar. 19, 1987, at V1.

66. From *Chung yang jih pao*, International Edition, Mar. 12, 1987, at 1.

67. CNA, Mar. 19, 1987, as cited in FBIS, Mar. 19, 1987, at V2-V3.

68. "Emergency Decree Zapped in Vote by ROC Leaders," *The Free China Journal*, July 13, 1987, at 1.

69. CNA, July 16, 1987, as cited in FBIS, July 17, 1987, at V1.

70. CNA, July 14, 1987, as reported in FBIS, July 15, 1987, at V2. An additional 23 prisoners, many of them dissidents, were released on July 14; on July 15, 70 others, including 30 dissidents, were transferred from military to civilian prison. The dissidents had their sentences cut in half and prisoners in for life had theirs reduced to 15 years. The Associated Press, July 15, 1987.

71. "Foreign Currency OK; ROC Controls Lifted," *The Free China Journal*, July 13, 1987, at 1. According to the article, 19 laws limiting the flow of foreign exchange in Taiwan have been abolished. Government approval

will still be required to bring more than $10,000 dollars into the country and Taiwanese companies must have at least $10,000,000 NT (about $322,000) in order to invest in overseas projects and must also provide proof that their liabilities do not exceed three times their capital. Six other regulations remain in place, including those that safeguard against black market foreign exchange trading and give the government authority to screen large remittances, require registration of foreign debt, and monitor operations of banks designated to deal in foreign exchange. Certain foreign currency regulations that come under the authority of other government ministries are also to be revised, and the Economics Ministry will revise regulations governing investments in Taiwan by overseas Chinese and other foreign interests, overseas investments by Taiwan firms, cooperative ventures, and administration of export processing zones.

72.   *The Washington Post,* July 15, 1987, at A16, A18. According to Asahi News Service, 219 of the Legislative Yuan's 319 members are 'lifetime' members who nominally represent the pre-1949 provinces of mainland China; the remaining 100 members are elected every three years. Parliamentary functions under Taiwan's constitution are carried out by the National Assembly, a unicameral body whose primary task is to elect the president and vice president; the Legislative Yuan, the formal lawmaking body; and the Control Yuan, which monitors the administration. Asahi News Service, July 15, 1987.

73.   *The Washington Post, supra* note 72.

74.   *Newsweek, supra* note 2, at 23.

Conclusions

INIS L. CLAUDE, JR.

This volume has presented five case studies of the use by governments of extraordinary powers to deal with what they have considered, or purported to consider, crises jeopardizing the order and security of the societies over which they rule. The ultimate purpose of collecting case studies in this way is to enable us to formulate generalizations, or to test pre-existing generalizations, or to determine whether generalizations are possible about the issue to which the cases pertain. One may discover that all the cases point to the same broad conclusion or share essential characteristics, or that each of them is unique. Whether or not our cases support the development of a general theory about constitutional emergency powers or the viability of limited government in a setting of domestic unrest and international turmoil, they do offer us the opportunity and incentive to muse about these problems. What can and should we learn from these case studies?

Strictly speaking, the issue of constitutional emergency powers arises only in relation to governments enshrining the principle of constitutionalism, which requires that rulers be restricted in what they do and in how they do it. Constitutionalism is often, and with some logic, linked closely with democracy, but either may in principle exist without the other; the essence of constitutional government has to do with the limits that it accepts rather than with the origins that it claims. Absolutist governments are, by definition, free at all times to exercise such authority as they may wish, and therefore have no need of special grants of authority to deal with crises. Systematically limited governments, by contrast, are certain from time to time to face emergencies with which they are ill-equipped to cope. According to Frederick M. Watkins, "the need for emergency powers is implicit in the very nature of constitutional government. The need is directly proportional, indeed, to the effectiveness of legal checks in controlling the activities of statesmen."[1] As Watkins reminded us, constitutionalism is a relative concept. It is evident that the five states considered in this book vary greatly in the nature and degree of the limitations under which their governments normally operate, but all of them are in some sense constitutional, as distinguished from absolutist, systems.

We are concerned, then, with exceptional powers, above and beyond those routinely available to governments, for dealing with exceptional situations, which is the way we characterize crises or emergencies. Typically, we think of an emergency as a temporary situation requiring urgent response, and we therefore conceive constitutional emergency powers as short-term authorizations to act in ways normally forbidden, to be invoked occasionally and relinquished after brief periods. The cases detailed in this volume remind us, however, how varied are the emergencies that plague governments in today's world. All of these cases deal with persistent difficulties rather than clearly transient ones, and Israel and Northern Ireland in particular might be said to confront permanent emergencies. In the latter case, the measures taken by the British government are exceptional in a spatial rather than a temporal sense, in that they apply to the seemingly interminable problems of a particular segment of the United Kingdom. As Professor Dowty notes, the duration of Israel's crisis may justify a distinction between the chronic emergency that has come to be regarded almost as normal and the acute emergency that arises sporadically. Crises obviously vary greatly not only as to frequency and duration but also as to severity, the nature of the threat that they pose, and the source from which they arise. They may be economic, or political, or military in character. Their manifestations may range from political dissent through rebellion, civil war, subversion, and terrorism to invasion by a foreign power. Israel's sharpest challenges appear to derive from neighboring states and the occupied territories rather than from its own body politic, while Northern Ireland's arise mainly out of the animosities of its two domestic communities, and the crises in the three other states under examination more conspicuously blend internal and external origins.

If crises were almost infinitely variable, so indeed are the special arrangements of governmental systems for dealing with them. The business of government is largely routine, having to do with meeting the ordinary requirements of society, but crises arise in all societies as inevitably as unpredictably, and every government, of whatever type, must somehow gear itself to meet unusual challenges. The need for special arrangements is a function in part of the anticipated character and severity of emergencies. South Korea, for instance, has greater reason to fear invasion than does New Zealand, and Italy is more likely than Denmark to experience acute class struggles. It is also a function in part of the adequacy of the authority normally available to the government. In some systems, government must call upon constitutional reserves for authority to act in ways ordinarily proscribed—as in Taiwan and South Korea, for instance—while in others, such as the United Kingdom, special legislation for dealing with emergencies can be enacted by the usual processes. A distinction can be made between the emergency scheme historically associated with civil law societies, the state of siege, and that associated with common law societies, martial rule.[2] Our cases suggest, however, that modern governments tend to mix features of those classical schemes and produce arrangements adapted to the unique circumstances and peculiar traditions of the individual state. Professor Evans invokes the concept of political culture in explaining Italy's response to terrorist activity, and the responses of Britain and Taiwan to their difficulties are clearly non-Italian. Governments are limited in various ways and to various degrees, and they are challenged in equally varied fashion. Hence, they differ markedly in their methods of undertaking to deal with the challenge of crisis.

Perhaps the most difficult and important issue related to the case studies presented in this volume is how one should evaluate the results of the exercise of constitutional emergency powers. What constitutes success and failure?

Formally, of course, the purpose whose fulfillment should serve as the criterion of success is the preservation of the order of the society being assaulted—the avoidance of the overturning or disintegration of the political and legal system, the restoration of social stability, the elimination of system-threatening violence, the defeat of enemies of the state, domestic or foreign. Constitutional emergency powers entail the use of radical measures for conservative ends. This purpose of maintaining the integrity of state and society is consistently espoused by governments resorting to special emergency arrangements, which, after all, are designed with that end in view.

By this criterion, all of our cases are in considerable measure success stories. None of the political systems in question has been shattered by domestic revolutionary upheaval or conquered by foreign enemies. We should note, however, that this standard of success is a fairly modern one. Many gradations exist between the extremes of order and disorder, and success in the sense suggested here means not the elimination but the control of violence, not the extinguishing but the damping of social conflagrations, not the solution but the management of troublesome problems. If one objects that constitutional emergency schemes seem then only to deal with symptoms without remedying the underlying causes of social and political malaise, the appropriate reply is an acknowledgement of the truth of this assertion, with a reminder that short-term crises must be dealt with before long-term problems can be tackled. When fire breaks out, one needs to postpone the lecture on fire-prevention and get on with the fire-fighting! An honest response will also point out that, although containing violence is a prerequisite for correcting the conditions that give rise to it, success in containment does not guarantee that such fundamental improvement can or will be achieved, and it may even weaken incentives to attempt that task. Or it may be that the vital energies of societies are so exhausted by the exertions of coping with crisis—one thinks of the British in Northern Ireland and of the Israelis in the occupied territories—that there is little to spare for investment in work on long-term solutions.

The judgment that all of our cases illustrate the successful use of emergency powers to deny victory to enemies of the social order might be qualified by noting that in the first two of the instances treated in the chapter on South Korea (designated by Professor Kim as Cases #1 and #2), disorder led to the transfer of political power. In the first instance emergency powers did not prevent President Rhee from being forced to resign, and in the second instance they were used not to save the legitimate government but to shore up the position of the regime that seized power in a military coup. Were these successes for constitutional emergency powers? Judgment of that issue must ultimately depend on whether one interprets these instances as mere changes of government or as revolutionary alterations of the political system; the criterion of success is not the protection of the government of the day but the preservation of the political system and social order.

For our purposes, the importance of these two Korean instances lies in the reminder that there is no clear and indisputable line between the two objectives of defending particular governing elites and defending the states and societies over which those elites preside. Governments always claim to resort to emergency measures in order to defend the order of their societies. May they not sometimes be engaged instead in saving their own political hides? As observers, we may argue about particular cases but we will surely agree that *some* governments are cynical enough to mask their desperate efforts to retain and even increase their power behind the facade of claims to take heroic action for the defense of public order and the integrity of the nation. Moreover, the confusion between the two objectives of solicitude is not necessarily the product of deliberate and dishonestly motivated obfuscation. Rulers often come to *believe*, not merely to claim, that their survival in office is vitally important to the safety and welfare of their states, and, indeed, this assumption is not invariably false. The interests of king and kingdom are sometimes inextricably interwoven. One of the highest hopes of the American Founding Fathers was that the constitutional system of their devising would so harness the political interests of office-holders that the pursuit of those interests would conduce to the public good. A regime's commitment to self-defense is not automatically to be presumed incompatible with, or neglectful of, its obligation to serve its state. Even if its main figures do not fall into the select category of truly indispensable leaders, the system's stability may require the frustration of violent efforts to overthrow its government. In short, the relationship between the defense of government and the defense of the socio-political order is marked both by the disingenuous representation of the former as the latter and by the genuine identification and merging of the two concerns.

An alternative test of the success of constitutional emergency powers focuses on the degree to which democratic freedoms and basic human rights are spared interference during periods of crisis. Governments, concentrating as they do on the objective of security and stability, are obviously unlikely to adopt this focus, but it is attractive to academic observers and those who might be described as professional civil libertarians or members of the human rights community. In his chapter on Israel, Professor Dowty, doubtless motivated in part by the urge to evaluate charges made by civil libertarians, devotes considerable attention to the question of whether security measures have impinged excessively on the enjoyment of legal protection and normal liberties by Palestinians and Israelis; in so doing, he indicates awareness of, though not necessarily agreement with, the notion that the crucial question about such measures is not whether they protect the state but whether they are respectful of human rights. Finding Israel's response to crisis reasonably successful according to either criterion, Professor Dowty has no occasion definitively to choose the one or the other. What we might call the human rights test, or the law and liberty tests, is frequently adopted not only by the groups mentioned above but also by unfriendly partisans, when they believe that they can convict the state under discussion, in the propaganda arena if not in an impartial court, of having failed that test, and by observers who have no particular reason to share in a government's concern for the security of its state. One can most readily choose the human rights test, articulating the primacy of the dignity and freedom of human beings over the claims of Leviathan and stressing reliance on the rule of law rather than on military and police power, when the socio-political system in question appears not to be seriously challenged or when the maintenance of its integrity is not high on one's list of priorities.

In some instances, the adoption of the human rights test is not so much a matter of subordinating the security interests of the regime and system to this higher value as it is an indication of the repudiation of those interests as illegitimate. In short, opposition to constitutional emergency powers or sharp criticism of the manner of their use *may* derive from and reflect opposition to the survival of a given regime or political system. This brings us back to the central point that emergency arrangements are inherently conservative devices, schemes for defending the status quo. Revolutionaries, however they may be motivated, are bound to be critical of the efforts of target governments to maintain order. Their criticism of harsh and arbitrary measures may be indicative of solicitude for the success of revolution rather than for the flourishing of human rights and democratic freedoms. For instance, the Arab world is probably more anti-Zionist than pro-human rights, and the IRA is probably more anti-British than pro-democratic. In some cases, however, zeal for undermining a regime or system may reflect a genuine commitment to the values of constitutionalism and democracy, expressed in the conviction that only a revolutionary change can end the suppression of those values. One might argue, for instance, that friends of democracy must support the trouble-makers, not the order-keepers, when regimes such as that of South Korea's President Rhee come under attack. In the extreme case, the objectives of defending stability and order and of upholding and promoting human rights are diametrically opposed to each other.

No government can be expected to take or to acquiesce in the view that it should be overthrown or that the society over which it presides should be disrupted. Governments of every sort, whether constitutional or authoritarian, therefore consider it necessary and legitimate to put the defense of the status quo against violent or subversive assault ahead of other considerations. This does not necessarily indicate indifference or contempt for human rights and freedoms—although of course some rulers as well as some revolutionaries are guilty of such contempt—but it clearly confirms Professor Garnett's proposition that "When the state totters toward the 'war of every man against every man,' the Hobbesian preference for security and order over freedom and justice is a natural response." When genuinely constitutional regimes resort to emergency measures that violate the normal rights of their citizens, they do so reluctantly, with the conviction that some sacrifice of those rights is justified to meet the necessity of maintaining order, and with the intention of minimizing both the extent and the duration of this deviation from ordinary constitutional arrangements. It may be that in the short run, as Professor Garnett suggests, democratic governments can survive only if they are willing to undertake undemocratic means to save themselves.

What about the long run? Critics of the use of constitutional emergency powers are legitimately concerned about the corrosive effects of frequent resort to those special arrangements upon the rule of law and free institutions, and especially the effects of long-continued reliance on them. Political habits, like others, are easy to form and difficult to break, and emergencies of such duration as we find in the cases of Israel, Northern Ireland, and Taiwan seem likely to foster habitual expectations of harsh and arbitrary actions by governments. One might argue that the situation never returns entirely to the constitutionally normal state after the invocation of emergency powers, and that the frequent and prolonged exercise of those powers gradually changes the exceptional into the ordinary, the emergency action into the routine procedure.

Against the reading of the probabilities we must cite the conviction of those who defend resort to emergency measures that the long-term possibility of genuine constitutionalism, of reliable respect for the decencies that define free and open societies, depends upon the maintenance of order and stability by officials who are wiling to use and careful not to abuse those extraordinary measures. According to this view, the risk of using emergency powers too timidly and too late is at least as serious as the risk of using them too readily and too freely, so far as the fate of rights and freedoms is concerned. The temporary suspension of certain guarantees is regarded less as a threat of permanent damage to the structure of constitutionalism than as a contribution to the security that is required for the long-term soundness of that structure. From this perspective, order and human rights are not in opposition, but what is requisite for order is essential to human rights.

The five case studies presented in this book are drawn from Asia, the Middle East, and Europe. They deal with greatly differing constitutional systems and governmental elites, struggling to contain and manage a considerable variety of threats to order and stability. For all their differences, these cases converge in offering confirmation of certain basic points. They tell us that the urge for security qualifies the demand for freedom, and that exceptional threats to security tend to generate support for exceptional restrictions on freedom. They tell us that the line between the necessary and proper use of emergency powers and the abusive exploitation of those powers is difficult both to agree upon and to adhere to, and they suggest the need for caution, lest efforts putatively designed to save and promote constitutionalism lead in practice to its being undermined. But they also suggest that limited governments can be equipped and enabled to cope with crises without destroying their commitment to constitutionalism, and that success in defending social and political order may provide the opportunity for the flourishing of the liberal values associated with constitutional democracy.

ENDNOTES

1. Frederick M. Watkins, *The Failure of Constitutional Emergency Powers under the German Republic* (Cambridge, Mass., 1939), p. 135.

2. See Carl J. Friedrich, *Constitutional Government and Democracy*, revised edition (Boston, 1950), pp. 575-77; Frederick M. Watkins, "The Problem of Constitutional Dictatorship," in C. J. Friedrich and E. S. Mason, eds., *Public Policy* (Cambridge, Mass., 1940), pp. 344-58.

Editor and Contributor Information

INIS L. CLAUDE, JR. is Edward Stettinius Professor Emeritus of International Relations at the University of Virginia.

ALAN DOWTY is Professor of Political Science at the University of Notre Dame.

ROBERT EVANS is Professor of Government & Foreign Affairs at the University of Virginia.

J. C. GARNETT is Chairman and Professor of Political Science at the University of Wales.

TAO-TAI HSIA is Chief of the Far Eastern Law Division at the Library of Congress.

YOUNG C. KIM is Deputy Director of the Institute for Sino-Soviet Studies at George Washington University.

SHAO-CHUAN LENG is Compton Professor of Government and Foreign Affairs and Chairman of the Asian Studies Committee at the University of Virginia.

KENNETH W. THOMPSON is Director of the White Burkett Miller Center of Public Affairs and J. Wilson Newman Professor of Governance at the University of Virginia.

WENDY ZELDIN is Senior Editor of the Far Eastern Law Division at the Library of Congress.

Index

INDEX

CASE INDEX (Israeli courts)